# Educating Immigrants

Edited by Joti Bhatnagar

ST. MARTIN'S PRESS NEW YORK

**Library of Congress Cataloging in Publication Data**
Main entry under title:

Educating immigrants.

    Includes index.
    1.    Children of immigrants—Education—Addresses, essays, lectures.
I. Bhatnagar, Joti.
LC3745.E38    1981                 371.97            80-22023
ISBN 0-312-23711-1

To Rita and Anuj

who, despite everything,
seem to have prospered in the new land

# CONTENTS

## ACKNOWLEDGEMENTS

This book is the result of help and encouragement from many sources. I am thankful to the authors of the individual chapters who undertook their writings and revisions, often at very short notice. Tammi Rossman helped me with editorial work with cheerful efficiency and magnificent assurance. Ronnie Braendel, Beverly Black, Barbra Whitehouse and Joele Barbot assisted me with typing and keeping in contact with authors spread over four continents. Leonidas Bombas helped me with proofreading and indexing.

I would like publicly to acknowledge my indebtedness to Arpi Hamalian, Susanne Probst and my wife Sheela, from whom I learned a great deal through discussion and critical evaluation of the material, some of which finally found its way into the book.

# 1 INTRODUCTION

**Joti Bhatnagar**

Human migration is as old as the human race itself. The social structure, political organisation and ethnic composition in three of the world's six continents — North America, South America and Australia — have been radically altered through mass migration in the last four hundred years. Although it dates further back, mass migration in the other three 'older' continents also had a great impact. For example, Aryans migrated from somewhere in Europe to India in about 1500 BC, thus completely changing the course of development of Indian languages, culture and civilisation. Many nations in Asia and Africa (such as South Africa, Rhodesia, Israel, Jordan, Lebanon) have been transformed through large-scale immigration in the last hundred years.

After the Second World War economies of the Western countries expanded at an unusually fast rate. This expansion led to such an increase in demand for manpower that in the late 1950s and early 1960s there were, in many European countries, many more job openings than there were people to fill them. For example, to meet its manpower needs, London Transport had to send recruiting teams to the West Indies. Most receiving countries viewed immigrant workers as a good way to supply the needs of the economic system. Immigrant workers at first often came alone, but their families soon followed. It came as a surprising discovery that immigrant workers and their families needed housing, health care, social services and educational facilities. No advance planning had been done to meet these needs. The arrival of a large number of immigrant children, largely from the relatively non-industrialised parts of the world, into urban centres of Europe and North America caused serious problems. The children and their parents were psychologically unprepared for the transition, just as the school boards and the local education authorities were caught without any sound educational policies regarding these children — with disastrous results for all concerned. A number of policies were developed on a trial-and-error basis with a number of trials and a number of errors. Although a number of countries in Western Europe were facing the problem, there was surprisingly little co-operation and exchange of ideas. The situation regarding consultation and exchange of ideas seems to have improved in the last few years, largely through the efforts of bodies such as UNESCO and the European Economic Community.

Published works (e.g. *International Review of Psychology 1976*, vol. 25, no.3) indicated that there is a large common element in the problems faced by the immigrant child in the various countries of Europe and North America. With this in mind I organised a symposium under the title 'Socio-personal and Academic Adjustment of Immigrant Children in European and North American Schools'. Under the chairmanship of Professor R. Taft, a world-renowned expert in the field of adjustment and integration of immigrants, the symposium took place at the International Congress of Applied Psychology in Munich, West Germany during the summer of 1978. Participants from Britain, Canada, France, Sweden and the United States presented papers and looked into the following controversial issues:

1. Whether immigrant children are unevenly distributed and thus form a high proportion of the population in some schools? Is their academic, social and emotional adjustment affected by this? Is the academic performance of the local children affected by the presence of a large number of immigrant children in some schools?
2. The relationship between linguistic behaviour and adjustment. Does speaking a language other than English, French or Swedish (as the case may be) at home, with friends, parents or siblings have any bearing on the adjustment of immigrant children?
3. The relationship between the adjustment and self-concept of immigrant children and concomitants of positive self-concept.
4. The role and validity of psychological tests for measuring the ability, aptitude and attainments of immigrant children.
5. The concept of cultural pluralism and its bearing upon the adjustment of immigrant children.
6. Social relations of immigrant children and their relationship with academic and personal adjustment.

The symposium removed any doubts about the value of international co-operation in developing policies regarding the education of immigrant children — a problem faced by many countries in the world. Since a book examining the problems and prospects of the education of immigrants across the world had not been published it was decided to invite participants at the symposium, together with authors from Australia, Germany, Israel and the Middle East, to contribute a chapter each to *Educating Immigrants*. This book encompasses several major receiving countries in Australia, Asia, Europe and North America. Without making the book extraordinarily long, it would have been very difficult to include all the major immigrant receiving countries of the world. South America, sub-Saharan Africa and some Asian countries (e.g. Thailand, India, Hong Kong), which have also received a large number of immigrants in recent years, were left out.

This book covers some interesting combinations of migrant populations and receiving countries. Immigration into Israel has been primarily for ethnic reasons. Jews all over the world regard Israel as their 'homeland' and many have chosen to emigrate there. Immigration of Jews into Israel does not involve any racial problems. On the other side of the coin, many Palestinians who have lived in Israel and continue to live there consider themselves to be strangers in their own land. As Professor Hamalian points out in her chapter, in a sociological sense, they have become immigrants in their own land. The Middle East presents an interesting case of population movements in an area where migration has always been a time-honoured tradition. But the oil-based boom in economy can no longer be managed solely through the traditional sources of migrant manpower. Immigrants to oil-rich economies such as Kuwait and Saudi Arabia now come from far-away places like Korea, Europe and North America. The bulk of immigrants in both Sweden and Switzerland come from neighbouring countries and language problems are their major concern. Britain, France and the Netherlands have received a large number of immigrants from their ex-colonies. These include European settlers in the colonies, who decided to return to their 'homeland' when the colonies attained independence, and citizens of the newly independent colonies, who decided to seek a better economic future in the 'mother country'. Racial, ethnic and language problems have been in the forefront of difficulties facing immigrants. Australia, Canada and the United States are all 'countries of immigrants'. Since the Second World War each of these countries has received millions of immigrants and, until recently, all three placed strict limitations on the admission of non-whites. In Canada, 'multiculturalism in a bilingual framework' is the official government policy. The concept of multiculturalism is also gaining ground in Australia and the United States. Germany has been neither a colonial power nor a 'country of immigrants'. It has traditionally been a source of immigrants. In common with other European countries, it has, nevertheless, received a large number of immigrant workers, mainly from Turkey and Southern Europe. Hamburg is now the third largest Turkish city in the world.

Most immigrant workers in Switzerland and Germany are on work permits renewable at the government's pleasure. The work permit does not carry a right to permanent residence. Many are uncertain whether their work permit will be extended or whether they will have to leave for their home countries, and this has been at the forefront of their problems. 'Living with packed suitcases' creates a serious dilemma for their children's education. Should the children be educated for work in Germany or the environment back home? What should be the language of instruction? If they learn German they might not fit into the labour market back home, and if they do not learn German they will find it impossible to find a job in Germany. Solving the problems regarding the length of stay does not necessarily solve the dilemmas facing immigrants and their children, as experience in Britain, Canada and the United States would suggest. In these countries most immigrants are accepted for permanent stay – they do not face anxiety and insecurity about possible deportation. Yet education of immigrants still poses serious questions. Should schools assimilate or integrate them? Should we encourage them to maintain their language and culture? If so, how? Would it not be better for their social mobility if they spoke English from day one and concentrated all their energies on mastering the English language? What is the difference between assimilation and integration? Since the terms 'assimilation', 'adjustment' and 'integration' are often used in the literature dealing with immigrants, it might be worth while to clarify these terms.

Assimilation refers to the adoption by the immigrant of the mannerisms, language, traditions, cultural mores and values of the host society. Over a period of time the immigrant becomes indistinguishable from the members of the host society. His original language and culture are all but forgotten.

Adjustment refers to the process through which the immigrant learns to live in harmony with his new environment. It implies coexistence of the old values and traditions with the new. It means that one has to make concessions to the requirements of the new society but it does not necessarily involve giving up cherished cultural values.

Integration implies adjustment on the side of both the immigrant and the host society. If a society admits a number of individuals with different cultural backgrounds, it no longer remains what it was before such admission. Although the immigrant will have to do most of the adjusting, some adjustment on the part of the host society will be required. Only when there is a willingness to do this will that integration be achieved. Integration also requires emotional adjustment and social acceptance of each other, on the part both of the immigrant and of the host society. It implies that the immigrant will integrate his old culture with the new, that the two cultures will be made compatible in his personality. The host society, on its part, will also accept, not only intellectually but also emotionally, the significance of the culture which the immigrant brings to his new land. Integration implies a multicultural society, a society based upon an explicit assumption that its cultural mosaic consists of many constituent elements, the contribution of minority groups no less valuable than that of the majority. A society based not only upon mutual coexistence, but upon respect and understanding between the various elements of the cultural mosaic, will permit true integration of immigrants. This, in turn, will lead to the development of a truly free, democratic and egalitarian social structure, to the benefit of all. Obviously, integration would be the ideal state, although no society seems to have come even close to achieving it.

Education systems reflect the social values of the society of which they are a part. In the following chapters an attempt will be made briefly to outline the number and type of immigrants, the immigration policies and the social climate in which the immigrants find themselves. In this setting an attempt will be made to evaluate the responses that have been made in the various countries to meet the challenge of providing suitable education for immigrant children.

# 2 EDUCATION OF IMMIGRANTS IN AUSTRALIA

**Ronald Taft and Desmond Cahill**

The first white settlers arrived in Sydney from Britain in 1788 to found
a prison colony to replace those lost in America. Subsequently, free
immigration was permitted and by 1850 there were 300,000 settlers
almost entirely from the United Kingdom. It is estimated that there were
300,000 aborigines on the whole continent at the time of the white
invasion, but their numbers substantially declined as they succumbed to
disease, murder, starvation and expulsion. Today the total population of
Australia is over 14 million. Of these, 3,500,000 (25 per cent of the
total population) were born elsewhere, and approximately 150,000
persons identify themselves as aborigines. The place of the aboriginal
peoples in Australian society, and in particular their education, is
largely outside the scope of a book on immigrant education, despite
the importance of the topic.

After the discovery of gold in 1851 the rate of immigration increased
greatly. By 1900 there were 3,750,000 Australians, almost entirely of
Anglo-Celtic origin, and by 1947 the population was 7,500,000. At
that time, Australia had received very few of the Scandinavian, Italian,
Slavic and Jewish immigrants who were so typical of the influx into the
USA in the late nineteenth and early twentieth centuries. The few
children who did not speak English on arrival were distributed in small
numbers around the schools where they gradually became inconspicuous,
although there were a few exceptions where small concentrations of the
one nationality congregated in a district. It was expected that the
immigrant children would be assimilated into the prevailing Anglo-
Celtic-Australian culture of the school systems, and there were few
doubts about this philosophy, except for those raised by the case of
the Germans and a few Chinese children.

There were 40,000 Chinese in Australia in the 1850s, but most of
these returned home or died without issue. The Germans, on the other
hand, who also came in similar numbers, settled as families and set up
their own private (Lutheran-sponsored) schools with German as the
language of instruction, thus pioneering bilingual education in the
country. Some of these schools switched to English in the late nineteenth centure because this language was considered by the parents to
be more favourable for the children to establish themselves in the wider

Australian community. Most of the German language schools, however, retained German as the language of instruction until World War I, at which time they were forced by laws that were passed in each State of Australia that made mandatory the use only of English for instructional purposes. This 'patriotic' law still stands on the statute books of two of the States, but today it is dormant and unlikely to be used to interfere with any bilingual or non-English instructional programmes in schools.

Before looking at the more recent immigration picture, it should also be mentioned that immigrants of Irish origin, who constituted perhaps one-quarter of the 'British' immigrants, attended almost exclusively their own private schools which constituted the separate Roman Catholic system and which provided an 'ethnic' type of education for this English-speaking minority.

## Post-war Immigration to Australia

A drastic change occurred in 1948 in the type of immigrants coming to Australia, and this was to have considerable implications for the education of their children. The previous, relatively exclusionist attitude towards people of non-British origin was abruptly modified by Australia's acceptance of 170,000 European refugees between 1948 and 1951, mainly from Poland and the Baltic States. This was followed by significant numbers of voluntary immigrant Dutch, Germans, Italians and Maltese during the 1950s and early 1960s, and Greeks and Yugoslavs during the late 1960s and early 1970s, as well as small numbers from many other countries. In the meantime, British immigrants continued to arrive at a steady rate, and over a million have arrived since 1945. During the long period of post-war economic growth, which has greatly diminished since 1974, the Australian government actively recruited immigrants with offers of assistance, frequently in conjunction with the governments of the countries of emigration. Amongst Australian policy makers, the assumption has always been that migration is oriented towards permanent settlement of families rather than individual guest-workers. Immigrants are free to choose their place of residence and enclave settlement is not encouraged.

The current official policy calls for 90,000 new arrivals per year, selected on the basis of family reunion, economic contribution or potential adaptability to Australian society. New Zealand citizens and refugees (at least 10,500 per year) constitute special cases, but are

Table 2.1:   Birthplace of Overseas Persons Resident in Australia

| Birthplace | '000 | | '000 |
|---|---|---|---|
| United Kingdom | 1,070.2 | Canada | 14.5 |
| Italy | 280.1 | Russia | 14.5 |
| Greece | 152.9 | Latvia | 13.4 |
| Yugoslavia | 143.6 | France | 12.0 |
| Germany | 107.6 | Ukraine | 11.4 |
| Netherlands | 92.1 | Portugal | 10.2 |
| New Zealand | 89.8 | Mauritius | 9.9 |
| Poland | 56.0 | Chile | 9.9 |
| Malta | 55.9 | Indonesia | 9.3 |
| Eire | 47.4 | Finland | 9.1 |
| India | 37.5 | Singapore | 9.0 |
| Lebanon | 33.4 | Hong Kong | 8.8 |
| USA | 31.5 | Uruguay | 7.8 |
| Egypt | 30.1 | Denmark | 7.0 |
| Hungary | 27.2 | Switzerland | 6.5 |
| Austria | 23.2 | Burma | 6.3 |
| Cyprus | 21.6 | Japan | 6.2 |
| Malaysia | 19.9 | Fiji | 6.0 |
| China | 19.5 | Philippines | 5.9 |
| Turkey | 19.5 | Israel | 5.3 |
| South Africa | 15.6 | Argentina | 5.2 |
| Czechoslovakia | 15.5 | Roumania | 4.6 |
| Papua New Guinea | 15.5 | Sweden | 4.2 |
| Spain | 15.4 | Estonia | 4.7 |
| Sri Lanka | 14.9 | Belgium | 4.0 |

| | |
|---|---|
| Total born overseas | 2,718,832 |
| Total Australian population | 13,548,448 |

These figures are extracts from the official 1976 Census. Since then, substantial numbers of Lebanese and Vietnamese refugees have entered the country.

included in the total. A relaxation of the early policy that excluded persons of non-European ancestry began in 1966, and the present policy officially proscribes any discrimination on the grounds of 'race, colour, nationality, descent, national or ethnic origin or sex'.

The composition of the recent immigration intake has been approximately one-quarter from the United Kingdom, one-sixth from the Middle East and South Asia (mainly Indian and Lebanese), one-quarter from East Asia (mainly Vietnamese and ethnic Chinese) and one-third from other widely scattered places. Thus, the composition of immigration to Australia in the past 30 years has completely transformed Australia from a homogeneous, English-Scottish-Irish community into a heterogeneous nation composed of many of the cultural and linguistic streams of the world. So far, however, there are very few residents of African Negro background, and obviously there are many peoples in the world who have not yet come to Australia.

Table 2.1 lists 50 countries that have constituted the birthplace of at least 4,000 residents of Australia. One out of every nine of the Australian population was born in a non-English-speaking country, the largest groups being Italian, Greek and Yugoslav. From the point of view of education, it is more significant to note that one out of every six schoolchildren has at least one parent whose mother tongue is not English. The proportion is much higher than this in some of the cities, since the settlement of immigrants has been almost entirely urban. Thus, in the city of Melbourne, with a total population of 2,750,000, approximately one-quarter of all schoolchildren have a non-English-speaking parent, and one in three has a parent who was born overseas.

Here, in summary form, are some of the features of the present immigration picture in Australia that have an influence on education:

1. While Australia has always been a country of immigration, it is only in the past 30 years that there has been a significant influx of non-English-speaking people. Consequently, the school systems have been relatively inexperienced in coping with children from non-English-speaking homes.

2. The number of settlers arriving in the past ten years has varied from a peak of 185,000 in 1969-70 (98,000 from non-English-speaking countries) down to a low of 52,750 in 1975-76 (29,500).

3. The immigrants vary widely in their level of education, depending on the nationality concerned. On arrival, the bulk of them have

primary education only, and some are effectively illiterate in any language despite a requirement of literacy in the selection process. Tertiary level education is more typical of refugees than of voluntary immigrants.

4. The nationalities and languages of the immigrants arriving in any year are heterogeneous and are constantly changing from one time to another, according to conditions in the countries of origin. Compared with some other countries of immigration, it is significant for the education of immigrants in Australia that there is little long-term continuity in the immigration of any one national or language group.

5. The residential distribution of immigrants is not random. On arrival, immigrants tend to live in groups in specific districts of the main urban areas, but mobility is quick and most new immigrants move on within a few years to areas of second and third settlement. In this process they become more dispersed in the general community, and their children have frequent changes of school. Areas of high immigrant density tend to change their typical national character every few years, and there are very few localities anywhere in Australia where persons of any one national background constitute as much as 50 per cent of the population.

6. Because the policy favours family rather than single-worker immigration, about one-third of the arrivals are under 15 years of age, i.e. potential schoolchildren. It is estimated that approximately 15,000 newly arrived children without a knowledge of English are joining schools in Australia each year. Possibly another 30,000 children with minimal knowledge of English begin school at the start of each academic year.

7. Among the services provided for government-sponsored immigrants is the privilege of staying for up to one year in a 'Migrant Reception Hostel', where accommodation and meals are available at a reasonable cost. As a result of this scheme it is possible to bring initial advisory services to them and to arrange for appropriate interpreters and consultants to be available. Another effect is that the regular schools in the neighbourhoods have to cater to a continually changing complement of newly arrived children of varying national backgrounds who remain for a short period only.

8. The proportion of Roman Catholics among the immigrants has consistently been substantial, and many of the children have been enrolled in fee-paying Catholic schools from the time of arrival. Thus, parochial schools in areas of high immigrant density have carried a relatively heavy burden in the task of absorbing immigrant children.

## Ethnic Attitudes in Australia

Thirty years ago, the Australian community held comfortable ethno-
centric and xenophobic attitudes. It was assumed that only a few
immigrants, mostly British, would be admitted, and that all would
quickly be assimilated to the prevailing, 'superior' Anglo-Celtic-
Australian way of life. Attitudes have varied since then according to
the economic trends of the time, but a gradual over-all trend towards
increasing liberalism has occurred. Taft presented a consolidated
account of Australian public opinion surveys since 1948 on attitudes
to immigration in general and to particular nationalities, and opinions
on their integration.[1] The responses indicate that the Australian public
differentiates less today than previously between British, Northern
European, Eastern European, Southern European and non-European
immigrants as suitable residents for the country. Table 2.2 sets out the
proportions of the public who have a positive attitude towards the
immigration of various groups and those who would exclude them
entirely. It shows decreasing discrimination against all nationalities and
especially against Negroes. Differential discrimination still exists and
at the time of writing, a combination of a high level of unemployment
and the strong pressure from would-be Indochinese refugees has stirred
up considerable antagonistic attitudes again. In a recent survey in the
State of Victoria, 31 per cent of the adult public were described as
'conscious bigots', and 18 per cent as 'unconscious bigots'.

Attitudes towards integration and multiculturalism have also been
measured. The survey of Irving Saulwick and Associates makes clear
that most Australians favour the proposition that immigrants 'should
be encouraged to fit into the community as soon as possible'.[2] Fifty-
four per cent of Australian-born people favoured this, compared with
46 per cent of all immigrants. On one of the two alternative choices,
'migrants should be left to fit in at their own pace', Taft comments:

> Considering everything, there is a greater acceptance of Government
> assistance for pluralism than there used to be, especially by young
> well-educated Australians, but the assimilation model for the inte-
> gration of immigrants is still a strong one, and is even favoured by
> many immigrants themselves.[3]

The attitudes of schoolchildren towards newcomers reflect those of
their parents. Thus, Martin and Meade report that 83 per cent of high
school students of Australian origin in Sydney endorsed the statement,

Table 2.2: Attitudes Towards the Immigration of Selected Nationalities in Australia

| | Melbourne 1948 (Oeser-Hammond) | | | Australia 1964 ASRP-Huck | | | Melbourne/Sydney 1971 Saulwick—*The Age* | | |
|---|---|---|---|---|---|---|---|---|---|
| | Free [a] immigration | Let in only a few | Exclude | Free immigration | Let in only a few | Exclude | Free immigration | Let in only a few | Exclude |
| English | 91 | 7 | 2 | 91 | 6 | 3 | 79 | 18 | 3 |
| Irish | 65 | 19 | 16 | 83 | 13 | 4 | – | – | – |
| Italian | 21 | 33 | 46 | 46 | 31 | 23 | 48 | 41 | 11 |
| Chinese | 32 | 44 | 24 | 17 | 50 | 33 | 36 | 45 | 19 |
| Negroes | 10 | 13 | 77 | 17 | 36 | 47 | 32 | 34 | 34 |

a. All figures are percentages. Free immigration = 'allow them to come', 'try to get them to come'.

'having a lot of migrants has not been so good for this country'.[4] In contrast, only 12 per cent of students of Greek background endorsed this. It should be noted, however, that these negative attitudes are not necessarily accompanied by hostile actions or social exclusion of immigrants in the school, although the attitudes are conveyed verbally.

## The Organisation of Education in Australia

Before attempting to describe the system of educating children from immigrant backgrounds in Australia, a brief explanation should be given of the school education system. The basic administrative unit is each one of the eight states and federal territories, which range in total population from five million in New South Wales down to 100,000 in the Northern Territory. The public school system is administered by a highly centralised state education department with little local autonomy. There is also a Catholic office of education to co-ordinate the various separate Roman Catholic schools in each state. There is a considerable number of other independent private schools, most of which have an affiliation with a religious denomination. The Catholic and other independent schools cater to 20 per cent of all primary students and 25 per cent of secondary students, despite the tuition fees that they all charge. The division of schools into levels differs from one state to another, but typically the schools cover 13 years of education from the ages of five to eighteen. They are divided into seven years of primary or elementary schooling and six of secondary schooling.

A complication of great importance to the education of immigrant children arises from the increasing role of the federal government in education, when it has traditionally been the responsibility of the States. In 1945 the Commonwealth Office of Education was established, partly to advise the Australian government on the subsidising of schools in the states, and also, since the immigration programme was viewed as a federal matter, the office took responsibility for the special education of immigrants (at first only for providing schools in immigrant residential centres and for setting up adult programmes). Later, the granting of direct financial aid to schools (including all private schools) by the federal government led to the organisation of a permanent Schools Commission under the direction of the Minister for Education, to advise on the disbursement of the aid in relation to policy. This body eventually became responsible for the extensive Child Migrant Education Program.

**Programmes for Immigrant Family Education**

*Adults*

At the beginning of the post-war intake of non-English-speaking immigrants in 1948, for obvious practical reasons attention began to be paid to the need to teach English to adults. Programmes were introduced to teach them on board ship during the three-week trip, or even before embarkation. Reading and correspondence courses were organised, and part-time continuation courses were provided. Later, in 1969, full-time intensive courses were introduced on a limited scale for professionally qualified immigrants. These programmes have been subsequently extended and new initiatives have been introduced. The types of programmes now available are as follows.

*Full-time Courses*. Intensive courses conducted for 320 hours over eight weeks are provided for professionally qualified immigrants to facilitate their employment in positions relevant to their qualifications. Accelerated courses conducted for 300 hours over ten weeks are provided for immigrants with a sub-professional, technical or trade background. Since November 1977, special on-arrival courses have been conducted for refugees from the Middle East and Indochina. The Galbally Report on *Migrant Services and Programs* recommended that full-time courses aimed not only at English language learning but also at the development of cultural competence must be substantially increased, and the federal government is presently implementing this recommendation. During these full-time courses, students are paid a modest living allowance — currently 18 per cent of the total adult migrant education programme budget is spent on these allowances.

*Part-time Courses*. Part-time courses range from 10 to 20 weeks and from 6 to 20 hours per week, depending on the needs and circumstances of the student clients and the purpose of the course. Some are conducted during the day, others at night.

*Continuation Courses*. Continuation classes enable a student to commence learning English on a part-time basis at his or her convenience. They are held for two hours, twice weekly on week nights, in schools, church halls, etc. The Galbally Report has recommended they be replaced with restructured certificate courses of different lengths and levels of difficulty.

*Correspondence Courses*. This programme consists of preliminary courses (available in Italian/English and Greek/English) and main courses of 120 lessons, based on a programme called 'Learning English' which is broadcast each morning by the national broadcasting network.

*Courses in Industry*. These courses, 36 hours in length over a six-week period, are given at the place of work for unskilled and semi-skilled workers. They are designed to develop elementary communication skills and the ability to read safety signs, and also to give information on services provided for employees.

*Home Tutor Scheme*. In this scheme voluntary 'tutors', after a short training course, go to the immigrant's home once or twice a week on a one-to-one basis. The scheme is aimed mainly at immigrant women who are isolated at home.

The number of immigrants participating in these courses has increased from 28,000 (part-time) in 1952 to 105,000 in 1977-78 (over 5,000 of them full-time). Expenditure in real terms has burgeoned in the past eight years with a fourfold increase. In addition to these courses, the migrant educational television service presents a programme, 'You Say the Word', once a week, which is watched by an estimated quarter of a million persons.

*Children*

*Education for Assimilation*. Until recent times, the official policy concerning the absorption of immigrants was one of total assimilation or Anglo-conformity. No possibility of a long-term linguistic or cultural rival was admitted, ethnic distinctiveness was not encouraged and it was considered that the quicker the assimilation to the pre-eminent Anglo-Saxon core culture, the better for the unity and uniformity of the Australian nation. The school system reflects the prevailing philosophy of the country, so that, at the time when assimilation was the prevailing orientation, the schools embodied this as well and, when this orientation became modified, so did that of the schools. A much quoted comment by a respected Australian school principal represents the attitude of the Australian school system to immigrant children during the 1950s and 1960s:

The child must learn to think in English from the start ... English is to be the basis of all instruction. It is the avenue to mutual under-

standing. It is the key to the success of the whole immigration
project ... English must be spoken to the pupils and by them, all
day and every day, in every activity, in school and out of it.[5]

It was expected that tolerance for and acceptance of the newcomers,
or 'New Australians' as they were euphemistically called at that time,
would lead them to learn about the Australian way of life and to
adopt it as quickly as possible, especially the use of the English language. Newly arrived children were inducted into regular classrooms,
often at a level below their age equivalent, or into vocationally oriented streams, and were then treated like all other children whether
they knew English or not. One rationale for this procedure was the
belief that children, resilient by nature, adapt quickly, and assimilation would be hindered by any labelling or by differential
treatment.

In response to suggestions that immigrant children had special
problems, a federal committee of investigation reported in 1960 that
teachers claim that Australian children 'have accepted the newcomers
naturally and without reservation', that 'about 97 per cent' of the
immigrants settle down well and that they are, as a group, 'above
average in scholarship'.[6] The committee did allow, however, that
some (24 per cent) are handicapped in English. The findings of the
committee were subjected to criticism, partly on methodological
grounds and partly because the report emphasised the successes rather
than the failures and problems that clearly existed among the immigrants.

*Transitional Phase: 1965-75.* The continuing arrival of large numbers
of non-English-speaking children from poorly educated, low-skilled
families in the 1960s led to a distinctive shift in emphasis from the
adaptation successes of immigrant children to a concern with their
problems. This shift was also caused by a public concern about
educational issues in general and by a movement from a teacher-
centred to a child-centred philosophy of education. An increasing
number of educationists expressed concern about the handicaps that
beset immigrant schoolchildren. Limited knowledge of English was
seen to be hampering their academic progress, and their cultural
distance from the Anglo-Australian milieu of the Australian classroom
was thought to be giving rise to socio-emotional problems as they
struggled to resolve the conflict of living in two different worlds, that
of the home and that of the school.

Since the states could not adequately cope with the problems of integrating the immigrant children, the federal government introduced its Child Migrant Education Program (CMEP) in 1970. The programme was totally orientated towards ESL teaching and was initially conceived as a stop-gap measure to cover the backlog of children who had a handicap in English due to their immigration to Australia. Not surprisingly, the CMEP opened a Pandora's box of new realisations, greater difficulties, fresh insights and new initiatives. Within four years, the programme was greatly expanded, major research projects were being planned and teachers' training colleges were beginning to grapple with the issues of educating children in a multilingual and culturally pluralist society. The expansion of the programme can be visualised from the figures: whereas in 1970 $ 1.8 million was allocated for the programme, by 1977 the figure had jumped to $ 26.4 million — a huge increase even allowing for the halving of the value of the Australian dollar through inflation. Through the CMEP it became possible to finance the training and payment of 'migrant English' teachers for public, Catholic and independent schools at both primary and secondary levels according to need, and to provide equipment, materials and (later) accommodation. The number of specialist teachers employed under the CMEP grew rapidly from 246 in the first year to 2,095 in 1974, but there were practical problems from the beginning. The teachers were required to be qualified for registration, and hence were usually from a monolinguistic background, living in areas that were distant from those in which most of the immigrant families lived. Many were seeking part-time work only, especially the female teachers. It has been found that those teachers who want full-time work tend to prefer regular classroom teaching to special migrant English teaching because of the extremely limited career prospects of the latter positions. Their employment is further complicated by the fact that they represent federally sponsored officers in a state education system, and the states have usually put their needs in the general teaching service ahead of the migrant English classes. The training consisted on a four-week course which was not a compulsory requirement for employment, plus the possibility of voluntarily attending a further two-week, in-service course.

Materials for use by the teachers have been provided by the federal government, but many teachers complain that these are inadequate. There are few linguists in Australian universities, and they have little interest in applied linguistics, so that scholarship and research on second language acquisition have been rather limited. The ESL programmes in the schools all took the form of 'withdrawal classes', whereby immigrant children are instructed for between one and five hours per week in special classes consisting of children of mixed ages and language backgrounds, by teachers who are unlikely to know the mother tongue of any of the students. The CMEP was geared in particular to providing a basic introduction to English for newly arrived schoolchildren, but it soon began to provide for the children a general orientation into the Australian community, for example through field trips. Many of the teachers became involved in the family life of the children and established contact with the parents. The programme developed a momentum of its own, and demand grew for the extension of the classes to longer-standing immigrant children from non-English-speaking homes, even if they had been born in Australia. As Martin puts it: 'It "flushed out" children whose educational difficulties were being ignored or accepted as irremediable or a sign of backwardness, and it unintentionally helped widen the very concept of migrant education.'[7] As the programme expanded, however, some disenchantment quickly surfaced because it was felt that the periodic withdrawal of the children from the classroom context meant that they were underexposed to informal language learning and, more importantly, that they became labelled as remedial.

Today, the withdrawal system is less common than formerly and is being replaced by other methods, especially language enrichment programmes whereby ESL teachers work in the classroom alongside the classroom teachers in a team effort. Although this is not included in their official function, their task is as much remedial, in that they help not only first- and second-generation children from immigrant families but even Australian children whose English language level is deficient.

The transitional phase has also witnessed an explosion in the numbers of 'ethnic schools', as ethnic communities have become conscious of the danger of the extinction of their national heritage. While only a small number of ethnic schools exist on a full-time basis, the norm is the part-time ethnic school, established by ethnic communities, often under religious sponsorship, very much along the lines of the Jewish cheders that have existed for many years. Classes are conducted outside normal school hours, either in the late afternoon or at the weekend when children are often reluctant to be in a class when their Australian peers are free to play. A government-sponsored report estimates that there are as many as 600 ethnic community schools throughout Australia with a total enrolment of 50,000 students, but it is generally considered that these figures are very conservative estimates.[8] The groups mainly involved in this area are the Greek and Italian communities in particular, plus German, Polish, Ukrainian, Latvian, Hungarian, Estonian, Jewish and Arabic groups — although over 30 different linguistic communities have organised schools and special classes.

The schools' aim is to preserve cultural heritage and create a sense of ethnic identity through a study of religion, history, geography, etc. While most of these schools cater to primary schoolchildren, several prepare adolescent students for language subjects at the university matriculation level. The popularity of the schools with the ethnic communities, if not with the pupils themselves, suggests that they perform an important function, but there are serious problems with them. Finances are short, teachers unqualified and the methods and equipment out of date compared with the regular school system. The schools have been seen by many teachers as a threat to their own sphere of influence and have been attacked on the grounds that they divide the children's education as well as overburden them. Nevertheless, two states have provided small subsidies to ethnic schools for teaching community langauges to secondary school students.

*Education for a Culturally Pluralist Society*. As the Pandora's box, initiated by the CMEP, became more widely opened, educationists began reflecting on the nature of Australia's heterogeneous population, the cultural imperialism implicit in the Anglo-conformist stance and the loss to Australia in squandering the cultural and linguistic resources of Australia's immigrant peoples. As a result of a number of influences, a reorientation began in this stance towards that which accepted the reality of Australia's ethnic heterogeneity and the positive value of encouraging multiculturalism. The influences for change during the late 1960s and early 1970s were manifold: the increasing salience of the non-British communities and the pressures emanating from them for the retention of their languages and cultures, the rise of concern in overseas countries such as Canada and the USA with the needs of ethnic minorities and the influence of some academics and other public figures who advocated a multicultural view of Australia.[9] The most notable example was Mr Al Grassby, who was Minister for Immigration from 1972 to 1974.

An in-depth discussion of the educational consequences of multiculturalism was provided at an important symposium at the University of Melbourne.[10] In the symposium, Smolicz made a threefold distinction between migrant education (the teaching of English as a second language), multicultural education (the teaching of community languages and knowledge of ethnic cultures to all Australian students) and ethnic education (the teaching of specific ethnic languages and cultures to members of the particular ethnic group). He favoured a place for all three aspects in the formal education system.

It has been characteristic of the present stage of immigrant education that the concept of multiculturalism has been advocated for Australia without any clear picture of what is implied by it or even whether the term is intended as a description *of* Australian society or a prescription *for* it. In an attempt to clarify the issues involved, Bullivant proposed the term 'polyethnic' to describe Australian society and called for a completely new approach to curriculum planning to prepare students for this conception of society.[11] In an expansion of this viewpoint, Cahill suggested that, in a polyethnic country like Australia, the formal education system must ensure that all students possess three facets of citizenship:

1. survival knowledge for living in a complex, highly technological society;
2. ethnic self-awareness in so far as students can be made aware of their own cultural and linguistic heritage;
3. transcultural consciousness, which implies an understanding of the fundamental similarities among human beings and an acceptance and understanding of other socio-cultural groups.[12]

While the attempts to formulate the meaning and implications of multiculturalism are proceeding, there have been important developments in the education system, although some of them have been more theoretical than actual. Government inquiries were set up in 1973 and 1974 to look into the problems occurring in schools of high immigrant density[13] and the teaching of ethnic languages in schools.[14] This latter report advocated more support for the teaching of ethnic or community languages in the schools. These inquiries were associated with the report of the Schools Commission, the body which is the major source of finance for the schools. It advocated the promotion of bilingual education, the teaching of community languages in schools and the aspects of multiculturalism in general. One of the practical outcomes has been an extension of the use of ethnic aides in schools as support for teachers, but this programme is still very limited in its applications, owing to financial stringencies.

The Australian Ethnic Affairs Council, established in 1977 under the chairmanship of Professor Jerzy Zubrzycki, published guidelines for

*Australia as a Multicultural Society.*[15] In the area of education, it recommended that:

1. the intensive English language centres be expanded, especially those for newly arrived children;
2. a review be made of ESL methods and techniques;
3. schools be given incentives to develop bilingual education, community languages and ethnic studies programmes and to infuse the curriculum in general with the reality of the pluralist nature of Australian society;
4. part-time ethnic schools be given support, teacher training institutions be encouraged to recruit teachers with non-English-speaking backgrounds and all students be made aware of the implications of a multicultural and multilingual education system;
5. educational materials presently used in Australian schools be reviewed in the light of the multicultural perspective.

To complete the picture of the official endorsement of multiculturalism, the Galbally Report on *Migrant Services and Programs* unequivocally recommended support for a multicultural Australia and advocated the expenditure of $ 50 million in the next three years, including $ 5 million for multicultural education and $ 12.35 million for ESL for children and adults.[16] With unprecedented alacrity, the Australian government immediately endorsed the entire programme, and the Schools Commission is investigating how the funds should be spent on multicultural education. To date, the proposals being made largely refer to the expansion of the teaching of community languages in schools, the involvement of the migrant communities in these programmes and the preparation of materials.[17] Characteristically, the committee referred to the community languages as 'Australian languages other than English', thus endorsing the concept of Australia as a multilingual country, although this clearly challenges the acceptance of English as the only official language.

At the secondary level, some schools have introduced such language programmes, but this movement has not flourished as quickly as might have been expected, even allowing for the expected bureaucratic inertia. The non-English language traditionally taught at secondary level in Australian schools has been French and, due to the excess of French teachers combined with a lack of qualified teachers in other languages, only a minority of children from non-English-speaking backgrounds are presently studying their first language at school, though their number is growing. While shifts in attitude have taken place, the vast majority of Australian elementary school teachers believe that first language maintenance will have detrimental effects upon English language development. According to a recent survey (1975), only 1.4 per cent of primary school students from non-English backgrounds were studying their own language at school and, at secondary level, 11 per cent. At the elementary school level, a number of schools in high-density immigrant areas in both the government and Catholic parochial systems have introduced community language programmes, especially in Greek and Italian, but usually for only an hour or two each week. For example, in South Australia, Italian, Greek, German, French, Spanish, Polish and the aboriginal Pitjantjatjara have been introduced into various schools.

One important contribution to Australian bilingual programmes in the 1970s has been the work of Marta Rado in the development of social science curricula units for the 10-14 age group.[18] These units, which are largely self-contained, are available in Arabic, Croatian, Greek, Italian, Serbian, Spanish and Turkish, and additional units are in preparation. Unfortunately, the development of the units in the languages of the newer immigrants has lagged behind, due to continual changes in the nationality of the new arrivals. The rationale for the project in the first place was to facilitate the continuing education of new arrivals during the transition period of their learning English, but the units have, in fact, found their main use in bilingual education with ethnic groups of longer standing.

A change-resistant factor at work in this area has been the overwhelming monolingualistic tradition in Australian society which has meant that languages other than English have never been taught at the elementary level.[19] This remark is especially applicable to the introduction of bilingual education.

Bilingual programmes have also been severely retarded by a gross lack of suitable resource material. Ethnic language bookshops that have recently developed have imported material that is not always useful in the Australian context. Under a grant from the Curriculum Development Centre, an Italian bilingual project team has begun to prepare suitable resource material for these programmes. Projects for the other major community languages are in the planning stages, but recent budgetary constraints have prevented their continuance. Qualified bilingual teachers are rare and their English language competence is often too poor to be acceptable. There have been suggestions that teaching competence needs to be redefined so that immigrant teachers can make a worthwhile contribution, but teacher training institutions and teacher unions are reluctant to make the necessary adjustments, although some courses do exist for retraining foreign teachers to work in the Australian context.

There have been some other interesting innovatory programmes of a multicultural, multilingual nature during the 1970s. A team from La Trobe University, under the leadership of Leslie Claydon, constituted a task force to carry out action research in schools in a district of high immigrant concentration.[20] The team members studied the life of the parents and analysed the relationship between the school staff, the students and the parents, and their mutual attitudes. The aim of the programme was to increase the consonance and understanding between school, home and community by involving the parties concerned in the research process.

Individual schools in all states have experimented with various aspects of multicultural education, e.g. teaching of some of the relevant languages and attempting to involve the community in the school. The 'Ten Schools Project' in the Adelaide area of South Australia represents an ambitious and well-funded project designed to transform the total school environment in its attitude towards cultural pluralism. The project (there are now 30 schools) designed and implemented programmes in the areas of ethnic studies, community language and ESL and also fostered frequent and effective communication between the school, the immigrant parents and the wider community. As with all the early programmes, no thoroughgoing assessment of the project has been carried out, but the impression gained from contact with the organisers is that it has been partially successful. Schools were initially drawn to it because it offered them financial assistance, itinerant specialist teachers and other help in dealing with children from non-English backgrounds. The South Australian Department of Education has prepared an ethnic studies programme dealing with six of the larger ethnic groups (Italian, Greek, German, Dutch, Croatian and Polish), for use with children in the 10-14 age group, and further material is in the course of preparation.

## Some Australian Research on Immigrant Education

Parallel with the rise of the awareness that the education of non-English-speaking immigrants involves special problems, research activity into immigrant education has been burgeoning. Nicoll indicates the following number of research reports in Australia on this subject: before 1960, 3; 1960-64, 2; 1965-69, 21; 1970-74, 64.[21] The major topics of these researches were classified as: migrant achievement — 27; socio-cultural (ethnic) influences on education — 36; bilingualism — 13; adult migrant education —13. A typical study of achievement is one that investigates how long immigrant children stay at school and how well they perform; a socio-cultural study may be concerned with emotional or social problems encountered by children in the process of adapting to life in Australia, their self-concept and their national identifications; studies of bilingualism deal with such subjects as linguistic factors in the acquisition of English, and the maintenance of the mother tongue.

A selection of the more important of the recent studies will now be described. These consist mainly of large-scale surveys of a variety of immigrant groups, using tests of abilities, teacher ratings, self-descriptions, personality inventories and attitude questionnaires. The studies have in the main been conducted by university staff members of the Australian Council for Educational Research and were funded by government-endowed commissions. The Education Research and Development Committee (ERCD) of the Australian Department of Education has a high-level panel for initiating financial support for research in multicultural education in all its aspects and for determining priorities in this area.

*Study of City Youth*

In 1969 a survey was conducted of teenagers living in the metropolitan area of Sydney, the population of which at the time was 2,750,000.[22] Care was taken to sample systematically the age group 12 to 20, both those who were still full-time students and those who were not. The 'Australians' and the 'migrants' who were still attending schools were compared on a number of demographic, ability, attitudinal and self-concept measures. For this study, 'migrant' was defined as any child of foreign-born parents who had experienced some primary schooling in Australia. Very few of the children were recent arrivals, and 30 per cent of the migrant sample had a British background.

Comparisons on a number of variables between various nationalities are set out in Table 2.3. The term 'mixed' refers to children whose two parents had differing national origins. It is notable that the first five nationalities on IQ (Otis Higher) were those whose parents used English to a high degree — universal in the case of the Anglo-Australian and British groups, of course. The Maltese were exceptional in that they spoke a fair amount of English but were lower on IQ and SES than

Table 2.3:  IQ Results and Responses to Attitude Questions by Nationality (Listed in rank order).

|  | IQ (Mean) | SES Parent Occupation | Critical of school [a] | Like school | Value Education | Amount of English spoken |
|---|---|---|---|---|---|---|
| Holland | 111 | *Australia* | Malta | Germany | Germany | Mixed |
| *Australia* | 111 | Asia | UK | Greece | Asia | Holland |
| UK | 111 | Mixed | *Australia* | Yugoslavia | *Australia* | Malta |
| Mixed | 109 | UK | Germany | Asia | Holland | Poland |
| Asia | 106 | Holland | Mixed | Malta | UK | Asia |
| Germany | 106 | Germany | Greece | S. Italy | Mixed | Germany |
| Poland | 105 | Greece | Poland | UK | Yugoslavia | N. Italy |
| Greece | 104 | Malta | S. Italy | Poland | Greece | Yugoslavia |
| Malta | 103 | N. Italy | Asia | N. Italy | Poland | S. Italy |
| N. Italy | 102 | Poland | N. Italy | Mixed | N. Italy | Greece |
| Yugoslavia | 101 | Yugoslavia | Yugoslavia | Holland | S. Italy | |
| S. Italy | 100 | S. Italy | — | *Australia* | Malta | |

a.  Programming error omitted Holland from this table.

Source;  W. F. Connell *et al.*, *12 to 20: Studies of City Youth* (Hicks Smith, Sydney, 1975).

some of the groups that spoke less English, notably Germans and Greeks. The Maltese valued education less than the other groups and were more critical about the schooling that they were receiving. (These findings for the Maltese are parallel to those reported by Taft and Cahill in their study of newly arrived Maltese children; see below.) The Germans were highest on their liking of school and their belief in the general value of education. The Greeks, Yugoslavs and Poles stressed the utilitarian value of education rather than its value *per se*. It is notable that all of the immigrant groups professed to like school more than did the Australians and there was a positive relationship between the time that the families had been in Australia and their resemblance to the Australians' low level of liking school. The higher liking for school of the immigrants compared with Australians was matched by a greater tendency to remain at school until the completion of secondary education, i.e. to matriculation level for entering higher education.

The Southern European and Asian youth had a greater preference for spending leisure time with their family rather than friends, than had the Northern Europeans and Australians, and they were likely to prefer other immigrants as their friends. On the Rosenberg scales of self-image there were few differences between immigrant groups and Australians, but the Southern Italians reported the least satisfactory self-concept of all groups. The authors attribute differences between the immigrants and the Australians to language, socio-economic class and cultural factors rather than to the fact that their families had migrated.

*Education and Occupational Aspirations of Immigrant Children*

Between 1967 and 1975, Taft carried out a series of investigations of the aspirations of youth in the State of Victoria for their ultimate occupation.[23] There were three main samples involved:

1. boys in their last two years of secondary school whose subsequent careers were followed up, in some cases for six years;
2. a representative sample of secondary school students in the year in which they intended to relinquish their full-time schooling — this study provided an index of the respondents' actual school careers to date and of their aspirations;
3. a sample of students in the second year of high school (8th grade) deliberately selected from schools containing a high density of newly arrived immigrants.

The overall picture that emerged from these studies was the same as that reported by Connell *et al.*, i.e. the children of non-English-speaking (NES) immigrants remained at school longer than did Australians of similar class background.[24] Here is a summary of the findings:

1. The educational aspirations of the students of NES origin were higher than those of Australians, especially in the working class, and the NES males had considerably higher aspirations than did the NES females.
2. NES immigrants who had arrived only recently had relatively lower expectations than immigrants of longer standing.
3. Greeks and Yugoslavs, both males and females, and Italian males had relatively high aspirations, irrespective of their occupational class. Jews, who were almost all middle class, had extremely high aspirations, and Italian females and Maltese of both sexes had low ones. (Other immigrant nationalities were not represented in sufficient numbers to reveal any reliable trends, but there was evidence that the children of former refugees with a high educational background, such as the Latvians, had high educational aspirations and considerable success.)
4. Children of working-class NES immigrants were not as successful academically (based on competitive scholarships, the matriculation examination and the student's progress in tertiary institutions) as were students with an Australian or an English-speaking immigrant background. Middle-class NES immigrants were quite successful, especially the girls, who achieved at a level which was superior to that of Australian girls or boys — an intriguing and perhaps very significant finding.
5. There was agreement between the NES students and their parents on their educational plans in nearly three-quarters of the cases and, where there was disagreement, it was the parents who tended to have the higher aspirations.
6. The sex, class and national differentials in occupational aspirations were similar to those in educational aspirations.

The results suggest that many of the children of immigrants will receive an education up to senior secondary or tertiary level and will achieve a middle-class occupation. Some will become business proprietors and thus achieve middle-class occupational status even without having a higher education. Considering the working-class status of most of their fathers, and the educational handicaps of a non-English-speaking background, this represents a significant upward mobility.

### The Experiences of Immigrant Schoolchildren in Secondary School

Martin and Meade conducted a three-year follow-up study of a large representative sample of 9th grade students in public high schools in Sydney.[25] Interviews were carried out with the students, their parents and their teachers, and ability tests and examination results were obtained. Just over half of the sample (57 per cent) had two Australian-born parents, 22 per cent had two parents from non-English-speaking countries (NES) and the others were children either of English-speaking immigrants (ES) or of mixed parentage.

The results confirmed some of the findings that were reported in Taft's studies of the educational aspirations of children in Victoria (see above) and Connell *et al.*'s studies in Sydney, namely, that a greater proportion of the NES children remained at school until the matriculation year than did Australians or ES immigrant children. The aspirations of the NES children played a bigger part in determining their school retention than did IQ, SES or academic success, whereas the relationship was the opposite for the Australians. The high aspirations of the NES children reflect those held by their parents which take little account of the child's ability or school performance. It is not surprising that the NES children watch less TV and study for longer hours than the others.

On the whole, the NES children were lower than those from English-speaking homes on SES and IQ scores (verbal and quantitative tests), but some of the national groups had higher school achievement than the Australians and ES immigrants. Of the larger national groups, the school performance of the Greek children was particularly high and that of the Lebanese and Maltese rather low. It should be noted, however, in interpreting these performance results, that the Catholic and independent school systems which were not represented in the sample would account for a disproportionate number of better students from certain of the national groups.

Martin and Meade conclude

> that some children of non-English-speaking origin reveal an unusual degree of maturity and perception that appears to be related to their coming to terms with the immediate personal experience of living in an ethnically plural society. These students emerge as the advantaged ones compared with the uptight and defensive Australians.[26]

The authors also state that

Somewhere between the stunting and liberating effects of migration are patterns of coping that may seem outwardly normal and undramatic but which, on the part of students of non-English-speaking backgrounds, require remarkable insight (that is, grasping clues to rewarded and punished behaviour) and immense self-control and hard work.

This often takes the form of parent-directed, strict conformity to the requirements of the school's authority structure.[27]

## The Adaptation and Adjustment of Newly Arrived Immigrant Children

In 1974 Taft and Cahill studied the characteristics and attitudes of members of families who had just arrived in Melbourne from South American countries or from Malta or the UK.[28] Interviews were conducted with all of the schoolchildren in the sample, irrespective of age, within a few weeks of their arrival, and again a year later and two years later. The children's parents and teachers were also interviewed. In this way it was possible to record the experiences of the families in the initial stages of adaptation, their reactions to them and the strategies used to cope with them. It was also possible to study early aspects of their acculturation and, in particular, their acquisition of English.

Perhaps the outstanding finding was that there were relatively few serious social and emotional problems encountered by any of these national groups, even in the initial period of their commencing school in Australia. The South Americans naturally had difficulties in learning English, and this affected their academic performance but not their socio-emotional adjustment. Even after two years, the academic and linguistic adjustment of the schoolchildren was still below the Australian average, although they had made greater progress in approaching it in the second year after their arrival than in the first. This suggests that the first year might be viewed as a period of preparation for the 'take-off'. The academic adjustment problems of those who arrived in their adolescence were more severe than those of the younger ones, and three-quarters of them dropped out as soon as they reached the minimum leaving age. The children had more difficulty in adapting to written English than oral, which they presumably picked up in both the formal situation of the classroom and informally from their English-speaking peers. The acquisition of written English was particularly retarded in the children who had changed their school frequently, but oral English was unaffected. The Maltese children, who were bilingual on arrival, failed to make up much of their deficiency in either oral or written English by two years and, unlike the South American and British children, they tended to become somewhat alienated from Australian society. Thus, the two national groups differed in their academic adjustment.[29]

Factors in the home background of the South Americans were investigated in relation to the children's language acculturation. It was found that the status characteristics of the parents (occupational level, education level, etc.) were poor predictors of the children's competence in English, while process mechanisms within the home environment (press for general learning, press for English language development, press for adaptation to Australia, press for ethnicity maintenance) were more relevant but still quite limited in their effect. The parents who seemed to enhance their children's English language competence were those who, themselves knowing some English upon arrival, set about the learning of English by attending courses and increasing their own competence, and who provided for their children a warm, emotionally supportive environment and suitable educational environment through positive but not over-demanding encouragement and concrete assistance in educational tasks like homework and through the availability of books and other educational aids.

The results of this study could indicate that parents whose coping with their present situation implies a clear goal with realistic strategies, i.e. personal competence, are the ones whose children adapt to the language requirements of Australian schools, rather than the parents who are able to provide a model of competence in English. The children of newly arrived immigrants do not rely on the home for teaching them English directly, but only for providing them with the intellectual resources for tackling the task.

## The Abilities and Achievement of Immigrant Children

In the last decade, the Australian Council for Educational Research has completed two major projects directly related to the academic and linguistic achievement of children from immigrant backgrounds. In a study conducted in 1971, de Lemos gave a battery of tests to a representative sample of primary schoolchildren in Melbourne on the basis of grade levels (Grades 2, 4 and 6) rather than age levels, and conducted lengthy interviews with the immigrant parents.[30] Her major finding was that there were consistent differences in performance between children from English-speaking and non-English-speaking backgrounds at the three grade levels studied. These differences were more marked on the language tests than on the non-verbal and arithmetic tests, and there was some tendency for the differences on non-verbal and arithmetic tests to decrease from Grade 2 to Grade 6, but not those on vocabulary and verbal comprehension tests. It was further found that there were significant differences in both verbal and non-verbal tests between children whose parents had lived in Australia for less than five years and those whose parents had resided in Australia for longer than five years.

Other results showed:

1. a consistent trend, particularly at the Grade 4 and Grade 6 levels, for higher test scores to be associated with greater use of English in the home environment;
2. a difference in most test scores, especially language, for immigrant children from homes where the reading background was higher than immigrant children where the reading background was lower (this last finding was also true of a home environment index based on the physical conditions of the home);
3. higher scores for children from Northern European backgrounds than those from Eastern and Southern Europe — the mean scores of this Northern European group were higher on most of the tests than those of the Anglo-Australian group.

The second major ACER project is Bourke and Keeves's literacy and numeracy study which examined a nation-wide sample of 10- and 14-year-old children.[31] As in de Lemos's study, the use of English at home was related to the students' performance in both reading and numeration tests (Table 2.4). Students with no English spoken in the home performed the worst as a group, while those from homes where English only or English and a Northern European language were spoken did best; the difference in performance between the two groups was greater for fourteen-year-old students than for ten-year-olds. It was largely the students from homes where English and a Southern European language were spoken, or where no English was spoken, who were the most seriously disadvantaged. While mastery by students from immigrant backgrounds was relatively greater in numeration than in reading, mastery of reading in English was correlated with the mastery of number work.

The findings of the ACER, like those of Taft and Cahill,[32] may have more to do with the general resources transmitted by the parents to the children[33] than with the more narrow provision of enculturation in the English language, but this question needs further investigation through the use of other research designs.

Table 2.4: Reading and Number Mastery of Students in Australian Schools

| Languages spoken in the Home | Percentage achieving mastery in each group | | | |
| | 10-year-olds | | 14-year-olds | |
| | Reading | Number | Reading | Number |
|---|---|---|---|---|
| English only | 54 | 76 | 74 | 76 |
| English and Northern European | 52 | 80 | 67 | 75 |
| English and Southern European | 40 | 66 | 53 | 62 |
| English and other | 40 | 64 | 54 | 64 |
| No English | 25 | 54 | 49 | 64 |

Source: This table is a combination of Tables 10.3 and 10.9 in S. Bourke and J. Keeves, *Australian Studies in School Performance: Volume III, The Mastery of Literacy and Numeracy: Final Report* (AGPS, Canberra, 1977).

## Reprise and Assessment of the Immediate Future

In thirty years the orientation of the Australian government and people towards immigration and the integration of immigrants has changed rapidly. These changes have resulted in some reorientations in the education system. In 1948, Australia, for the first time, began to accept the validity of non-British immigration on a large scale and, more recently, of non-European entry into Australia. ESL classes for adults were subsidised by the federal government from the start, although the number of these classes was always insufficient, and in 1970 it was finally accepted that an ESL programme for children should also be developed and supported. The growth of this programme and the diversification of its methods have been dramatic since then, and the demand has rapidly changed from transitional ESL programmes for newly arrived children to remedial and enrichment programmes for second-generation children. It seems likely that it will be realised more and more that the demand for an expansion of the latter programmes is asking for something which is not specifically a problem for immigration authorities, and that language remediation and enrichment should be available across the curriculum for all schoolchildren irrespective of their origin. Transition programmes will, however, continue in one form or another for newly arrived children, including the increased use of intensive courses, especially at secondary school level, possibly with more use being made of bilingual teachers, although practical considerations will be a limiting factor.

The future of other aspects of education in a multicultural society is less clear even though multiculturalism has now been officially adopted as government policy. There is little doubt that programmes aimed at the learning and maintenance of some of the languages of the immigrant communities will be expanded, but whether this will produce the effect of maintaining the language is debatable, due to resistance by the school system and suspicion by some members of the ethnic communities that first language maintenance may be detrimental to English language development. To what extent this movement will affect the monolingual Anglo-Australians remains to be seen, since foreign language teaching is a contracting rather than an expanding part of the curriculum.

Yet, the response of many primary and secondary schools to the needs of the heterogeneous school populations has not moved beyond the ESL stage. The interest in bilingual education in some quarters has been real but, notwithstanding some interest by schools in the idea, Quinn found in a recent survey 'not a single programme of serious bilingual education'.[34] The constant reiteration of closer co-operation between the 'trinity' of home, school and child in the case of immigrant families is often viewed as either too difficult or as a waste of time, even though the employment of bilingual aides has alleviated the situation to a limited extent. At the tertiary level, the universities have displayed a marked reluctance to establish departments in the languages of the more recently arrived immigrant groups, especially in those languages and cultures that are more distant from the mainstream Anglo-Australian culture.

Moreover, educationists, especially at the lower levels of decision making, remain confused and unsure about the exact nature of education in a multicultural society. For some, it is basically a renewed and vigorous ESL programme aimed at all children from non-English homes; for some who are imbued with a folk interpretation of culture, it is merely the study of Italian cuisine, Greek dancing, Turkish customs, etc.; and for others, it involves nothing more than the study of the history and geography of the countries from which immigrants have come. Educational programmes and resource materials have been designed and taught on the basis of these three alternative but shallow conceptions of multiculturalism which Geneva Gay has fittingly called 'benevolent multiculturalism'.[35]

Because the concept is so often interpreted in this narrow way, Bullivant has now denounced the term as conceptually bankrupt.

Neglected or glossed over are the low socio-economic positions of many ethnics, their lack of access to social rewards and economic resources, the prejudice and discrimination shown towards them by the dominant host society, and similar power-conflict issues.[36]

This review of the conceptualisation of multiculturalism raises some intriguing questions, but our inquiry suggests that the ambiguities associated with a multicultural policy call for a radical rethinking of the whole structure of the school system in relation to the community and of the ways in which the school and home can become better integrated.

As the research reviewed in this chapter seems to indicate, except for three groups which seem to be at greater risk than others — children from certain national backgrounds, children of low IQ from low SES background and newly arrived immigrant adolescents — children from immigrant families, on the whole, adapt to the social and intellectual demands of their schools by playing the game according to the rules set down by the Anglo-Australian majority. They have high educational aspirations and some success in projecting themselves into middle-class occupations, mainly through higher education. Consequently, even though they may well eventually abandon their cultural and linguistic heritage or lose any strong identification with their ethnic communities, they will take their place in the general Australian society. It remains to be seen whether the rapid developments of the past decade in the educational sphere will lead to greater numbers of bicultural individuals who will be at home with both their own ethnic origins and the wider Australian community.

It is our belief that children from non-English-speaking communities will be educationally treated more and more as an integral part of a heterogeneous society rather than as immigrants who need special support and attention simply because they are immigrants. The transitional needs of newly arrived immigrant families will, of course, continue to be met through special programmes largely outside of special multicultural programmes, but the latter will become more universal. The educational remediation, welfare services and special curricula that are being developed at present for members of ethnic communities will eventually come to be seen as but a special part of the over-all services provided for the general Australian population.

# Notes

1.   R. Taft, 'Australian Attitudes to Immigrants', in *Australia's Multicultural Society*, La Trobe University, Meredith Memorial Lectures (La Trobe University, Melbourne, 1978).

2.   *The Age*, November 1977.

3.   Taft, 'Australian Attitudes to Immigrants', p. 19.

4.   J. Martin and P. Meade, *The Educational Experience of Sydney High School Students* (AGPS, Canberra, 1979), Report no. 1.

5.   J. Martin, 'The Education of Immigrant Children in Australia, 1945-1975', in C. Price and J. Martin (eds), *Australian Immigration: a Bibliography and Digest* (AGPS, Canberra, 1975), no. 3, Part 2, p. 12.

6.   *First Report on the Progress of Migrant Children in Australia* (Commonwealth Immigration Advisory Council, Canberra, 1960).

7.   Martin, 'The Education of Immigrant Children', p. 36.

8.   *Report of the Committee on Teaching of Migrant Languages in Schools* (AGPS, Canberra, 1976).

9.   J.J. Smolicz, 'Ethnic Cultures in Australian Society: a Question of Cultural Interaction', in *Melbourne Studies in Education* (Melbourne University Press, Melbourne, 1976).

10.   *Melbourne Studies in Education.*

11.   B. Bullivant, 'Education for the Polyethnic Society', *The Forum of Education*, vol. 36 (1977), pp. 27-31.

12.   D. Cahill, 'Dialectical Polyethnicity: A Contemporary Model to Understand Ethnic Interaction and Culture Contact', *Ethnic Studies*, vol. 1 (1977), pp. 1-13.

13.   *Report of the Inquiry into Schools of High Migrant Density: 1974 Study Based on Schools Selected in New South Wales and Victoria* (Australian Department of Education, 1975).

14.   *Report of the Committee on Teaching of Migrant Languages in Schools* (Australian Department of Education, AGPS, Canberra, 1976).

15.   *Australia as a Multicultural Society* (Australian Ethnic Affairs Council, AGPS, Canberra, 1977).

16.   F. Galbally *et al.*, *Migrant Services and Programs* (AGPS, Canberra, 1978).

17.   Report of the Committee on Multicultural Education to the Schools Commission, *Education for a Multicultural Society* (Canberra, February 1979).

18.   M. Rado, 'Bilingual Education', in L. Claydon, T. Knight and M. Rado, *Curriculum and Culture* (George Allen and Unwin, Sydney, 1977).

19.   W. Bostock, 'Monolingualism in Australia', *Australian Quarterly*, vol. 45 (1973), pp. 39-52.

20.   L. Claydon, *Renewing Urban Teaching* (Cambridge University Press, London, 1973).

21.   P. Nicoll, *Directions for Research in Migrant Education* (Commonwealth Department of Education, Canberra, 1977).

22.   W.F. Connell, R. Stroobart, K. Sinclair, R. Connell and K. Rogers, *12-20: Studies of City Youth* (Hicks Smith, Sydney, 1975).

23.   R. Taft, 'The Career Aspirations of Immigrant School Children in Victoria', *La Trobe Sociology Papers, no. 12* (Department of Sociology, La Trobe University, Melbourne, 1975).

24.   Connell *et al.*, *Studies of City Youth.*

25.   Martin and Meade, *The Educational Experience of Sydney High School Students.*

26.   Ibid., p. 19.

27.   Ibid., p. 18.

28. R. Taft and D. Cahill, *The Initial Adjustment of Schooling of Immigrant Families* (AGPS, Canberra, 1978).

29. Martin and Meade, *The Educational Experience of Sydney High School Students.*

30. M. de Lemos, *Study of the Educational Achievement of Migrant Children* (Australian Council for Educational Research, Melbourne, 1975).

31. S. Bourke and J. Keeves, *Australian Studies in School Performance: Volume III, The Mastery of Literacy and Numeracy: Final Report* (AGPS, Canberra, 1977).

32. Taft and Cahill, *The Initial Adjustment to Schooling of Immigrant Families.*

33. T. Kotler and S. Hammond, 'The Outcomes of Resource Use in Migrant Families', *Human Relations*, vol. 28 (1975), pp. 49-62.

34. T. Quinn, 'Second Language Acquisition Research in Australia: Perspectives and Directions', paper prepared for the Education Research and Development Committee, Australia, 1979.

35. G. Gay, 'Changing Conceptions of Multicultural Education: Educational Perspectives', *Journal of the College of Education*, vol. 16 (University of Hawaii, 1977), pp. 49.

36. B. Bullivant, 'The Challenge of Pluralism for Australian Education', paper delivered at the University of Tasmania, 1979.

# 3 SOCIAL, PERSONAL AND ACADEMIC ADJUSTMENT OF ETHNIC MINORITY PUPILS IN BRITISH SCHOOLS

**Gajendra K. Verma and Kanka Mallick**

The termination of Britain's colonial empire has resulted in quite fundamental social and economic changes which could not have been foreseen before 1947. However, it became clear soon after the Second World War that Britain could no longer remain an imperialist power. During its colonial rule, Britain has been responsible for the forced migration of slaves from Africa to the Caribbean and for the migration of workers from India to Africa and the Caribbean. Tinker has shown that the lot of these workers was hardly better than that of slaves.[1] It was not anticipated that some day large numbers of workers from the former colonial territories would actually undertake voluntary migration to Britain.

Before 1961, migration to Britain from the former colonial territories was unrestricted. But the traces of the ideology of colonialism still remained in the minds of some sections of the British population. Although there are countervailing indices, it would be hard to resist the proposition that British social policy has become markedly racist over the past two decades, a trend reflected not only in the legislation governing immigration, but in the changing rhetoric of political party spokesmen. Labour Party views, in particular, have moved steadily to the right in pursuit of electoral safety, a process convincingly documented by Moore.[2] Party differences have narrowed as they compete for a kind of middle-ground stance which Downing and Schlesinger scathingly term 'reasonable racism'.[3] However, the reactionary forces in British politics were successful in persuading both Labour and Conservative governments to implement restrictive policies. In recent years, entry permits have been issued to those people from the Indian subcontinent who have professional qualifications, e.g. doctors. Immigration visas have also been granted, no doubt reluctantly, to refugees of Asian origin who were expelled from Uganda in 1972. Before the strict immigration controls were introduced between 1962 and 1971, workers from the West Indies, Pakistan and India were allowed to come to Britain in order to fill the semi-skilled and unskilled jobs which the indigenous workers were not keen to tackle. A large majority

47

of these people work in factories, especially in the textile industry. It is interesting to note that professional people from the Indian subcontinent, particularly doctors, are still granted visas but on a smaller scale.

Britain is only beginning, it seems, to come to terms with the fact of multi-ethnicity and cultural diversity. Because the majority of migrants who came to Britain in the sixties were young (and therefore fertile), there is each year an increasing number of children from ethnic minority groups in British schools. Due to such population changes, the characteristics of the school population in many parts of the country have undergone considerable change. Today, children of various ethnic minority groups are found throughout the English school system. Bullock rightly comments that 'many schools in multi-cultural areas turn a blind eye to the fact that the community they serve has radically altered over the last ten years and is now one in which new cultures are represented'.[4] What this effectively means is that Britain is becoming an increasingly multiracial and multi-ethnic society, and in schools the cultural and ethnic mix in terms of religious, cultural and racial background is very diverse.

It should be mentioned that, generally speaking, whenever a reference is made to the immigrant communities in Britain, the explicit assumption is that the reference is to the 'coloured' immigrants — blacks and browns — that is, those who have come from 'New Commonwealth' countries in the Caribbean, India, Pakistan and Bangladesh. Britain's coloured population is less than 3.5 per cent of the total and of these just over 40 per cent are West Indians and most of the rest are Asians. Nearly three-quarters of the Asians and West Indians are concentrated in the urban areas of the West Midlands and Greater London.[5] According to census estimates, the total estimated number of immigrants is in the region of nearly three million. Of these, about 50 per cent are white immigrants from Europe, the Old Commonwealth and Ireland. The other half have come from the New Commonwealth countries of the West Indies, Asia, Africa and Southeast Asia. The number of New Commonwealth immigrants now living in Britain is estimated to be as follows: Asians, 618,000; West Indians, 236,000; Africans, 30,000. The forces which brought migrants from the West Indies and the Indian subcontinent appear to have been the lack of employment and economic opportunity in their home countries, the availability of jobs in the UK and the active recruitment of black and Asian workers by some industries in Britain.

Government policy on immigration to Britain in the post-war years has changed from *laissez-faire* to the strict and often selective control of certain immigrant groups. There has always been a hard core of racism in British society which has advocated the suppression, control and eventual repatriation of all non-whites.[6] Many hold a broadly assimilationist policy, suggesting that immigrants will be accepted but only if they conform to British custom and way of life and give up their 'alien custom' of dress, language and religion. A minority of the population, however, take a liberal view advocating a pluralistic society, suggesting that Britain should not completely assimilate New Commonwealth immigrants but should allow them autonomy in regard to dress, customs and religion, which are basic human rights. They strongly argue that the immigrant groups bring with them new perspectives which are of positive value to British society.

There seems to be a paradox in the assimilationist policy. The West Indians are closer to British culture and institutions, yet they have suffered considerable discrimination in education, employment and housing. Similarly, young Asians who were educated totally in Britain and who speak perfect English have been the target of discrimination in many spheres of life. For example, in a recent survey of graduates in engineering at universities and polytechnics in Leeds and Manchester, it was found that Indians who had received all their education in Britain still found great difficulty in finding employment as compared to their white peers.[7] This continued rejection has created considerable feelings of alienation and resentment on the part of young West Indians, Indians and Pakistanis.[8] Thus, the responses of the indigenous community have been, on the whole, a critical stiffness and non-acceptance.

It is widely accepted that multicultural education faces a variety of problems including those presented by multilingualism, cultural differences between various groups and between pupils and teachers, adverse social pressures from the declining urban environments in which many ethnic minorities are forced to live, poor interethnic relationships in the school and the impact of widespread racial discrimination upon pupils in multiracial schools. In view of these and other problems, various kinds of questions are often raised with regard to the social, personal and academic adjustment of ethnic minority pupils. These problems of adjustment can only be fully understood by reference to social and cultural backgrounds.

## Social and Cultural Backgrounds of Asian and West Indian Communities

### The Asian Community

The term 'Asian' has been used to signify people mainly from the Indian subcontinent, i.e. India, Pakistan and Bangladesh (formerly East Pakistan), but the term also includes East African Asians.

The Asian immigration to Britain was at its peak in the sixties. The poor prospects for jobs in their own countries motivated Asians to migrate to Britain. The high wages for unskilled labour in Britain provided one of the chief attractions. The East African Asians came to live in Britain because the Africanisation programmes forced the Asian community to leave East Africa. The vast majority of the early Asian immigrants were young men who had left their families and dependants behind. Most of these people were unskilled and had no proficiency in English. They found the hardest and least well-paid jobs in the big industrial cities; these jobs had no promotion prospects and had been abandoned by the native white working men. When they had settled down to their jobs they brought their families over to England, and this has led to the growth of large minority communities in some cities. One of the contributing factors in the increasing tendency to settle and call for families was the legislation controlling immigration. It is worth mentioning here that more than half of the Asian children are British born and have never seen their parents' country of origin.

The number of Asians in Britain is approximately one million. The majority of Indians in Britain are Hindu by religion; some are Sikh. The Pakistani (and also Bangladeshi) people differ in that they are Muslim. In many respects the social and cultural background of Pakistanis and Bangladeshis is not all that different from Indians. The main language groups of the Asian community are Gujarati, Punjabi, Urdu, Bengali and Hindi. Thus, several ideologies and value systems are represented in the Asian group. Another characteristic of the Asian immigrants is the limited extent of the areas from which they have originated. The two northwestern states of Punjab and Gujarat in India and about a half-dozen areas in the combined Pakistan and Bangladesh area have contributed the bulk of Asian immigrants.

The traditional family system in the Indian subcontinent is the joint/extended family, which plays an important role in the life of an individual in the community. Because of the nature of migration and immigration restrictions, the Asian extended family system in Britain is less common than in the country of origin. Nevertheless, where these networks exist, they can provide valuable support for the individual's personal and cultural identity. Any migrant groups who come to settle in a new country have some difficulty in adjusting to a new way of life. Asians in Britain, however, face particular problems because of their strong adherence to their own religion, language, customs and traditions.

*The West Indian Community*

The West Indians form the largest single group of New Commonwealth immigrants in Britain. English spoken with a particular dialect is the mother tongue of most of the West Indians. In many ways West Indians have been strongly Anglicised even before coming to England. They were the most assimilationist of all the coloured immigrants in the sense that they perceived England as their mother country and, unlike other ethnic groups they did not feel that they had to come to terms with an alien culture. In fact, they were least prepared of all the immigrant groups to meet prejudice and hostility in British society.

In the decade 1950 to 1960, when Britain was desperately short of unskilled labour, West Indian migration was at its height. They occupied the same sector of the labour market as did the Asian migrants. In the face of discrimination which operates in many spheres (employment, housing and social relations), the reaction of many blacks from the Caribbean has been one of alienation.[9]

## Problems of Adjustment of Ethnic Minority Children: Social, Personal and Educational

A glance through the literature reveals an endless list of meanings assigned to the term 'adjustment'. There is considerable overlap between the various meanings emphasised by different writers and, hence, the theories connected with them are ambiguous. However, one of the theoretical conceptualisations associated with the term 'adjustment' refers to feelings of being in harmony with one's environment — although this does not necessarily imply that the outlook of the person and his social environment are identical. The most widely used criterion with which to determine an individual's adjustment to his environment is his satisfaction with various aspects of life.[10] Immigrants in any society face many kinds of social, personal and educational problems. Adult migrants face problems mainly in the areas of housing, employment and education. They also experience processes of resocialisation that may result in changed patterns of behaving and living, or in adherence to traditional beliefs and practices. Some changes at the levels of personality and social relationships are also involved in migration.[11]

The processes of socialisation and resocialisation are viewed somewhat differently in the case of the children of immigrants. Although they face similar problems of adjustment to those faced by their parents, they do not have the same level of confidence and maturity.

The problem of identity, particularly evident in young Asians, is now of increasing concern to educationists and social workers in Britain. There is now more resistance to the simplistic views of assimilation or integration which pervaded official British thinking in the 1960s. Although this school of thought remains important, the idea of plural accommodation, as reflected in multicultural education, seems to be gaining ground. The hard core of racism also survives, as can be seen in the racial riots of East London and Southall.

The most difficult problem for black and Asian children seems to be their identity development. They face hostility and discrimination from the indigenous population in many aspects of life, prejudices that their parents have experienced and perhaps tolerated. The second-generation youngsters, however, are not prepared to accept discrimination as an inevitable part of British society. Because of stressful experiences in the process of socialisation — both at school and in a wider society — they may be baffled about their self-identity, and often they ask questions such as, 'Am I English or not?', 'Am I a West Indian?', 'Am I a Pakistani?'. They begin to cast doubts on their identity and may even deny the reality of their skin colour and their place in the community. The confusion and conflict of identity of immigrant children has been described by Milner in his book *Children and Race*.[12] He conducted an experiment with 300 children, aged five to eight years. They were shown dolls or pictures, one representing their own racial group and the other the dominant group in the immediate environment. When asked the question, 'Which doll looks most like you?', 48 per cent of the West Indian children and 24 per cent of the Asian children chose the white doll. It is interesting to note that 58 per cent of the West Indian children and 45 per cent of the Asian children maintained that the doll that looked like them was 'bad', and 82 per cent and 77 per cent said the doll that looked like them was 'ugly'; 78 per cent and 48 per cent respectively felt the white doll was the 'nicer' of the two. Milner, on the basis of his study, concluded that black British children generally show a strong preference for the dominant white group and a tendency to devalue their own group.

The realisation and recognition of the identity and culture of the ethnic minority children are not only important to the child's self-image, his intellectual functioning and social behaviour, but also crucial for his occupational and social adjustment.

The initiative in this direction has come from the European Economic Community, of which Britain is now a member. The EEC has emphasised the importance of giving instruction to the children of migrants in their traditional language, incorporating their culture and religion. To incorporate this policy, experiments supported by the EEC are being carried out in some British schools, but there is still resistance from British teachers to the widespread acceptance of this policy.[13] The Netherlands have long practised a policy of pluralism, giving particular attention to the cultural autonomy and personal identity of ethnic minority groups. This policy has been based on the assumption that pluralism is necessary not only as a basis for tolerance but also as a means of ensuring that the minority groups are socially happy, healthy and hard working. Bagley, in a study of the Dutch plural society, has shown that identity and cultural conflicts diminish the capacity of any group for successful economic and social adaptation.[14]

## Children of Immigrants in British Schools

Changed characteristics of the school population in recent years have posed challenges for both teachers and educational planners, problems which they have not always been willing to face. Although pupils with New Commonwealth backgrounds constitute a small proportion of the total school population in Britain as a whole, their concentration in certain urban areas tends to account for a large proportion of ethnic minority children in many schools. A survey by Townsend and Brittan[15] showed that these children constituted approximately 3.3 per cent of the total school population in the country, on the basis of a definition provided by the Department of Education and Science. The figure included those who came with their parents, those who came later and, more recently, growing numbers born in Britain. This proportion will continue to rise because of the younger age structure of the immigrant population. As indicated earlier, there has been a steady increase in the number of West Indian children attending English schools. A few of these came with their parents from the West Indies, many others joined one or both parents already settled here and a large majority were born here. A common factor among most West Indian children is poor housing, since their parents tend to live in multiple-occupied houses where facilities have to be shared or are absent. The deprivation of the West Indian population lies in their experience of overcrowding and sharing of houses, their high unemployment levels and concentration in manual jobs, their low incomes and their lack of educational qualifications. A report by the Community Relations Commission states that

the frustration experienced by West Indians at their inability to compete on equal terms in Britain due to colour prejudice and their lack of acceptance by the white community leads to a lack of confidence and rigidity on the part of the older generation in enforcing West Indian standards.[16]

There is research evidence that a high proportion of West Indian mothers rely on substitute care for their children from an early period.[17] This seems to be related to their home circumstances. Most West Indian mothers work to raise family income and to support children and this leads to problems of child care. The West Indian mother's choice of a babysitter is not determined by the number of children the sitter has in her care (and all that this implies), but largely by the price charged. As babysitting conditions have far-reaching effects on the child's future progress at school, poor environmental stimulation limits the West Indian child's ability for language development and acquisition of ideas and concepts that he or she will encounter in the classroom at the age of five. The West Indian child who spends his pre-school years receiving inadequate intellectual stimulation is representative of the culturally deprived children mentioned by Pringle who 'have lost the race long before starting school'.[18] Lack of emotional stimulation is an even greater hazard for West Indian children.[19]

A report given to a conference in London, organised by the World Organization for Early Childhood Education, drew attention to the fact that an increasing number of West Indian children were referred to the Psychiatry Department of Kings College Hospital and other child guidance clinics suffering from a condition which resembles autism.[20] Further investigations of those cases showed that the symptoms of aloofness, apathy and little or no speech reflected maternal deprivation and lack of emotional and intellectual stimulation. The West Indian children are subjected, on the one hand, to a high degree of stress and, on the other, to lack of opportunity and unequal treatment in the wider British society; they become confused in their identity and may develop poor self-esteem.[21] We can propose a number of reasons for this, among them biases in the school system, linguistic factors, family difficulties, the educational background of the parents and cultural conflicts within a wider society — all these factors seem to contribute to underachievement among children of West Indian parents. The Inner London Education Authority, when testing the reading standards of ten-year-old children, found that West Indian children had a mean reading score four points below the mean for children of indigenous unskilled workers.[22] The poor performance of many West Indian children in London schools is of great concern to the West Indian community as well as to the government, and reflects the multiple deprivations that many West Indian families suffer.

A more recent study by Driver seems to contradict the common view that the general level of school achievement among all West Indian pupils is consistently low.[23] The results of his study with secondary school pupils indicated that West Indian girls do well in CSE examinations and their level of motivation is remarkably high. Further, his results showed that social pressures within the West Indian community have played an important role in the educational difficulties and underachievements among West Indian boys. These difficulties were intensified by teachers who failed both to appreciate what the boys and their families expected of them and often to discern and respond adequately to the expressed concerns of such pupils in their classroom.

The second-generation Asians, like the West Indians, are going or already have gone through the British educational system. They were either born in Britain or joined their parents as young dependants. The majority of young Asians who came as dependants are from rural areas of the Indian subcontinent; and coming from India to Britain, from a simple way of life in a village to a modern technologically advanced urban area, can be a traumatic experience for many of them. Some but by no means all Asian immigrants have language and communication problems and fewer qualifications for good employment. Those who speak little English tend to be employed in manual jobs with low income. These people minimise their language disadvantage by living in areas with a high concentration of fellow countrymen. This tends to reinforce the Asian patterns of living in extended families with large numbers of dependants. One important factor for children learning English at schools is what language they speak at home. Some educationists are of the opinion that any language used at home other than English hinders the process of learning English at school. This applies especially to Asian children, because most of them speak their mother tongue at home instead of English. A study of language proficiency in a multiracial junior school for children aged seven to eleven years showed that Asian children who spoke some English at home had a distinct advantage in terms of general language skills and scholastic achievement over those who had never or had hardly ever done so.[24] A more recent view is that Asian children should speak their traditional language first, as a means of fostering identity, with gradual introduction to English. This has been a policy for many years in

Wales, and there are now a number of mother tongue teaching projects in languages such as Punjabi, Gujarati and Italian.

A recent report by the Community Relations Commission stated that West Indians were more disadvantaged than Asians because of a less secure sense of identity and an increased cultural confusion.[25] However, both West Indian and Asian youngsters were considered to be at a considerable disadvantage, being caught between their minority cultural origins and their experiences of growing up in a white racist society.

## Academic Achievement of Ethnic Minority Pupils

The findings of many studies and research reports clearly imply that the British educational system has failed to meet the needs of ethnic minority children, has ignored their linguistic backgrounds and strengths and has discriminated against them in various ways. This fact has resulted in an increasing alienation of such children from the British school system, a decline in academic attainment and an increasingly aggressive outlook towards a social system which is rightly seen as profoundly racist.[26] The evidence of racism can be seen in many aspects of life. At least half the population in Britain expresses prejudiced attitudes to a serious degree,[27] and there is a considerable amount of racial discrimination based not on foreignness but on colour of skin.[28] Schools discriminate by transferring disproportionate numbers of ethnic minority pupils, mainly West Indians, to schools for the educationally subnormal and by allocating them in disproportionate numbers to lower streams in secondary schools. It is true that in the primary school some children of West Indian parents do not achieve well at the initial stages. Because of the children's poor performance, teachers come to have negative perceptions and low expectations of them and may, in turn, teach them in uninteresting ways. This 'teacher expectation effect' has been established by many well-designed studies in America,[29] and obviously exists in British schools.[30] Children react negatively to negative labels; but poor achievement and poor behaviour are seen by the teachers as confirmations of their initial negative expectations. Prejudices of teachers have been documented in many studies.[31] Although the social background factors of black children are responsible for their initial poor performance in British schools, their future status in society is progressively moulded through the negative and prejudiced attitudes of teachers who fail to meet the linguistic and cultural needs of many black children. In secondary schools, ethnic minority pupils become more aware of the real nature of a society which discriminates strongly against black people. They begin to question the value of acquiring qualifications which are probably useless as long as employers practise racial discrimination in employment selection.

Previous work on the academic achievement of ethnic minority pupils in English schools showed the following pattern: immigrant pupils were either concentrated in the lower streams, or, in the case of West Indians, were over-represented in schools for educationally subnormal children, or did less well academically than white pupils, or scored lower on intelligence or ability tests. Perhaps the only exception to this pattern is Houghton's finding which showed that there was no significant difference in the test scores of black and white pupils, both groups coming from deprived backgrounds.[32] Further, he found that both were significantly underfunctioning relative to national norms for the test. In a partial replication of this study, Bagley administered the Stanford-Binet test to a group of black and white pupils aged seven to ten in English schools.[33] Subjects were specially selected for stability and quality of home background, the underlying hypothesis being that black children who came from stable working-class or lower-middle-class homes would not be intellectually disadvantaged. Both black and white children tested had IQ levels above those expected from the national norms, suggesting that social disadvantage rather than race was the major factor in underachievement. A major difficulty of assessment in multiracial schools is that most of the tests are culturally/ethnically biased against ethnic minority groups because of language difficulties, unfamiliarity with the subject-matter, or the form of testing.[34] For example, tests of intelligence, aptitude and personality are constructed and standardised for one particular ethnic group but are used for other ethnic and racial groups.[35] Generalisations from the results of these tests have often given rise to a wide variety of misleading interpretations, especially when these results are interpreted by those who have little understanding of the populations. Further research from the Inner London Education Authority has shown that length of education in England is more important in determining primary school achievement than either length of residence in Britain or being born in Britain.[36] Yet there is also evidence that, even with full education in England, the achievement of West Indian pupils is significantly below that of the indigenous white population. Little concluded that the levels of achievement of West Indian pupils could be improved by the implementation of special programmes of education beginning in the pre-school period. Wiles's study of a boys' comprehensive school in South London found that, of the coloured immigrant children who had their entire education in Britain, a somewhat higher proportion was in the top stream than was the case with the native children, but that those who did not have their entire education in Britain were overwhelmingly in the bottom two streams.[37]

There is some evidence of increasing acculturation for Asian families when their length of residence in Britain is longer. This is reflected in the increased scholastic performance of Asian pupils, particularly at the secondary school level. Durojaiye, in a study of Manchester, found that, if the mother in an Asian family had a knowledge of English, this was most likely to be associated with an efficient command of English in her children, a necessary prerequisite for the high level of scholastic achievement which many of these Asian children manifested.[38]

Ghuman's study with Punjabi Sikhs in Birmingham and Nottingham demonstrated that Punjabi children who have had full schooling in England showed a similar pattern of abilities to those of their English counterparts.[39] Their educational performance, as suggested by Ghuman, is due to school-based educational experiences. What was most striking in his results is that the cognitive functioning of the Punjabi boys in Birmingham was much closer to that of their English counterparts than it was to the cognitive functioning of boys in Punjab. Ghuman explains these differences in terms of social environment. His sample from Punjab lived in a rural environment where the social system is based on face-to-face interaction, the network of relationships is limited and the communication is mostly direct. Consequently, there are relatively fewer demands placed on the children to use abstract styles of thinking. In contrast, children in the British educational system, including the children of Punjabi migrants in Birmingham, receive an education which is intellectually much broader than that of a rural education in India, a kind of education which prepares pupils to adopt a wide variety of roles in society. Dove conducted a survey among 15- and 16-year-old pupils at three London comprehensive schools to find out 'how do immigrant school leavers see their future in terms of further education, training and jobs?'.[40] In all, 545 boys and girls took part in the inquiry, which included both first- and second-generation immigrants. She reported that the Asian pupils more often stated that they enjoyed school than did the West Indian and white teenagers. She also found that the Asian and West Indian pupils set a high value on acquiring paper qualifications – in some cases higher than their white counterparts. More whites than immigrants were eager to leave school as soon as possible without taking examinations. The results showed that more than 90 per cent of the Asians and 80 per cent of the West Indians wanted to take CSE or 'O' level GCE, while as many as 63 per cent of the Asians wanted to stay on at school until they had 'A' levels.[41] These findings clearly suggest that children of immigrant parents are willing to work hard to achieve occupational success. Writing about the implications of her research findings, Dove comments: 'It also helps to cast doubt on the racial stereotype of the fun-loving, indolent West Indian, thrown at the bottom of the occupational ladder because he is unwilling to strive for success.'[42]

The findings of the studies outlined above seem to indicate that, given the right kind of educational experiences, children from traditional societies are capable of developing the mental abilities which are valued by contemporary Western society.

We may speculate that Asian children going through the British educational system come to acquire not only Western styles of cognition, but also many of the prevalent attitudes and values of the society in which they have settled. A study by Taylor has thrown some light on this aspect.[43] His sample of investigation consisted of Punjabi boys in their adolescent years, most of whom had grown up in the northern English city of Newcastle-on-Tyne. The youngsters in Taylor's study were fluent in English, although they spoke Punjabi at home with their parents. In school they were strongly motivated to succeed and they performed at a higher scholastic level than their English counterparts. Their parents had a strong psychological orientation to Punjab, their country of origin, but their children stood half-way between traditional Punjabi culture and British culture (Taylor titled his study, *The Halfway Generation*). In a comparison of the cultural assimilation of different religious groups among the Punjabi sample, Taylor found that Hindus and Sikhs had made the most cultural transition, while Muslims had made very little. His respondents were of the opinion that they did not wish to give up their Punjabi identity, but they did want to liberalise the traditional village and family regime. The findings of Taylor's study clearly suggest that the second-generation Asians, while accepting many English cultural values, still wish to retain their strong family ties.

## Self-esteem of Pupils in Multi-ethnic Schools

The term self-esteem is frequently used in discussions about multi-ethnic education, but often without reference to empirical studies. However, if the concept of multi-ethnic education has any significance, it must refer to self-esteem levels of minority groups, for it is ultimately bound up with the individual's behaviour and attitudes in many areas of inter-personal relationships. Self-esteem is largely an evaluative dimension, measuring how the individual feels about himself and about himself in relation to others. Self-esteem is defined as the extent to which an individual has positive feelings towards himself, particularly with respect to achievement and social relationships. Self-esteem develops through interaction with others and is likely to be reflected in the individual's behaviour. Self-esteem is a crucial and pivotal concept in understanding multi-ethnic interactions. The assumption is that in multi-ethnic schools particular levels of self-esteem may emerge both from interactions and from the structural organisation of schools. Coopersmith, writing about self-concept, suggests that individuals not only form mental pictures of themselves; they also develop feelings and attitudes about the quality and content of that image. 'The self-concept is the symbol or the image which the person has formed out of his personal experiences, while self-esteem is the person's evaluation of that image.'[44]

The studies of self-esteem and related concepts with respect of minority adolescents in British schools have produced interesting but sometimes contradictory findings. In part, this could be due to the different methods of measuring self-esteem. It could also be due to specific factors in the school and community which influence self-esteem in particular ways. Our own study, looking at the levels of self-esteem of the three major ethnic groups in British schools, may be particularly valuable in obtaining a more comprehensive over-all picture of the self-esteem of blacks and Asian pupils.[45] In all, some 1,900 pupils aged 14 to 16, belonging to various ethnic groups in 39 schools in London, the Midlands and the North of England, were studied. Details of this research programme are published elsewhere.[46]

The 39 schools involved in the programme ranged from heavily multiracial schools to schools in rural counties of rather static and homogeneous population. We were not researching multiracial education as such, but education within a multiracial society.

A large battery of tests was administered before the teaching began and after it had ended. The results of this study are reported else-where.[47] For the purpose of this paper we examined the results of the questionnaire. Approximately 1,000 pupils belonging to the three ethnic groups were studied. Of these 1,000, 141 were black (West

Indian) and 137 were Asian pupils. In the analysis, first of all, profiles of the self-esteem characteristics of the three ethnic groups were compared. The results showed that, in general, self-esteem levels of Asian pupils do not differ significantly from those of their white counterparts. With regard to the comparison of self-esteem between black and white pupils, the black boys have significantly poorer self-esteem than their white counterparts: the mean self-esteem score for black boys is 22.35, standard deviation of 10.62; for the white boys, 17.65, SD 9.64 (a higher score on the Coopersmith scale indicates poor self-esteem). The difference between the black girls and the white girls is not significant, however: the mean score for black girls is 18.67, SD 10.39, and for the white girls, 18.94, SD 10.13. It is interesting to note that the black girls have significantly better self-esteem than have black boys. The over-all patterns indicated that white and Asian groups were closer with respect to their self-esteem profile than they were to the black group. Also, Asian and white groups had higher levels of self-esteem than the black pupils.

Further analysis of data was carried out to explore levels of self-esteem in Asian and black pupils in relation to their proportions in the school classes. No significant difference was obtained in the case of Asian pupils — their self-esteem was independent of ethnic concentration. The results showed that the self-esteem of black male pupils did vary with ethnic concentration, being highest in classes with middle levels of concentration (between 10 and 25 per cent blacks). The self-esteem of black girls was highest in classes with high levels of concentration (more than 30 per cent blacks) and poorest in lower levels of concentration (less than 10 per cent blacks).

The results of this study showed that the level of self-esteem in male blacks in particular is below those of female blacks, Asians and whites. This poor self-esteem may be a result of an historical situation in which the ravages of slavery have led to a matriarchal and authoritarian family system which devalues males and also to the continuance of severe racial discrimination against black males in many spheres of life. For example, McIntosh and Smith found that male blacks applying for junior clerical posts were discriminated against in 48 per cent of cases; female blacks applying for similar posts were discriminated against in 22 per cent of cases.[48] The knowledge of racial discrimination in society filters to the schools and depresses motivation and increases alienation.

If our sample represented a fair picture of the teenagers in multi-ethnic schools, the findings of this study may have a number of implications for multi-ethnic education. In the multi-ethnic schools, particular levels of self-esteem may emerge from the interactions and the structural organisation of the school. The school can modify or enhance particular levels of self-esteem.

In the real world of the classroom, pupils of various ethnic groups navigate a careful journey through the narrow straits of community feelings. Still, the fate of multicultural education in Britain seems to be one of promise and fulfilment. Pupils from ethnic minority groups do not need to bargain away their identity to pay the price of an adequate education. The school is in command of those factors which can contribute to harmonious, multicultural, multi-ethnic classes, by means of such strategies as training and working closely with parents and the community. This, in turn, can exert an important influence on self-esteem. In a racist society, the multi-ethnic classroom seems to be one of the few places able to exert such an influence.

Some of the pupils in the 39 schools involved in a study of curriculum strategies designed to change racial attitudes did not in fact show any favourable attitude change. We found that a group of variables — alienation from school and teachers, poor academic achievement, jaundiced view of life and poor self-esteem — was associated with this resistance to classroom teaching. Put another way, it is those pupils who have adequate levels of self-esteem and who are not alienated from school and teachers who are most likely to benefit from teaching about race relations. Highly prejudiced pupils tend to be resistant to such teaching, and perhaps for them an individualised approach, involving counselling which is not directly related to their racist attitudes but to the underlying social and psychological problems which are at the root of their prejudiced attitudes, is needed.

The relationship between prejudice and self-esteem in ethnic minority groups in British schools is more complex. Although we have constructed what appears to be a valid scale of anti-white attitudes, it is not clear whether expression of anti-white attitudes is a function of personal maladaptation or a realisation that the sources of racism and discrimination in British society are the attitudes and behaviours of white people.[49] We have found a significant correlation between poor self-esteem and anti-white attitudes in West Indian males; but in West Indian females the relationship is significant in the opposite direction. In other words, black girls with high levels of self-esteem tend to be anti-white, while the opposite is true for black males. Hypothetically, the attitudes of these high self-esteem girls might be said to be based on an objective appraisal of the facts of racism in British society, while the attitudes of the boys are based on extreme levels of alienation which are also associated with poor self-esteem. We should bear in mind that it is black males rather than black females who have to bear the brunt of occupational and social discrimination in British society.

## Concluding Remarks

In this paper we have tried to review the complex factors which contribute to a consideration of the social, personal and academic adjustment of ethnic minorities in British schools. It is evident from the discussion that the educational problems of black and Asian children constitute an issue closely bound up with larger social issues and cannot therefore be considered in isolation. We are faced not only with a narrowly based school population, but with a multiracial, multicultural situation. Educationists and social workers would agree that, in a sense, the plight of these children is essentially similar to the plight of indigenous socially and educationally disadvantaged children in slum and decaying inner-city areas. Unfortunately, ethnic minority children have to face the additional problems of colour prejudice and language adaptation. Thus, the educational difficulties of black and Asian children cannot be separated from questions of multiple deprivation in the minority community — poor housing, concentration in manual work, low incomes, lack of facilities for pre-school and after-school activities, poor youth employment prospects and many other factors. But we must also remember the special issues related to implicit or explicit racism as advocated by the three kinds of attitudes identified — the rejectionist view, the assimilationist view and the view supporting cultural pluralism. Studies in Britain and America have shown that education, especially intercultural, has a marked effect on the social and personal development of the individual. It can both exacerbate and relieve the problems of plural societies.[50] The education system has so far not come to terms with the fact that Britain is a plural or multicultural society. Most teachers would seem to support the concept of 'integration', yet in practice they are working towards a naive kind of 'assimilation'. In principle, educators and politicians seem to endorse the idea that minority group children should be allowed to retain the culture of their parents and maintain their own cultural and ethnic identity (cultural pluralism). However, there has been little curriculum change to make this possible. The two issues which preoccupy teachers in multiracial schools are language and the curriculum. Both seem to be closely linked with the concept of 'integration' (defined as the acceptance on equal terms of culturally discrete groups). No one would deny that the acquisition of English language and literacy is of considerable importance for minority group children if they are to have equal chances of success in school and in the world of work, but there is increasing emphasis in theory, if not in practice, on teaching English as a second rather than as a first language to some minority groups.

According to CRC Reports, teachers in multiracial schools agree that ethnic minority pupils are at a particular educational disadvantage due to language difficulties and the problems of adaptation to life and values in English society.[51] These teachers further point out that another difficulty in multiracial schools is related to differences in ideas about purposes of education, schools and the role of the teacher.

The sad fact that emerges from the studies reviewed in this paper is that many ethnic minority children are performing at a level significantly below that of English children and, although the length of education in the UK appears to be a significant factor in determining primary school performance, many environmental factors which can depress performance still remain important. Much of the evidence suggests that it is children of West Indian origin who are doing least well in school and who leave school with the lowest and fewest qualifications. This, combined with continued racial discrimination, accounts for the high unemployment rate among West Indian youths, which is twice the national average.

Ballard and Holden found that even those coloured British students who had managed to progress to higher education suffered considerable difficulties in obtaining employment compared to their white counterparts, and they concluded that many of them would have to accept jobs in a lower sector of the employment market than their skills and qualifications warranted.[52] The prospect of an expanding coloured population occupying low-status jobs, or alternatively failing to find employment at all, has serious implications for educational policy and research.

Education of ethnic minority children does not consist merely of the imparting of the English language and of academic skills. It also involves deep understanding of the social and cultural backgrounds of these children and a constant effort on the part of the teacher to help the children understand and respect each other's cultures in the plural or multicultural society that Britain has now become. The teacher is a vital link between cultures and subcultures for whom these differences pose a special challenge. In order to provide different kinds of learning experiences the teacher must have an understanding and appreciation of the social and cultural diversity of ethnic minority groups. Bullock suggests that 'this should receive attention in both initial and in-service teacher training'.[53] It is unfortunate that, as the results of an NFER Survey showed, a significant proportion of the overwhelmingly white native teaching force perceives minority ethnic groups in Britain in hostile and stereotyped terms.[54]

Teachers have a real contribution to make in multicultural education. The success of multicultural education, in the final analysis, depends on teachers who are trained and well motivated to teach in multiracial classrooms. This, in turn, is linked to the question of future patterns of teacher education — i.e. the question of the restructuring of teacher education programmes, with a particularly greater emphasis on in-service training programmes.

In recent years, some colleges of education, polytechnics, institutes of higher education and university departments of education have taken initiatives to begin and promote courses which give orientation in multicultural education. Perhaps the most ambitious course of this nature is one leading to a B.Ed. degree offered by the City of Birmingham polytechnic. Unfortunately, such courses are still rare.

In-service training programmes should be organised to help teachers to understand both the historical background and current situation of ethnic minorities in Britain and the concept of multicultural education, to examine the curriculum of their subject areas in order to avoid historical, religious and cultural bias in presentation, and to produce teaching materials relevant to the cultural and linguistic character of the school population. The need for such training is well illustrated by work carried out on the evaluation of curriculum innovation in multicultural education.[55] The findings clearly indicated that the use of teaching materials aimed at increasing the pupils' understanding and tolerance of each other's cultures was likely to be successful in the hands of those teachers who were themselves sympathetic to the idea of multicultural education. The evaluation showed that only a minority of teachers hold liberal views in this respect. Provision for in-service teacher training and a greater emphasis in their training programmes on both attitudes and professional skills seem to be the solution to many of the educational problems faced by ethnic minority children.

Another solution to the problem would be to employ more teachers from ethnic minority groups. A survey conducted a few years ago showed that Aylestone High School in the London Borough of Brent had pupils from 52 different national origins. About a thousand of the 1,350 students were from a Caribbean background, but most of them were born in Britain. Eight of the teaching staff of about 100 were black. This gross imbalance between black and brown children and black and brown teachers in most inner urban, multiracial schools has been a matter of grave concern for several years.

Although the flow of teachers from the West Indies and the Indian subcontinent into the UK has been almost stopped because of immigration controls, a substantial number of qualified immigrant teachers (recognised by the Department of Education and Science) are not employed in schools. Some of these teachers do not want to take on the arduous task of teaching the often rebellious indigenous British pupils in inner-city schools, but many have been unable to obtain teaching jobs because of the discrimination and prejudice of local education authorities. There is evidence to show that even those who have completed additional courses at British institutions have found considerable difficulty in obtaining employment.[56] One of the crucial factors in their unemployment seems to be the conservatism and, indeed, the prejudice of administrators and some head teachers in British schools.[57]

It must be pointed out that teachers currently being trained to teach in British schools will be teaching fewer and fewer 'immigrants'. Rather, they will be teaching young black or brown Britons, born in the UK, who will be demanding the same educational and occupational chances as their white counterparts. If their legitimate demands are denied, they will surely suffer as individuals. But, in addition, British society as a whole will suffer at social, political and economic levels.

## Notes

1.   H. Tinker, *A New System of Slavery: The Export of Indian Labour Overseas 1830-1920* (Oxford University Press, London, 1974).

2.   R. Moore, *Racism and Black Resistance in Britain* (Pluto Press, London, 1975).

3.   J. Downing and P. Schlesinger, 'Racist at the Ministry', *The Guardian*, 23 November 1976.

4.   E. Bullock, *A Language for Life* (HMSO, London, 1975).

5.   S. Walker, 'The Immigrants: Yes we can live in Peace', *Reader's Digest* (1978).

6.   C. Bagley, K. Mallick and G. Verma, 'Pupil Self-esteem: a Comparison of Black and White Teenagers in British Schools', in G. Verma and C. Bagley (eds), *Race, Education and Identity* (Macmillan, London, 1979); C. Bagley, *Social Structure and Prejudice in Five English Boroughs* (Institute of Race Relations, London, 1970).

7.   R. Ballard and G. Holden, 'The Employment of Coloured Graduates in Britain', *New Community*, 4 (1975), pp. 325-36.

8.   C. Bagley and L. Young, 'Identity and Alienation in Young Blacks in Britain', unpublished.

9.   Ibid.

10.   R. Taft, 'Migration: Problems of Adjustment and Assimilation in Immigrants', in P. Watson (ed.), *Psychology and Race* (Penguin, Harmondsworth, 1973).

11.   S. Allen, *New Minorities, Old Conflicts: Asian and West Indian Migrants in Britain* (Random House, New York, 1971).

12.   D. Milner, *Children and Race* (Penguin, Harmondsworth, 1975).

13.   *The Times Educational Supplement*, 12 December 1975, 16 July 1976 and 22 October 1976.

14.   C. Bagley, *The Dutch Plural Society: A Comparative Study of Race Relations* (Oxford University Press, London, 1975).

15.   H.E.R. Townsend and E. Brittan, *Organisation in Multi-racial Schools* (Slough NFER, Windsor, 1972).

16.   Community Relations Commission, *Urban Deprivation: Racial Inequality and Social Policy: A Report* (HMSO, London, 1977).

17.   C. Bagley, 'The Background of Deviance in Black Children in London', in G. Verma and C. Bagley (eds), *Race and Education Across Cultures* (Heinemann, London, 1975).

18.   K. Pringle, *Deprivation and Education*, 2nd edn (Longman in association with the National Children's Bureau, London, 1971).

19.   W. Bushell, 'The Immigrant (West Indian) Child in School', in V.P. Varma (ed.), *Stresses in Children* (Unibooks, Leicester, 1974).

20.   Ibid.

21.   C. Bagley, G. Verma, K. Mallick and L. Young, *Personality, Self-Esteem and Prejudice* (Saxon House, Farnborough, 1979).

22.   A. Little, 'The Educational Achievement of Ethnic Minority Children in London Schools', in Verma and Bagley (eds), *Race and Education Across Cultures*.

23.   G. Driver, 'Cultural Competence, Social Power and School Achievement: West Indian Secondary School Pupils in West Midlands', *New Community*, 5, no. 5 (1977).

24.   E. McEwan, C. Gipps and R. Sumner, *Language Proficiency in the Multi-Racial Junior School* (NFER, Windsor, 1975).

25.   Community Relations Commission, *Urban Deprivation: Racial Inequality and Social Policy*.

26.   Bagley *et al.*, *Personality, Self-Esteem and Prejudice.*

27.   Ibid.

28.   J.K. Bhatnagar, *Immigrants at School* (Cornmarket Press, London, 1970).

29.   R. Rosenthal, 'The Pygmalion Effect Lives', *Psychology Today*, 7 (1973), pp. 56-63.

30.   W. Pidgeon, *Teacher Expectation and Pupil Performance* (NFER, Windsor, 1969).

31.   E. Brittan, 'Multi-racial Education II — Teacher Opinion on Aspects of School Life', *Educational Research*, 18 (1976), pp. 182-91.

32.   V. Houghton, 'Intelligence Testing of West Indian and English Children', *Race*, 8 (1966), pp. 147-56.

33.   C. Bagley, 'Social Environment and Intelligence in West Indian Children in London', *Social and Economic Studies*, 30 (1971), pp. 420-30.

34.   G.K. Verma, 'Attitude Measurement in a Multi-ethnic Society', *Bulletin of the British Psychological Society* (November 1979).

35.   G.K. Verma, 'The Democratisation of Test Construction: A Response to the Problems of Educational Measurement in a Multi-Ethnic Society', paper

presented at the International Conference on Testing, 1977.

36.    A. Little *et al.*, 'The Education of Immigrant Pupils in Inner London Primary Schools', *Race*, 9 (1968), pp. 439-52; Little, 'The Educational Achievement of Ethnic Minority Children in London Schools', in Verma and Bagley (eds), *Race and Education Across Cultures.*

37.    S. Wiles, 'Children from Overseas (2)', *Institute of Race Relations Newsletter* (June 1968).

38.    S. Durojaiye, 'Social Context of Immigrant Pupils Learning English', *Educational Review* (1972).

39.    P. Ghuman, *The Cultural Context of Thinking* (NFER, Windsor, 1975).

40.    L. Dove, 'The Hopes of Immigrant Schoolchildren', *New Society* (April 1975).

41.    In Britain, school leaving examinations consist of either Certificate of Secondary Education (CSE) or General Certificate of Education (GCE). The latter can be taken at either the Ordinary or 'O' level or the Advanced or 'A' level. GCE 'A' level is normally a prerequisite for university entry.

42.    Dove, 'The Hopes of Immigrant Schoolchildren'.

43.    J.E. Taylor, *The Halfway Generation* (NFER, Windsor, 1976).

44.    S. Coopersmith, 'Self-concept, Race and Education', in Verma and Bagley (eds), *Race and Education Across Cultures.*

45.    G. Verma and K. Mallick, 'Self-esteem of Black, Asian and White Adolescents in Multi-ethnic Schools', *The New Era* (July 1978); Bagley and Young, 'Identity and Alienation in Young Blacks in Britain'.

46.    L. Stenhouse, G. Verma and R. Wild, *Problems and Effects of Teaching About Race Relations* (forthcoming, London, 1981).

47.    G.K. Verma, 'Some Effects of Curriculum Innovation on the Racial Attitudes of Adolescents', *International Journal of Inter-Cultural Relations*, 1, no. 3 (1977).

48.    N. McIntosh and D. Smith, *The Extent of Racial Discrimination* (Political and Economic Planning, London, 1974).

49.    C. Bagley and G. Verma, 'Inter-ethnic Attitudes and Behaviour in British Multi-racial Schools', in Verma and Bagley (eds), *Race and Education Across Cultures.*

50.    Bagley, *The Dutch Plural Society.*

51.    Community Relations Commission, *Urban Deprivation: Racial Inequality and Social Policy.*

52.    Ballard and Holden, 'The Employment of Coloured Graduates in Britain'.

53.    Bullock, *A Language for Life.*

54.    Brittan, 'Multi-racial Education II − Teacher Opinion on Aspects of School Life'.

55.    G.K. Verma and C. Bagley, 'Changing Racial Attitudes in Adolescents: an Experimental English Study', *International Journal of Psychology*, 8 (1973), pp. 55-8; Verma, 'Some Effects of Curriculum Innovation on the Racial Attitudes of Adolescents'; G.K. Verma and C. Bagley, 'Measured Change in Racial Attitudes Following the Use of Three Teaching Methods', in Verma and Bagley (eds), *Race, Education and Identity.*

56.    *The Guardian*, 8 September 1973; *The Times Educational Supplement*, 3 October 1975, 19 September 1975 and 15 August 1975.

57.    M. Jackson, 'Recruiting Minority Group Teachers', *Teacher Education and Community Relations*,11 (1974), p. 1; M. Jackson, 'The D.E.S. Didn't Seem to Know Much About Us', *The Times Educational Supplement*, 18 July 1975.

# 4 MULTICULTURALISM AND EDUCATION OF IMMIGRANTS IN CANADA

**Joti Bhatnagar**

Canada is a confederation of ten provinces and two federal territories. The British North America Act of 1867, which established the Dominion of Canada, defined areas that fell in the domain of the federal and provincial governments. Over some areas, such as national defence, the federal government was given exclusive jurisdiction. Over others, such as health care, provincial governments were given exclusive control. And in some areas, such as immigration, both federal and provincial governments were given authority. Education is a provincial responsibility. Thus, although there are many similarities, each province has its own education system. Consequently, one cannot talk about an education system in Canada; each province has enacted laws defining rights and responsibilities and administrative structures in the field of education. Since the dynamics of the education system can only be understood against a backdrop of general social currents and cross-currents, it is proposed briefly to review the structure of Canadian society and discuss the education of immigrants within that context.

There are three basic facts about Canada that have been influential throughout its history — its large land mass and relatively small population, its proximity to the United States and the relations between English-Canadians and French-Canadians.

Canada is the second largest country in the world, although much of its land mass is unsuitable for settlement. About 85 per cent of its 22 million inhabitants are concentrated in a 50-mile belt bordering the United States. Since its neighbour to the south has always been much more powerful economically, militarily, in terms of manpower and mass media, developments in the United States have had tremendous impact upon Canada's history, economy, values, attitudes and system of education. 'If America sneezes, Canada catches cold.' The last Canadian Governor General, Jules Léger, once remarked: 'We dream in French and English but we work and we entertain ourselves more and more in American.' Much of the Canadian economy is owned by Americans, and Canadian mass media are dominated by American productions to the extent that the Canadian Radio and Television Commission has had to enact regulations requiring a certain proportion of Canadian content in broadcasts from Canadian radio and television stations. Because of its broader economic base, higher standard of living and more hospitable climate, the United States have always received the largest proportion of people migrating from Canada. In order both to keep and indeed increase its population base and to settle the land, Canada has looked upon immigration as a valuable resource. Immigrants played a major role in the settlement of Western Canada in the early part of this century.

Canada has always been populated by ethnically heterogeneous groups. Before the 'discovery' of Canada by Europeans, the 250,000 to 300,000 people who lived in the territory that now constitutes Canada belonged to about 50 societies and dozens of linguistic groups. The French came during the sixteenth century and soon the French-Canadians in Atlantic provinces became differentiated from the rest as Acadians. Later, yet another distinct group, the Métis, emerged through interbreeding between the French and the Canadian Indians.[1] The British influx came during the eighteenth century, followed by smaller numbers of Germans and Dutch.

> The 1870-71 census, the first census after Confederation, revealed that the two largest groups in Canada at that time were the French with a total of 1,082,940 and the British – the English, Scots, Welsh, and Irish – with a combined total of 2,110,502. If taken separately, none of the latter outnumbered the French. There were 706,349 Englishmen, 549,946 Scots, 7,773 Welshmen and 846,414 Irishmen. Other groups were much smaller, the only sizeable one being the Germans with 202,991. There were 29,662 Dutch, 21,496 Negroes, then listed as 'Africans', and small groups of Swiss, Italians, Spanish, Portuguese, and other nationalities. The Ukrainians were not mentioned. The Chinese community probably already numbered several thousand and, concentrated in British Columbia, was not present in this census, as the province did not enter Confederation until 1871.[2]

Table 4.1 describes the proportion of the various ethnic groups in the Canadian population, as shown by the official census taken every ten years since the Confederation. In 1871, only 8 per cent of Canada's population belonged to a group other than the 'founding races'. The Germans constituted the only other ethnic group of any significant size. By 1971, the proportion of the population which was non-British and non-French had grown to 27 per cent, and the proportion has steadily increased since 1971.

Table 4.1: Ethnic Origins of the Population (Census Dates, 1871-1971)
(000)

| | 1871 | 1881 | 1901 | 1911 | 1921 | 1931 | 1941 | 1951 | 1961 | 1971 |
|---|---|---|---|---|---|---|---|---|---|---|
| Total European [a] | 3,433 | 4,147 | 5,171 | 7,006 | 8,569 | 10,134 | 11,243 | 13,583 | 17,654 | 20,764 |
| French | 1,083 | 1,299 | 1,649 | 2,062 | 2,453 | 2,928 | 3,483 | 4,319 | 5,540 | 6,180 |
| English | 706 | 881 | 1,261 | 1,871 | 2,545 | 2,741 | 2,968 | 3,630 | 4,195 | 9,624 |
| Irish | 846 | 957 | 989 | 1,075 | 1,108 | 1,231 | 1,268 | 1,440 | 1,753 | |
| Scottish | 550 | 700 | 800 | 1,027 | 1,174 | 1,346 | 1,404 | 1,547 | 1,902 | |
| Other British | 8 | 10 | 13 | 26 | 42 | 62 | 76 | 92 | 146 | |
| German | 203 | 254 | 311 | 403 | 295 | 474 | 465 | 620 | 1,050 | 1,317 |
| Italian | 1 | 2 | 11 | 46 | 67 | 98 | 113 | 152 | 450 | 731 |
| Jewish | | 1 | 16 | 76 | 126 | 157 | 170 | 182 | 173 | 297 |
| Dutch | 30 | 30 | 34 | 56 | 118 | 149 | 213 | 264 | 430 | 426 |
| Polish | | | 6 | 34 | 53 | 146 | 167 | 220 | 324 | 316 |
| Russian | 1[b] | 1[b] | 20 | 44 | 100 | 88 | 84 | 91 | 119 | 64 |
| Scandinavian [c] | 2 | 5 | 31 | 113 | 168 | 227 | 244 | 283 | 387 | 385 |
| Ukrainian | | | 6 | 75 | 107 | 225 | 306 | 395 | 473 | 581 |
| Other European | 4 | 6 | 24 | 99 | 214 | 261 | 284 | 346 | 711 | 842 |
| Asiatic | | | | | | | | | | |
| Chinese | | 4 | 17 | 28 | 40 | 47 | 35 | 33 | 58 | 119 |
| Japanese | | | 5 | 9 | 16 | 23 | 23 | 22 | 29 | 37 |
| Other Asiatic | | | 2 | 6 | 10 | 15 | 16 | 19 | 34 | 129 |
| Indians and Eskimos | 23 | 109 | 128 | 106 | 114 | 129 | 126 | 166 | 220 | 313 |
| Other and Unknown | 29 | 65 | 49 | 52 | 39 | 29 | 64[d] | 188 | 242 | 206 |
| Total — Canada [a] | 3,486 | 4,325 | 5,371 | 7,207 | 8,788 | 10,377 | 11,507 | 14,009 | 18,238 | 21,568 |
| % European | 98.5 | 95.9 | 96.2 | 97.2 | 97.5 | 97.7 | 97.7 | 97.0 | 96.8 | 96.2 |

a. Individual components may not sum to totals due to rounding. b. Includes Finnish and Polish. c. Includes Danish, Icelandic, Norwegian, Swedish. d. Includes 35,417 Métis.

Sources: M.C. Urquhart, (ed.), *Historical Statistics of Canada*, Macmillan, Toronto, 1971; *Statistics Canada, 1971 Census of Canada*, Catalogue no. 92.723, vol. 1, Part 3.

Table 4.2:   Immigration by Calendar Year, 1852-1976

| | | | | | | | |
|---|---|---|---|---|---|---|---|
| 1852 | 29,307 | 1884 | 103,824 | 1916 | 55,914 | 1948 | 125,414 |
| 1853 | 29,464 | 1885 | 79,169 | 1917 | 72,910 | 1949 | 95,217 |
| 1854 | 37,263 | 1886 | 69,152 | 1918 | 41,845 | 1950 | 73,912 |
| 1855 | 25,296 | 1887 | 84,526 | 1919 | 107,698 | 1951 | 194,391 |
| 1856 | 22,544 | 1888 | 88,766 | 1920 | 138,824 | 1952 | 164,498 |
| 1857 | 33,854 | 1889 | 91,600 | 1921 | 91,728 | 1953 | 168,868 |
| 1858 | 12,339 | 1890 | 75,067 | 1922 | 64,224 | 1954 | 154,227 |
| 1859 | 6,300 | 1891 | 82,165 | 1923 | 133,729 | 1955 | 109,946 |
| 1860 | 6,276 | 1892 | 30,996 | 1924 | 124,164 | 1956 | 164,857 |
| 1861 | 13,589 | 1893 | 29,633 | 1925 | 84,907 | 1957 | 282,164 |
| 1862 | 18,294 | 1894 | 20,829 | 1926 | 135,982 | 1958 | 124,851 |
| 1863 | 21,000 | 1895 | 18,790 | 1927 | 158,886 | 1959 | 106,928 |
| 1864 | 24,779 | 1896 | 16,835 | 1928 | 166,783 | 1960 | 104,111 |
| 1865 | 18,958 | 1897 | 21,716 | 1929 | 164,993 | 1961 | 71,689 |
| 1866 | 11,427 | 1898 | 31,900 | 1930 | 104,806 | 1962 | 74,586 |
| 1867 | 10,666 | 1899 | 44,543 | 1931 | 27,530 | 1963 | 93,151 |
| 1868 | 12,765 | 1900 | 41,681 | 1932 | 20,591 | 1964 | 112,606 |
| 1869 | 18,630 | 1901 | 55,747 | 1933 | 14,382 | 1965 | 146,758 |
| 1870 | 24,706 | 1902 | 89,102 | 1934 | 12,476 | 1966 | 194,743 |
| 1871 | 27,773 | 1903 | 138,660 | 1935 | 11,277 | 1967 | 222,876 |
| 1872 | 36,578 | 1904 | 131,252 | 1936 | 11,643 | 1968 | 183,974 |
| 1873 | 50,050 | 1905 | 141,465 | 1937 | 15,101 | 1969 | 161,531 |
| 1874 | 39,373 | 1906 | 211,653 | 1938 | 17,244 | 1970 | 147,713 |
| 1875 | 27,382 | 1907 | 272,409 | 1939 | 16,994 | 1971 | 121,900 |
| 1876 | 25,633 | 1908 | 143,326 | 1940 | 11,324 | 1972 | 122,006 |
| 1877 | 27,832 | 1909 | 173,694 | 1941 | 9,329 | 1973 | 184,200 |
| 1878 | 29,807 | 1910 | 286,839 | 1942 | 7,576 | 1974 | 218,465 |
| 1879 | 40,492 | 1911 | 331,288 | 1943 | 8,504 | 1975 | 187,881 |
| 1880 | 38,505 | 1912 | 375,756 | 1944 | 12,801 | 1976 | 149,429 |
| 1881 | 47,991 | 1913 | 400,870 | 1945 | 22,722 | | |
| 1882 | 112,458 | 1914 | 150,484 | 1946 | 71,719 | | |
| 1883 | 113,624 | 1915 | 36,665 | 1947 | 64,127 | | |

Source:   Department of Manpower and Immigration, *Immigration Statistics.*

Because of its role in the development of the nation, immigration policy has always aroused widespread controversy and considerable passion. Public debate on the subject in Canada has always been intensified by heated rhetoric and fiery accusations of racial discrimination. Yet the most striking feature of Canadian immigration policy through the years has been the absence of a general agreement about what immigration should be or should do.[3]

Until World War I, immigration policy was geared primarily for population growth to serve the interest of Canadian sovereignty and economic development. As a result of a policy initiated by Prime Minister Laurier's government, three million immigrants entered Canada between 1896 and 1914, including some 400,000 in 1913, the largest number ever recorded. New sources of immigrants emerged. Immigrants from the Ukraine, Hungary, Roumania, Russia and East Asia came in ever-increasing numbers. This permitted the settlement of the west, the building of the Canadian Pacific Railway and the general increase in the population base to keep Canada a viable sovereign state distinct from the United States. The large influx of workers also produced controversy culminating in the Immigration Act of 1910. This Act encouraged the immigration of farmers, farm labourers and domestic servants from Britain, the United States and northern Europe, while at the same time discouraging those who belonged to other nationalities unlikely to assimilate (euphemism for non-whites) and who consequently would prevent the building of a nation of like-minded people. For the first time, Canada imposed restrictions based on ethnic and racial categories. A 'head tax' was imposed to limit Chinese immigration, and a 'gentleman's agreement' was reached with the government of Japan to restrict the number of Japanese labourers entering Canada. Regulations established in 1918 prohibited entry to any immigrant who did not travel in a single vehicle or vessel from his native country to Canada. For example, if an immigrant had to take two ships in order to come to Canada, his entry was prohibited. The purpose of this rather strange regulation was to eliminate completely East Indian immigration, since there were no direct passenger steamship links between Indian and Canadian ports. The principle of selective immigration on the basis of race and country of origin continued to be the cornerstone of Canadian immigration policy until it was replaced by immigration regulations that came into force in 1967.

The period between the two world wars was an uncertain one for Canadian immigration, which rose considerably during the boom years of the twenties and fell sharply during the depression of the thirties.

Legislation was enacted in 1923 to exclude virtually all Chinese immigration, and the 'gentleman's agreement' with Japan was revised to limit Japanese to a maximum of 150 immigrants per year. During the 1920s, Canada established a list of 'preferred' and 'non-preferred' countries. The British, French and Americans were the most preferred immigrants. Northern Europeans were also welcome. Other Europeans were also admitted if Canada needed more immigrants than could be supplied by the 'preferred' countries. Non-whites remained inadmissible. Most immigrants in the 1920s settled either in the industrial and commercial centres or in the resource-based boom towns in Quebec and Ontario.[4] This was a shift from the agriculturally oriented immigration prior to World War I.

The period from the end of the Second World War to the present has been characterised by a much more diverse immigrant population in terms of education, occupation and ethnic origin. By 1950, three categories of people were accepted as desirable immigrants. The most desirable group consisted of citizens of the UK, Australia, New Zealand, the United States, Eire and France. The second category included relatives of individuals already resident in Canada. Other people could also be admitted if they were citizens of 'non-Asiatic' countries entering Canada with 'assured employment' as agriculturists, miners or lumbermen.[5] The only Asiatics to be admitted were unmarried children under the age of 18 and wives of Canadian citizens. The 1952 Immigration Act gave wide powers to the Minister of Citizenship and Immigration to prohibit the entry of immigrants on the basis of nationality, ethnic origin, 'peculiar cultural traits' and inability to assimilate. Quotas were fixed for least desirable immigrants. For example, immigrants from India were limited to a maximum of 300, from Pakistan to 100 and from Ceylon to 50 per year.[6] One federal minister after another spoke in Parliament to support these regulations because it had been 'scientifically proven' that Jews, blacks and Asiatics were unassimilable — something most social scientists even at that time regarded as nonsensical.

The rapidly expanding economy of the 1950s and 1960s demanded educated, professional and skilled manpower that could not be supplied by the 'preferred' countries. More liberal attitudes were sought by Canadians who found the blatantly racist policies of their government unacceptable and by ethnic groups determined to rescue their friends and relatives from political and economic conditions prevailing in many countries. In 1967, the government introduced regulations that produced a basic change in Canadian immigration policy. The new regulations retained the concept of selectivity of immigrants but the selection was to be based on educational background, skills, training and need for the individual in the Canadian marketplace rather than on race, ethnicity or country of origin. For the first time, discrimination on the basis of race or nationality was to be eliminated, and immigrants were judged solely on nine criteria — education and training, personal qualities, occupational demand, occupational skill, age, prearranged employment, knowledge of English and French, relatives in Canada and employment opportunities in the areas of destination.[7]

Changes in immigration regulation, together with structural changes affecting the national economies of both Canada and the sending countries, have significantly altered the pattern and composition of immigration. In 1956, 88 per cent of Canada's immigrants came from the United Kingdom and continental Europe. This dominance declined gradually and, by 1977, individuals from these countries accounted for less than 36 per cent of the immigrants arriving in that year. On the other hand, there has been a dramatic increase in the number of immigrants from Asia, Central and South America and the Caribbean. While, in 1956, immigrants from these countries accounted for less than 4 per cent of the immigrants in that year, the figure rose to over 45 per cent in 1977.[8]

Table 4.3: Canadian Immigration by Place of Last Permanent Residence (% of total immigration)

| | 1956 | 1961 | 1966 | 1971 | 1977 |
|---|---|---|---|---|---|
| United Kingdom | 30.6 | 16.5 | 32.5 | 12.7 | 15.7 |
| France | 2.3 | 3.3 | 4.0 | 2.4 | 2.4 |
| Italy | 16.9 | 19.7 | 16.2 | 4.7 | 3.0 |
| Germany | 15.8 | 8.7 | 4.8 | 1.9 | 2.0 |
| Other Europe | 22.7 | 24.5 | 18.7 | 21.0 | 12.4 |
| | 57.7 | 56.2 | 43.7 | 30.0 | 19.8 |
| Africa | 0.4 | 1.5 | 1.9 | 2.3 | 5.5 |
| India | 0.2 | 0.8 | 1.1 | 4.4 | 4.8 |
| Other Asia | 1.9 | 3.0 | 6.0 | 13.8 | 22.5 |
| | 2.1 | 3.8 | 7.1 | 18.2 | 27.3 |
| Australasia | 1.2 | 2.0 | 2.1 | 2.4 | 1.3 |
| USA | 5.9 | 16.1 | 9.0 | 20.0 | 11.2 |
| Central and South America | 1.0 | 2.0 | 1.4 | 4.6 | 8.0 |
| Caribbean | 0.8 | 1.8 | 2.1 | 9.0 | 10.4 |
| Other | 0.3 | 0.1 | 0.2 | 0.8 | 0.8 |
| Total | 100.0 | 100.0 | 100.0 | 100.0 | 100.0 |

Data sources: *Immigration Statistics, Canada* — 1956, 1961, 1966, 1971; *Employment and Immigration, Canada,* 1977.

Immigration since World War II has accelerated the trend for urbanisation: the vast majority of immigrants have settled in towns and cities. The three big cities — Montreal, Toronto and Vancouver — absorbed an overwhelming proportion of new immigrants, resulting in a large concentration of immigrants in these metropolitan areas. The 1971 census figures, our last official census, show that in Toronto, for example, close to half of the household heads were born outside Canada, another fifth had at least one foreign-born parent and 29 per cent were born in Canada and had both foreign-born parents. Figures published by the Toronto Board of Education show that, as of September 1976, more than 50 per cent of the 95,000 students served by the Board did not claim English as their mother tongue. A little over 10 per cent reported Italian as their mother tongue, about 5.6 per cent reported Portuguese, 6.1 per cent Chinese and another 14.1 per cent some other language. About 30 per cent of the students were born outside Canada. Of these, over 5,000 were born in Portugal, over 3,000 in Italy, over 2,500 in China or Hong Kong, over 4,900 in the Caribbean, over 2,000 in Greece, over 4,000 in other European countries, over 2,000 in parts of Asia and the Middle East and over 1,100 in parts of Central and South America. How does this concentration of immigrant children affect their education? Does it enhance or retard their academic performance, social integration, linguistic adjustment, self-concept? How does it affect the local Canadian children? Should we employ the policy of dispersal practised in some other countries? Unfortunately, research on these questions is almost non-existent in Canada.

Table 4.4 gives the occupations immigrants intended to undertake in Canada at various points in time. The occupational mix has changed significantly in the post-war period. During 1946-55, more than 20 per cent of immigrants intended to work in agriculture. By 1974-75, the proportion had declined to only about 2 per cent. A similar decline could be observed for labourers in that time period. By contrast, the managerial and professional occupations accounted for only about 7 per cent of the working immigrants between 1946 and 1955. In 1974-75, these occupations were named by 25 per cent. Immigrants in Canada today are widely represented throughout the occupational structure. Immigrants who intended to work in managerial and professional occupations had a high level of education before coming to Canada. Canada, thus, gained trained manpower without having to pay for the training. A study conducted for the Federal Department of Labour estimated that the value of education of all immigrants arriving in Canada between 1951 and 1961, measured in terms of costs that would have been incur-

Table 4.4: Immigration to Canada by (Intended) Occupational Group

| Occupational groups | 1946-55 | 1956-69 | Fiscal year 1971-72 | Fiscal year 1972-73 | Fiscal year 1973-74 | Fiscal year 1974-75 |
|---|---|---|---|---|---|---|
| Managerial [a] | 4,213 | 21,172 | 3,532 | 4,439 | 6,304 | 5,731 |
| Professional | 44,526 | 211,115 | 15,708 | 15,214 | 20,704 | 20,498 |
| Clerical | 46,788 | 132,268 | 9,072 | 9,074 | 14,438 | 15,334 |
| Commercial and financial | 25,731 | 38,626 | 2,404 | 2,526 | 4,254 | 3,966 |
| Service and recreation [b] | 69,447 | 131,586 | 6,179 | 7,039 | 11,687 | 11,656 |
| Transport and communication | 15,332 | 20,538 | 746 | 837 | 1,211 | 1,506 |
| Agriculture | 138,195 | 56,756 | 2,082 | 2,185 | 3,329 | 2,256 |
| Fishing, trapping and logging | 12,928 | 3,111 | 77 | 98 | 273 | 253 |
| Mining | 10,029 | 6,344 | 214 | 143 | 177 | 242 |
| Manufacturing, mechanical and construction | 200,611 | 328,455 | 15,045 | 16,078 | 33,169 | 30,263 |
| Labourers | 63,743 | 102,382 | 1,233 | 1,297 | 653 | 4,197 |
| Others | 9,255 | 6,751 | 1,976 | 2,677 | 5,529 | 6,483 |
| Total workers | 635,798 | 1,059,104 | 58,268 | 61,607 | 101,764 | 102,385 |
| Total non-workers | 586,521 | 985,721 | 59,300 | 63,120 | 101,546 | 114,226 |
| Wives | 252,347 | 379,035 | 20,823 | 21,640 | 29,754 | 32,810 |
| Children | 289,298 | 513,140 | 28,985 | 31,591 | 48,641 | 63,201 |
| Others | 44,876 | 93,546 | 9,492 | 9,889 | 23,151 | 18,215 |
| Grand total | 1,222,319 | 2,044,825 | 117,568 | 124,727 | 203,310 | 216,611 |

a. Available as separate occupational group since 1953 only.

b. Includes domestic servants.

Sources: Manpower and Immigration, *1972 Immigration*; Department of Manpower and Immigration, *Annual Reports*, 1972-73, 1974-75.

red in providing a comparable educational attainment in Canada, was
$5.9 billion.[9]

Canada is a country of immigrants. The changed pattern of immigration, particularly during the 1960s and 1970s, has helped to streng-
then the concept of Canada as also a land of minorities. From the first
census in 1871 to the last in 1971, no single ethnic group has been
shown to form a majority in Canada. At the present time, Canada has
approximately ten million British-Canadians, six million French-
Canadians and six million belonging to other ethnic groups, including
some 750,000 non-whites.

An historical account of immigration to Canada would not be complete without examining the attitude of the Canadian population
towards immigration and immigrants. A persistent feature of Canadian
public opinion over the years has been the negative attitude maintained
by members of the public who regard immigrants as posing an economic, social, cultural or political threat. Education has been regarded as
the most potent tool for assimilating the immigrants and thus reducing
the threat. Successive groups of immigrants, except the English, have
had to face prejudice and experience discrimination. The level of hostility towards a particular immigrant group seems to have increased in
direct proportion to the increase in their numbers. The Irish, the Central
Europeans, the Jews, the Southern Europeans and now the non-whites
have all been targets of inhospitable remarks. During the middle of the
nineteenth century, Canada was facing a rising tide of immigration from
Ireland. Here is what a Chief Superintendent of a school board in
Toronto had to say about the Irish immigrants:

> Many of these immigrants will doubtless add both to the intelligence
> and productive industry of the country. But is this the character of
> most of them? From their former wretched circumstances and still
> more wretched habits, they are notoriously as destitute of intelligence
> and industry as they are of means of subsistence. Their condition
> appeals to our own humanity; but their character justly excites our
> solicitude, and demands our practical attention. The physical disease
> and death which have accompanied their influx among us may be
> precursors of the worst pestilence of social insubordination and dis-
> order. It is therefore of the last importance that every possible effort
> should be employed to bring the facilities of education within the
> reach of the families of these unfortunate people, that they may
> grow up in the industry and intelligence of the country, and not in
> the idleness and pauperism, not to say mendicity and vices of their
> forefathers.[10]

The statement embodies all the basic ingredients of the anti-immigrant attitudes: labelling them as agents of vice, disease, disruption and social disorder; a condemnation of their habits, character and values; and education as the chief vehicle for uplifting them and especially their children to the Canadian level of morality and industry.[11] Immigrants from Central Europe, or 'stalwart peasants in the sheepskin coat' as they were popularly known in the early part of this century, were next to inherit this legacy which in modern times seems to have been passed on to the visible minorities, i.e. the Asians and the blacks.

What is the behaviour pattern expected from an immigrant before he will be considered assimilated and accepted as a full-fledged member of Canadian society? These expectations seem to have undergone a change over time. Until the early 1960s, Canada (including the Province of Quebec, where more than 80 per cent of the population is French speaking) was openly and unabashedly British. Assimilation into the Canadian version of British culture was the only hope offered to the immigrant. In order to get a fair shake, many immigrants not only had to adopt British customs and mannerisms but also had to change their names in order to conceal their ethnic identity. For some, especially the second-generation European immigrants, it was possible, for visible minorities it was not. And then came the sixties, a dozen years of upheaval in North America. In the United States there were campus riots, the destruction of black ghettos, the opting out of young people, the drugs, the rock music scene, the emergence of black power. In Canada things were less volatile and the change more subtle but just as, if not more, far reaching. The Province of Quebec underwent what has come to be known as the 'quiet revolution'. French-Canadians in that province increasingly began to identify themselves as Quebecois. No longer satisfied with a subservient role, they demanded a bigger role in business, government and industry.

At that time ethnic groups all across the globe were agitating against the British Empire, resulting in many cases in the birth of new independent nations. Many Quebecois claimed that Quebec was, in many ways, like a British colony and should therefore agitate to obtain full independence. In 1976, the Province of Quebec elected a Parti Quebecois government which is dedicated to taking Quebec out of the confederation. This has generally been regarded as the greatest political crisis in the history of Canadian confederation.

English Canada faced another challenge from a different quarter. A 'third force' emerged on the Canadian social and political scene. Inspired by the black power movement in the United States, the fall of the

British Empire and the rise of ethnics all over the world, people whose background was neither English nor French were getting fed up with the 'founding races' philosophy. No longer willing to play second fiddle, they demanded recognition of their cultural heritage, of their contribution towards the emergence of Canada as a modern industrial state and of their rightful place in the Canadian mosaic. It was claimed that government policies failed to meet the real needs of the immigrants, and that ethnic communities deserved a much better status and role in policy-making bodies.[12] The federal government's response to the situation was the setting up, in 1963, of the Royal Commission on Bilingualism and Biculturalism 'to enquire into and report upon the existing state of bilingualism and biculturalism in Canada and to recommend what steps should be taken to develop the Canadian confederation on the basis of an equal partnership between the two "founding races" '. The primary purpose of the Royal Commission was to inquire into English-French relations and to look into other ethnic groups in so far as they affected English-French relations. Many briefs submitted to the Commission soon made it clear that there was a host of ethnic groups who were interested in a multicultural and not a bicultural Canada. After several years of research and public hearings, the Commission published a volume on *The Cultural Contribution of the Other Ethnic Groups.*[13] This volume is a goldmine of research and information on topics such as integration, assimilation, discrimination, cultural heritage and language. The role of education in responding to the needs of new Canadians in a multicultural society is discussed. The recommendations made by the Commission in this volume were accepted in their entirety by the government.[14] As a response to the Commission's reports, the government developed the policy of 'multiculturalism within a bilingual framework'. The policy advocates cultural pluralism rather than cultural assimilation of ethnic groups. Prime Minister Trudeau put it in no uncertain terms:

A policy of multiculturalism within a bilingual framework commends itself to the Government of Canada as the most suitable means of assuring the cultural freedom of Canadians. National unity, if it is to mean anything in the deeply personal sense, must be founded on confidence in one's own individual identity; out of this can grow respect for that of others and a willingness to share ideas, attitudes and assumptions. A vigorous policy of multiculturalism will help to create this initial confidence. It can form the base of a society which is based on fair play for all.

In order to achieve this goal Trudeau proposed:

> First, resources permitting, the government will seek to assist all
> Canadian cultural groups that have demonstrated a desire and effort
> to continue to develop a capacity to grow and contribute to Canada,
> and a clear need for assistance, the small and weak groups no less
> than the strong and highly organized.
>
> Second, the government will assist members of all cultural groups
> to overcome cultural barriers to full participation in Canadian
> society.
>
> Third, the government will promote creative encounters and
> interchange among all Canadian cultural groups in the interest of
> national unity.
>
> Fourth, the government will continue to assist immigrants to
> acquire at least one of Canada's official languages in order to become
> full participants in Canadian society.[15]

Within the framework of this policy, Canada has 'two official languages
but no official culture'. It recognises that Canada consists of immigrants
from all parts of the globe and that the Canadian cultural mosaic contains many cultures, each making its own unique contribution. No ethnic
group, including the British and French ethnic groups, takes precedence
over another. The policy is based on the assumption that in order to
have respect for other cultures the individual must have confidence in
his own cultural foundations, and that all cultural groups are essential
to our society and should, therefore, be retained. It is, in short, a policy
of cultural democracy as opposed to a policy of cultural imperialism.

To implement this policy a new Cabinet post of Minister of State
for Multiculturalism was established, and two advisory bodies — the
Canadian Consultative Council on Multiculturalism and the Ethnic
Studies Advisory Committee — were set up. Programmes were developed
to award grants to meet certain needs of ethnic groups to maintain
their language and culture and to explore the possibility of establishing
one or more centres of Canadian ethnic studies. The official policy of
multiculturalism within a bilingual framework and its implementation
have aroused considerable interest. Several national conferences have
been organised and a considerable amount of literature has appeared.[16]
The literature was enough to justify publication of a bibliography of
works on the subject.[17]

In a detailed study of the socialisation of immigrant children in
Canada, Danzinger found that the single most important variable deter-

mining the 'position in the social structure for the majority of the male adults' is the achieved level of education.[18] Therefore, a great deal of effort for the implementation of multiculturalism has been in the field of education. Multiculturalism implies certain objectives for the education of immigrants. Thus, an immigrant child must:

1. become fluent in at least one of Canada's two official languages in order to participate effectively in a Canadian context;
2. be encouraged to retain his own language and culture and develop a sense of pride in his own cultural heritage;
3. be encouraged to feel that he does not have to be like an Anglo-Saxon in order to receive equality of educational and economic opportunities.

What has been done to meet these objectives?

### Learning of English/French as a Second Language

When an immigrant child comes to Canada, learning a Canadian language is his most obvious need, and this has received a great deal of attention. Mary Ashworth, who conducted a nation-wide survey of English language classes for immigrant children, classifies the great variety of these programmes into five categories.[19]

*Reception Classes.* Immigrant children are enrolled in reception classes to learn English on a full-time basis. They spend most of their day in the reception class but may be integrated with Canadian children for non-verbal subjects such as physical education, art and music. They are sent back to their normal class as soon as their English becomes adequate. The advantage of this type of arrangement is that children can concentrate on learning English without interruptions or diversions. However, unless care is taken to ensure that immigrant children have social interaction with Canadian children, the reception class can become an immigrant ghetto.

*Half-day Classes.* Under this arrangement, the child spends half the day in the new Canadian class learning English and the other half of the day in a regular class with children of his own age. Elementary schools with their flexible time-tables and open approach seem to find half-day classes quite acceptable, as these classes seem to give the child the best of both worlds, intensive language training along with opportunities for social interaction with other children. Secondary schools with modular or rotating time-tables are not nearly as happy with half-day classes. They tend to see them as an interruption of the student's academic studies.

*Withdrawal Classes with Itinerant Teachers.* In some areas such as the prairie provinces, the immigrant children are spread out thinly across the school districts, making it difficult to gather them all together in one place, and so the teacher travels from school to school, withdrawing students for varying periods of time. Some teachers serve as few as three schools a week, while others rush between 13 — no mean feat when one considers temperatures of often −50°C, howling winds and icy streets!

*Withdrawal Classes with School-based Teachers.* The alternative to itinerant teachers is to have the children travel to a central location to meet the teacher. Sometimes the children are transferred to the teacher's school until they have mastered English; sometimes they ride the buses perhaps three times a week from their own school to the teacher's school.

*Total Integration.* Some school districts in Canada, particularly those in the Maritimes, receive so few immigrant children that a special programme is not feasible. The child is therefore placed in a regular class and given whatever help the teacher can provide. Unfortunately, there are still quite a few administrators who, despite evidence to the contrary, follow a 'do nothing and the problem will disappear in time' approach.

Ashworth points out that one of the weaknesses of most language training programmes lies in the second phase of language learning. Once the student has mastered basic English and is enrolled in regular classes, there is seldom anything more than occasional help available to him. Despite the well-documented fact that language is far too intricate a system for a learner to master all its complexities in one year, that is the standard time which a child is expected to spend in a Canadian class. Problems of second-phase language learning are very acute in districts which have a high entry of students from Hong Kong at the senior high school level. In 1972, nearly 3,000 students entered Canada from Hong Kong to attend high school.

The language of instruction in Canada is English except in the Province of Quebec, where two parallel systems exist, one with French and the other with English as the medium of instruction from kindergarten to university. In 1966, the Parent Commission which inquired into the provincial education system had little to say about the needs of immigrant children.[20] Until the beginning of the 1970s no attempt was made to provide French language programmes for immigrants. In 1970, the Gendron Commission reported that the French language education system in Quebec has been unaware of immigrants' needs and has made no attempt to provide satisfactory programmes.[21] Hence, the new Canadians have tended to send their children to the English system of education. For example, in the early 1970s, only 25 per cent of Italian children in the Montreal Catholic School Commission were attending French language schools.[22] It was pointed out that the increasing propensity of immigrant parents to send their children to English language schools, coupled with the declining birth-rate among the French-Canadians, could upset the demographic balance in Quebec to the detriment of French-Canadians. Strong voices were raised by nationalist Quebecois to stop this trend. In 1977, the government of Quebec passed Bill 101 requiring all immigrant children, with certain exceptions, to attend French language schools. School boards in Quebec have now begun to give serious consideration to improving French as a second language programme.

### Retention of Language and Cultural Heritage

The Multiculturalism Branch of the Department of Secretary of State provides grants for ethnic groups wishing to maintain supplementary classes for teaching the language and culture of the ethnic group, or for support of other cultural activities such as dance, music, folk festivals and so on. Most of the language classes, however, are arranged either in the evening or on Saturdays. Children view these as extra work and are, on the whole, not very enthusiastic about them. To overcome this problem, many school boards have started language classes within the school system. Toronto, for example, offers German, Italian, Chinese, Hebrew, Polish, Portuguese, Russian, Ukrainian, Greek, Hungarian, Latvian and Croatian in its schools. Language classes by themselves, however, have been found to be insufficient. If immigrant children are to develop a pride in their cultural heritage, more than language classes are needed. Several school boards across Canada recognise and have begun to experiment with bilingual, bicultural programmes.

The Toronto Board of Education started an experimental programme in the fall of 1965 in the Main Street school. At first, 75 students over twelve years of age were enrolled. Many of the teachers involved in the programme were themselves bilingual or multilingual. The programme recognised that the problems of immigrant children go beyond linguistic difficulties. It emphasised communication, commitment and dialogue that would allow the immigrant child to become acculturated at his own pace.

> The real fact of life in this question of the new immigrant population in our school system is that the problem it presents is not, never has been, and never will be, a language problem. It is a cultural problem. Furthermore, it insists that the new immigrant's culture and ours be integrated, made compatible, in the personality of the immigrant himself. This means that there is only one valid principle to which the Board can look for its solution. The new immigrant must be provided with the opportunity and the possibility to effect the integration of his own culture with the new culture — which the school represents — for himself, on his own terms and in his own time.[23]

The methodology employed in the school is described by the principal:

> At Main Street there is a great deal of sharing of experiences. Teachers and students do things together — they work out projects together, they visit the community library, stores, and shops together, they eat their lunch together, they go on field trips together. The students are encouraged to talk about the way of life in their native land and of the changes Canada has meant for them and their families. There is no attempt to influence the students into adopting the clothes, food and responses of other young Canadians. The fact that a boy's lunch consists of a thick chunk of meat and a slab of bread instead of a ham or cheese sandwich and an apple should be, not a source of confusion and embarrassment, but an opportunity for an exchange of information and ideas — perhaps an exchange of food. The round lunch tables provide a setting for developing dialogue as a pupil eats with teachers and classmates. Here, as elsewhere in the school, the aim is not to assimilate these young people into our culture, but to integrate them.[24]

The school proved to be popular with immigrants and its enrolment increased. Despite its commendable aims, the students who attended the school did not produce any measurable gains. Evaluation by the Research Department of the Toronto Board of Education did not show any great differences between graduates of this school and those from a regular reception class.

In two mid-town Toronto public schools, 90 per cent of the children were of Chinese origin. In the early 1970s parents of these children began speaking out on the communication gap widening between themselves and their children — the children were, more and more, talking in English and becoming part of a new culture that seemed to be rejecting the older culture of their parents. There were after-school Chinese classes in the community, but they required a great deal of extra work and were too expensive for most families. The parents appealed to the school board, and after much discussion the programme began in 1974. The Board's document outlining the rationale of the bicultural programme states:

> The existence of such a program in the school would place a recognition of integrity and worth of the Chinese culture within the child's frame of reference. Secondly it would represent compatibility between the home and school rather than a cultural competition for the children's allegiance.[25]

In the first year, 300 students, including a few not of Chinese background, enrolled in the programme, which consisted of withdrawing the students from regular classes for half an hour per day for instructions in Chinese language and culture. The programme was evaluated a year after its inauguration. The researchers found that most students, parents and teachers agreed that the Chinese programme was successful in making students more aware of Chinese culture. The students' self-concept improved and their academic achievement did not suffer.[26] A similar Greek bilingual programme is now being run in two schools in East Toronto.

In 1973, an experimental Italian transition programme was started in a junior and senior kindergarten. In this programme, the children are initially taught their mother tongue — Italian in this case. They are then gradually introduced to English and are expected to catch up with regular classes in oral and written English by grade three. But are children who enter this programme deficient in English? The psychologists who evaluated the programme found that the children did not suffer in English language comprehension. Their self-concept improved.[27]

In early 1971, the Vancouver School Board, the University of British Columbia, the Metropolitan School Board and Khalsa-Diwan Society (an East Indian community organisation) got together to organise a programme for East Indian and other immigrant children in the summer of 1971. The programme, which included a variety of activities including field trips, arts and crafts, story time and the publication of a weekly newspaper, was staffed by 23 university and high school students, both East Indians and Caucasians. Evaluation of the programme showed a considerable difference between the pre- and post-test scores of the children.[28] Programmes of this nature appear to be extremely beneficial for immigrant children, particularly if they are run by organisers who are enthusiastic, competent and have an aptitude for cross-cultural work.

The government of Quebec initiated a project (Project d'Enseigne- ment de Langues d'Origine) to offer children of linguistic minorities the possibility of maintaining and developing their knowledge of the lang- uage and culture of the family. Three programmes, Greek, Italian and Portuguese, were developed by three production committees. The members of these committees belonged to the ethnic group concerned, had a thorough competence in the language and culture, had experience in teaching ethnic languages and were thoroughly familiar with the French language and the Quebec school system. The programmes were open to children who had knowledge of the language concerned and whose parents recognised themselves as belonging to the particular ethnic group. The programme was offered on a trial basis in the 1978- 79 school year in grade 1 in seven Montreal Catholic School Commis- sion schools, and consisted of teaching ethnic language and culture for half of the school time. Preliminary results indicate a general satisfac- tion on the part of children, parents, teachers and organisers of the programme.[29] The programme is being extended to grade 2 in the 1979-80 school year, when the results of the experiment might be published.

Culture conflict has been widely reported as a major problem facing immigrant children throughout the world.[30] In Canada, culture conflict has been found to be a serious problem with black students,[31] West Indians,[32] Greeks,[33] Koreans,[34] Moroccans,[35] Spanish-speaking Latin Americans,[36] Portuguese,[37] Chinese,[38] Italians,[39] and East Indians.[40] Through programmes of the nature described above, it is hoped that cultural differences will be viewed as an asset rather than a hindrance to the education of immigrant children. On the whole, this still remains a pious hope rather than an achieved reality. Much experimentation still needs to be done, but we seem to be moving in the right direction.

## Equality of Cultural Status

The third objective of giving equal status to all cultures remains more

elusive. It requires a general acceptance of the concept of multiculturalism by both the ethnic groups and the population at large. To judge the
mood of the nation on the subject, the federal government commis-
sioned two studies. The first, conducted by O'Bryan and his associates,
attempted

> to examine the main patterns of non-official language knowledge
> and use in Canada, and to ascertain whether there is a real desire to
> support the retention of such language as a viable source of cultural
> identity and preservation, among members of groups whose ancest-
> ral language is other than English or French.[41]

Because, if the ethnic groups do not wish to retain their language and
culture, the government is wasting its time pursuing its multiculturalism
policy. The study found quite extensive knowledge of non-official languages among first-generation immigrants, although such knowledge was
almost lost in the second generation. By the third generation it was not
a question of retention but of reacquisition. Without substantial assistance, the home language will be a fond memory for third-generation
immigrants. Because of the facilities available for language exercise,
language loss was slower in Toronto and Montreal than in smaller cities.
Support for the retention of non-official languages was found to be
very widespread among ethnic groups in big cities. Many ethnic groups
regarded ethnic cultural survival, and especially language survival, a key
concern which has very substantial social and emotional impact. No
serious opposition to the principle of cultural retention could be observed. Though support for language retention did decline among second-
and third-generation immigrants, this decline was much less marked
than the decline in language use. The data indicate that the 'current
rates of language loss are viewed as unsatisfactory not only by the
immigrants but also by their children and grandchildren'.[42] The study
found formidable evidence for a strongly felt need for cultural and
language retention both by those who retained the ancestral language
and by those who lost it. Most immigrants favoured public and not
ethnic schools as the preferred tool for language retention. There is

> very strong and clear support among many members of Canada's
> ethnic minority groups for inclusion of the non-official languages in
> the course of instruction and as vehicles of instruction in the public
> schools and especially in the elementary schools. This point should
> not be missed since it reflects a high degree of concern expressed by

many parents for the teaching of ancestral language to their children. Indeed, many said they would insist on their children taking the courses and almost all would encourage them to do so.[43]

The second study conducted by Berry and his associates was designed to answer the question 'whether all Canadians view cultural diversity as a valuable resource, and whether confidence in one's own identity is a prerequisite for accepting others'.[44] A national sample of 1,849 respondents was interviewed. Most respondents perceived the consequences of immigration as being more positive than negative, though concerns were expressed about the possibility of increasing unemployment and upsetting the balance between English- and French-Canadians. Most immigrants, including non-whites, were rated as acceptable, and those with skilled trades or high levels of education were considered most desirable. When asked about their behavioural intentions, respondents showed patterns of discrimination against immigrants.

> Discrimination was greatest against high status immigrants in a business relationship, and was least against low status immigrants in a business relationship. The combination of these results with those reported earlier suggests the following paradox. While highly educated and skilled immigrants are considered highly desirable for admission to Canada, there is some reluctance to use their services, especially if they are of high status.[45]

The study found a pecking order of preferences for ethnic groups: Northern Europeans, South and Central Europeans and non-whites, in that order. The study found little factual knowledge about multiculturalism in the Canadian population. Despite this lack of knowledge, attitudes towards multiculturalism were generally positive, although behavioural intentions were less so.

> This contrast in support between ideology and behavioural intentions may be understood in terms of the abstract through to concrete dimensions ... It may well be that Canadians think that the idea of multiculturalism is good, that some of the programs are fun, but that they do not want to get involved. Overall, however, the climate for multiculturalism is fairly positive; the ideological base is supportive, and there are some specific programs which appear to be generally highly acceptable.[46]

The study found that, on the whole, Canadians reject explicit racism, yet physical differences among groups are, nevertheless, important. 'Race appeared to be one of the basic dimensions in the structure of perception of ethnic groups.'[47] The authors conclude that, on the whole, the Canadian core is more tolerant than the core in most other multiracial societies and is relatively open to the concept of multiculturalism. Dr Berry and his colleagues employed a national sample. We get a different picture from studies done in high-immigrant areas. Richmond reported that blacks and Asians were four times more likely than whites to report employment discrimination and eight times more likely to report discrimination in housing.[48] Ramcharan found that 58 per cent of the West Indians claimed to have encountered employment discrimination, 37 per cent discrimination in housing and 16 per cent discrimination in other areas.[49] Head's study of the black community in Toronto showed that 59 per cent of the blacks reported some form of discrimination.[50] Recently, the Ontario Human Rights Commission Report notes that in 1976-77 'race related complaints made up 58 per cent of the commission's work load'.[51] The number of reported incidents of racial violence in public places such as subways, parking lots, on the street and so on have increased dramatically, and these have led to the creation of Metro Toronto's Task Force on Race Relations. Additional evidence of prejudice and discrimination of both the violent and subtle variety have been reported in briefs such as the Ubale Report submitted to the Human Rights Commission by the various ethnic groups.[52] More recently, Henry conducted a study to examine the dynamics of racism in Toronto. A random sample of 617 white residents of Toronto was given a specially constructed questionnaire. She found 16 per cent of the population to be extremely racist and 35 per cent inclined towards racism.[53]

Social climate in the community is reflected in the social climate inside the school. If the situation in high-immigrant areas such as Toronto is indeed as bad as the studies would suggest, there would be little chance of the immigrant child developing positive self-concept if his ethnic group was held in low regard. The school boards have attempted to remedy this, mainly through providing information to students and in-service training for teachers. The Toronto Board of Education, for example, has developed multi-media packages on Greece, Italy, the West Indies and various other countries for use with teachers, parent-teacher associations and students. The packages provide information on the cultural backgrounds of the various groups. At least four Canadian universities now offer programmes in multicultural studies, and more are like to follow suit.

One of the persistent elements militating against the development of a healthy self-concept among minority group children is the treatment of minorities in the textbooks used in classrooms. McDiarmid and Pratt undertook a content analysis of all social studies textbooks authorised for use in Ontario schools.[54] They noted that no research on the treatment of racial minorities in textbooks has been done in Europe and that, in the United States, the treatment of immigrants in textbooks was not studied until the Second World War. The researchers found that textbooks used in Ontario schools made scant reference to religious groups other than Christians. Immigrants, on the whole, received positive treatment, but Negroes and natives were treated in negative terms. An analysis of the pictures in textbooks revealed that natives, Asians and Africans were given negative treatment.

> A very high proportion of both Africans and Asians were shown engaged in manual work. Skilled or professional work seemed largely the preserve of whites, who accounted for almost three-quarters of those shown in this classification. There are scholars, engineers, and modern farmers in India, Malaysia, and Thailand, to choose just three countries. Portraying most representatives of other groups as primitive agriculturalists restricts important information which should be available for the students in our schools.[55]

There is evidence to suggest that school texts are important contributors to the development of ethnic attitudes among children.[56] If multiculturalism is to become a reality, much more work needs to be done in removing racial bias from the texts currently in use in Canadian schools.

Multiculturalism, the current official policy, is an exciting theoretical concept. It has never been seriously tried in a modern industrial state. Can it work? It depends upon the interpretation that is put upon the concept of language and culture maintenance. If it implies wholesale importation of cultures from all parts of the globe and an attempt to preserve them in an undiluted form, it is bound to fail. If, on the other hand, it means resisting total rejection of the old culture in favour of an uncritical acceptance of the new, if it means integration of the old with the new values, if it means not just being an Italian, or a Canadian, but an Italian-Canadian, it might succeed. The concept of multiculturalism is not without its critics. Porter maintains that cultural differences are exaggerated by English-Canadians in order to use them as an excuse for preventing minority groups from climbing the social ladder.[57] He maintains that the myth of cultural differences is the major obstacle in the way of equality of opportunity in Canada. Since multiculturalism implies maintenance of cultural differences, it will greatly help the cause of continuing English-Canadian monopoly over elite positions in Canadian society. To a certain extent Porter's criticisms are justified. A distinction could be drawn between a multi-ethnic pluralist society and an institutionally pluralist society. While there has been a great deal of discussion in Canada about the former, little thought has been given to the latter. In practice, English-Canadians, and to a lesser extent French-Canadians, still control the major institutions in Canadian society and, until every child in school has an equal opportunity to put his hands on levels of power, multiculturalism is likely to remain an empty slogan.

In conclusion, the education of immigrants poses two major problems. Firstly, there is a great lack of sound empirically based research. Much of our knowledge comes either from chance remarks of parents, teachers, principals, students, administrators and the like, or from anecdotal accounts published in the news media. Good studies are few and far between. Secondly, in common with other multiracial societies, Canada has not yet learnt how to avoid intergroup conflict, particularly prejudice and discrimination against visible minorities, or how to integrate rather than assimilate immigrant children into an educational system and society at large. A great deal of innovation, experimentation and evaluation needs to be done.

## Notes

1.  Jean Burnet, 'Myths and Multiculturalism', *Canadian Journal of Education, 4* (1979), pp. 43-58.
2.  Freda Hawkins, *Canada and Immigration: Public Policy and Public Concern* (McGill-Queen's University Press, Montreal, 1972), p. 34.
3.  Constantine Passaris, *Understanding Canadian Immigration* (The Canadian Foundation for Economic Education, Montreal, 1978).
4.  Dean D. Wood, *Multicultural Canada* (Ontario Institute for Studies in Education, Toronto, 1978), p. 15.
5.  George Rawlyk, 'Canada's Immigration Policy, 1945-1962', *Dalhousie Review*, 42 (3) (1962), p. 290.
6.  Ibid.
7.  Edith Ferguson, *Immigrants in Canada* (University of Toronto, Toronto, 1974), p. 17.
8.  Canadian Imperial Bank of Commerce, 'Canadian Population. Past Trends and Future Prospects', *Commercial Letter*, no. 2 (1979).
9.  Passaris, *Understanding Canadian Immigration*.
10.  A.E. Ryerson, 'The Importance of Education to a Manufacturing, and a Free People', *Journal of Education for Upper Canada*, 1 (1848), pp. 289-301, quoted in Keith A. McLeod, 'A Short History of the Immigrant Student as "New Canadian" ', in A. Wolfgang (ed.), *Education of Immigrant Students: Issues and*

*Answers* (Ontario Institute for Studies in Education, Toronto, 1975).

11.  McLeod, 'The Immigrant Student as "New Canadian" '.

12.  Ontario Economic Council, *Immigrant Integration: Our Obligations – Political, Social and Economic – to the 1,700,000 People Who Have Come to Ontario In the Past Quarter Century* (Ontario Economic Council, Toronto, 1970).

13.  Royal Commission on Bilingualism and Biculturalism, Report, vol. 4: *The Cultural Contribution of the Other Ethnic Groups* (Queen's Printer, Ottawa, 1970).

14.  Canada Parliament, House of Commons, 'Canadian Culture: Announcement of Implementation Policy of Multiculturalism within Bilingual Framework', 28th Parliament, 3rd session, 8 October 1971, *Debates 8.*

15.  Ibid.

16.  e.g. *Canada: Multicultural*, proceedings of a conference held at the University of Toronto (Citizenship Branch, Ontario Department of the Provincial Secretary and Citizenship, Toronto, n.d.); Sheilagh Dubois, *Conference on Multiculturalism in Education* (Ontario Association for Curriculum Development, Toronto, 1977).

17.  John R. Mallea and L. Philip, 'Canadian Pluralism and Education: A Select Bibliography', *Canadian Ethnic Studies* 8, no. 1 (1976).

18.  Kurt Danziger, *The Socialization of Immigrant Children, Part I* (Ethnic Research Programme, Institute of Behavioural Research, York University, Toronto, 1971).

19.  Mary Ashworth, *Immigrant Children and Canadian Schools* (McClelland and Stewart, Toronto, 1975).

20.  Royal Commission of Inquiry on Education, 'The Minority Ethnic Groups in the School System', in *Report of the Commission* (Alphonse Marie Parent, Chairman), vol. 3: *The Ethnic Groups* (Printer for the Province of Quebec, Quebec, 1966), pp. 107-14.

21.  Marilyn Reid and Lynne Guinet, *A Review of the Provisions in Vancouver Schools for New Canadians at the Primary Level*, Research Report 71-18 (Department of Evaluation and Research, Vancouver Board of School Trustees, Vancouver, 1971).

22.  K. McRoberts and D. Postage, *Quebec Social Change and Political Crisis* (McClelland and Stewart, Toronto, 1976), p. 137.

23.  Mel Lafountain, quoted in Toronto Board of Education, *We Are All Immigrants to This Place* (Toronto Board of Education, Toronto, 1976).

24.  Joseph L. Steriott, 'Experiments on the Main Street', *Toronto Education Quarterly* (1965-66), pp. 2-3, quoted in Toronto Board of Education, *We Are All Immigrants to This Place.*

25.  Toronto Board of Education, *We Are All Immigrants to This Place.*

26.  Ibid.

27.  Ibid.

28.  Janet L. Moody, *An Evaluation of the Khalsa-Diwan Moberly Program (Under the Mango Tree) Vancouver Summer 1971* (Vancouver School Board Department of Planning and Evaluation, Vancouver, 1971), p. 1.

29.  M. Bosquet, Personal Correspondence.

30.  Joti Bhatnagar, 'Education of Immigrant Children', *Canadian Ethnic Studies*, 8 (1976), pp. 52-70.

31.  Jeffrey L. Derevensky and Charles Lusthaus, 'Black and Immigrant Children in Montreal: A Curricular Comparison', paper presented at the Annual Meeting of the American Educational Research Association, San Francisco, April 1976.

32.  John Roth, *West Indians in Toronto: The Students and the Schools* (Board of Education for the Borough of York, Toronto, 1974).

33.    Eileen Mary Lewis, 'A Study of the Cultural and Language Problems of Greek Immigrant Children in Montreal', M.Ed. thesis, Bishop's University, 1973.

34.    Rimkyu, Lee, 'Sources of Information and Education Used by Korean Adult Residents in Vancouver', MA thesis, University of British Columbia, 1972.

35.    Marvin J. Godfrey, 'A Study of the Academic Achievement and Personal and Social Adjustment of Jewish Moroccan Immigrant Students in the English High Schools of Montreal', MA thesis, McGill University, 1970.

36.    Marcela S. Duran, 'Values and Education: A Study of the Spanish-Speaking Latin-American Children in the Junior Schools of Metropolitan Toronto', MA thesis, University of Toronto, 1975.

37.    Ana Maria Coelho, *Conflicts and Adjustments of Portuguese Youth in School, Home, and Community* (Ontario Ministry of Culture and Recreation, Toronto, 1973).

38.    Ramesh A. Deosaran, Edgar N. Wright and Thelma Kane, *The 1975 Every Student Survey: Student's Background and Its Relationship to Program Placement*, Research Service Report no. 138 (Research Department, Toronto Board of Education, Toronto, 1976).

39.    Robert Remnant, 'Italian Students in Toronto Schools: Equality in Difference', *CSSE Bulletin*, 2 (September 1974).

40.    Janet L. Moody, *Evaluation of the Punjabi-English Class at the Moberly Primary Annex for the 1973-74 School Year*, Research Report 74-18 (Department of Planning and Evaluation, Vancouver Board of School Trustees, Vancouver, 1974).

41.    K.A. O'Bryan, O. Kuplovista and J.A. Reitz, 'A Review of the Principal Results', in Canadian Consultative Council on Multiculturalism, *Conference Report – Second Canadian Conference on Multiculturalism* (Minister of Supplies and Services, Ottawa, 1978).

42.    Ibid.

43.    Ibid.

44.    J.W. Berry, R. Karlein and D.M. Taylor, 'Summary – Multiculturalism and Ethnic Attitudes in Canada', in Canadian Consultative Council on Multiculturalism, *Conference Report – Second Canadian Conference on Multiculturalism*.

45.    Ibid.

46.    Ibid.

47.    Ibid.

48.    A.H. Richmond, 'Black and Asian Immigrants in Britain and Canada: Some Comparisons', *Journal of the Community Relations Commission*, 4 (1976), pp. 501-23.

49.    S. Ramcharan, 'Adaptations of West Indians in Canada', unpublished PhD dissertation, York University, Toronto, 1974.

50.    W. Head and J. Lee, *The Black Presence in Canadian Mosaic* (York University, Toronto, 1975).

51.    Ontario Human Rights Commission, *Life Together: A Report on Human Rights in Ontario* (Queen's Printer, Toronto, 1977), p. 56.

52.    B. Ubale, *Equal Opportunities and Public Policy* (B. Ubale, Toronto, 1977).

53.    Frances Henry, *The Dynamics of Racism in Toronto* (York University, Toronto, 1978).

54.    A. McDiarmid and D. Pratt, *Teaching Prejudice* (The Ontario Institute for Studies in Education, Toronto, 1971).

55.    Ibid.

56.    F.O. Shirley, 'The Influence of Reading on Concepts, Attitudes and Behavior of 10th, 11th and 12th Grade Students', unpublished PhD dissertation, University of Arizona, 1966; F.L. Fisher, 'Influences of Reading and Discussion

of the Attitudes of 5th Graders towards American Indians', *Journal of Educational Research*, 62 (1968), pp. 130-4.

57.    J. Porter, 'Bilingualism and the Myths of Culture', *Canadian Review of Sociology and Anthropology*, 6 (1969), pp. 111-19.

# 5 THE EDUCATION OF IMMIGRANT CHILDREN IN FRANCE

**Martine Charlot**

In the course of its history, France has always welcomed considerable numbers of foreigners. At the beginning of the twentieth century, as a result of the colonial phenomenon, people of remote origin came to France and were employed in low-status jobs. After the First World War, which left an enormous gap in the French workforce, the influx of immigrant workers increased considerably. Europeans, especially Poles and Italians, responded to the need in France for miners, construction workers and farmers. Many of these workers started families in France, and their third- and even fourth-generation descendants have now been naturalised and totally integrated into French society. In addition to these Europeans, there were also many Russian and Armenian immigrants. Between the two world wars, the foreign population of France accounted for almost 7 per cent of the total population.

## The Migratory Influx of the Sixties

The slaughter of the First World War seriously affected the number of individuals who would ultimately come of working age at a time when France was in the process of rebuilding itself and accommodating to an era of accelerated industrialisation — just after World War II. If there were insufficient numbers of French youths to fill the jobs in such a rapidly expanding employment market, the colonies and the developing European countries (as they were modestly called), subjected to dictatorial regimes (Spain, Portugal) and suffering from unemployment, yielded a seemingly inexhaustible reserve of manpower. Until 1972, the influx of foreign workers to fill jobs in construction, metallurgy and farming was practically uncontrolled. Even the Algerian War (1954-62) hardly slowed the flow of Maghribans into France. Between 1960 and 1973, many Portuguese secretly crossed the Spanish and French borders *en masse*. After finding jobs, which was easy, they just stayed and regarded themselves as immigrants. At the time, social measures concerning housing were almost non-existent. Meanwhile, after anywhere from a few months to a few years, the foreign workers, who at the beginning had generally come by themselves, called their families or their fiancées or started new families. This produced a fair number of second-generation immigrants. As a result of the very liberal attitudes of the French authorities towards these workers, large numbers of young people of foreign origin brought up in France are competing with French youths for job opportunities, which have been limited since 1974.

Each year, many thousands of foreign workers do not return to France after their summer vacations, but the majority of them have permanently established themselves in France, especially after the immigration halt in July 1974. At present, a very large proportion of the newcomers (about 1,000 per month) are refugees from southeast Asia. A considerable number of these refugees are women, children and adolescents. It is necessary to note that the closure of immigration to workers was not accompanied by a similar closure of family immigration. Therefore, young children of all origins continue regularly to arrive in France.

The statistics concerning the foreign population in France are far from accurate. The two official sources show considerable variation. According to an estimate made by the Ministry of the Interior on 31 December 1977 (Table 5.1), the foreign population should be 4,236,994, or 8 per cent of the total population. On the other hand,

Table 5.1:  Principal Nationalities

| Portuguese | 881,985 | Tunisians | 176,154 |
|---|---|---|---|
| Algerians | 829,572 | Turks | 80,482 |
| Italians | 528,809 | Poles | 79,387 |
| Spaniards | 486,299 | Yugoslavs | 77,354 |
| Moroccans | 376,055 | Belgians | 64,891 |

according to the last census in 1975 (Table 5.2), the number of foreigners should be only 3,442,415, or 6.5 per cent of the population. It is almost certain that the figures provided by the Ministry of the Interior are overestimates and that those derived from the census are underestimates. Therefore, it would be appropriate to assume that the actual figure is about 3,900,000 foreigners, of whom 1,800,000 are working.

The distribution of workers by socio-economic status, according to the 1975 census, is given in Table 5.3. As is evident from this table,

Table 5.2: Total Population by Sex and Principal Nationalities according to the Census of 1975

| Nationality | Total | | Male | | Female | |
|---|---|---|---|---|---|---|
| | Number | % | Number | % | Number | % |
| Total population | 52,599,430 | 100.0 | 25,744,475 | 100.0 | 26,854,955 | 100.0 |
| Foreigners | 3,442,415 | 6.5 | 2,060,840 | 8.0 | 1,381,575 | 5.2 |
| of which: | | | | | | |
| Europe | 2,090,235 | 60.7 (a) | 143,670 | 55.0 (a) | 957,565 | 69.3 (a) |
| Spaniards | 497,480 | 14.5 | 262,365 | 12.7 | 235,115 | 17.0 |
| Italians | 462,940 | 13.4 | 260,440 | 12.6 | 202,500 | 14.7 |
| Portuguese | 758,925 | 22.0 | 408,530 | 19.8 | 350,395 | 25.4 |
| Yugoslavs | 70,280 | 2.0 | 40,720 | 2.0 | 29,560 | 2.1 |
| Africa | 1,192,300 | 34.6 | 829,895 | 40.3 | 362,405 | 26.2 |
| Algerians | 710,690 | 20.6 | 483,090 | 23.4 | 227,600 | 16.5 |
| Moroccans | 260,025 | 7.6 | 190,570 | 9.3 | 69,455 | 5.0 |
| Tunisians | 139,735 | 4.1 | 96,515 | 4.7 | 43,220 | 3.1 |
| Maltese | 12,530 | 0.3 | 11,275 | 0.6 | 1,255 | 0.1 |
| Senegalese | 14,920 | 0.4 | 12,735 | 0.6 | 2,185 | 0.2 |
| Asia | 116,915 | 3.4 | 76,445 | 3.7 | 40,470 | 2.9 |
| Turks | 50,860 | 1.5 | 37,790 | 1.8 | 13,970 | 0.9 |

a. These percentages represent the proportion of the total foreign population.

Table 5.3:    Distribution of Workers by Socio-economic Status

| Socio-professional category | Number | % |
|---|---|---|
| Farmers | 15,125 | 0.9 |
| Farm workers | 69,550 | 4.4 |
| Managers | 49,585 | 3.1 |
| Professionals and executives | 38,570 | 2.4 |
| Technicians and clerical | 40,955 | 2.6 |
| Workers | 86,010 | 5.4 |
| Foremen | 362,810 | 22.9 |
| Skilled workers | 776,810 | 49.0 |
| Miners, sailors and fishermen | 16,045 | 1.0 |
| Service industry personnel | 108,870 | 6.9 |
| Other | 20,010 | 1.4 |
| Total | 1,584,340 | 100.0 |

Source:    Recensement (INSEE).

the class of labourers is the most largely represented. In fact, the number of foreigners who have both professional qualifications and the opportunity of using them is very low. Like the preceding immigrant populations now in the process of naturalisation (Italian, Spanish), the Maghriban and Black African workers, often illiterate, occupy low-status jobs.

## Young Immigrants in the School System

For several years now, the proportion of children born to parents, at least one of whom is foreign, has exceeded 10 per cent of the total legitimate births. The proportion of foreign children less than 20 years of age has now reached about 7 per cent of the total number within this age group. Foreigners are unequally distributed throughout the country. There are very few in the western and central regions where there is little industrialisation. On the other hand, there are a great number of foreigners in Paris and in Ile-de-France. Thirty-six per cent of the total foreign population of France is concentrated in these regions. Whereas the foreigners constitute between 6.5 and 8 per cent of the total French population, they form 15.5 per cent of the population of these regions. In the Rhone-Alps area they account for 13.1

per cent of the country's foreign population and 11.6 per cent of the region's population, while in Provence-Côte d'Azur they constitute 9.2 per cent of the total French foreign population and 10.6 per cent of the area's population. There are also many foreigners in industrialised regions in the north and the east, and in the regions bordering Spain. According to the 1975 census, the cities most heavily populated by foreigners are: Paris (12 per cent of the total population), Lyon (11.8 per cent), Marseille (7.9 per cent), Lille (8.1 per cent) and Grenoble (12.8 per cent). It is important to note that, even in these cities or their suburbs, the concentration of foreign populations differs widely according to districts. For instance, in the suburbs west of Paris foreigners are poorly represented, while in the districts of the so-called *red belt*, the northwest and northeast, their proportion varies between 20 per cent and 30 per cent of the total population. Certain sectors of these more populated districts often consist of 75 to 85 per cent foreigners. Some towns are almost entirely populated by foreigners, a situation which, as we will see, has considerable consequences for the education of the children, and all the more so because of the propensity of these foreign families to have many children: it is not uncommon to see Algerian families with ten or more children.

Young immigrants are distributed throughout the French school system from the age of two and a half in pre-schools (for those born in France or who arrived very young) and up to the age of 16 (at the end of compulsory school attendance). A certain number of immigrant children continue their studies beyond the age of 16, some in the classical, modern or technical secondary schools and some in the pre-vocational and vocational streams. The distribution of these children in the public school system, according to the statistics of the Ministry of Education (1977-78), is given in Tables 5.4 and 5.5.

These statistics have the disadvantage of listing, under the same heading of 'foreigners', young people of very different origins: young Spaniards and Italians, not yet naturalised but very much integrated into French society and presenting no more scholastic difficulties than the young French of the same social milieu; young people born in France (who use French as their first language) and young people who have arrived recently; young people of privileged milieus (not many) and young people from disadvantaged milieus; young people from large families (North Africans and Black Africans) and young people from small families (Yugoslavs). Besides, such statistics do not consider children with French passports who often present scholastic difficulties, such as Moslem children of Algerian repatriates and children from the West Indies.

Table 5.4: Data from the First Stage (3 to 11 years)

Metropolitan France — 1977-78

| | | Foreign Students by Nationality | | | | | | | | | | | |
|---|---|---|---|---|---|---|---|---|---|---|---|---|---|
| | | Algerians | Moroccans | Tunisians | Other African countries | Spaniards | Portuguese | Yugoslavs | Italians | Other countries in the Common Market | Others | Total | % foreigners over total number |
| Pre-school | Number | 64,694 | 21,245 | 10,668 | 5,824 | 15,767 | 55,543 | 3,908 | 9,803 | 2,440 | 13,686 | 203,578 | 9.1 |
| | % | 31.9 | 10.5 | 5.2 | 2.9 | 7.7 | 27.2 | 1.9 | 4.8 | 1.2 | 6.7 | 100.0 | |
| Elementary | Number | 114,892 | 32,688 | 13,075 | 5,982 | 37,532 | 104,991 | 6,543 | 26,873 | 4,313 | 25,031 | 371,920 | 9.3 |
| | % | 30.9 | 8.8 | 3.5 | 1.6 | 10.1 | 28.2 | 1.8 | 7.2 | 1.2 | 6.7 | 100.0 | |
| Special | Number | 6,490 | 1,572 | 580 | 138 | 1,469 | 4,707 | 203 | 1,031 | 112 | 759 | 17,061 | 13.8 |
| | % | 38.0 | 9.2 | 3.4 | 0.8 | 8.6 | 27.6 | 1.2 | 6.0 | 0.7 | 4.5 | 100.0 | |
| Total | Number | 186,076 | 55,505 | 24,323 | 11,944 | 54,768 | 165,241 | 10,654 | 37,707 | 6,865 | 39,476 | 592,559 | 9.3 |
| | % | 31.4 | 9.4 | 4.1 | 2.0 | 9.2 | 27.9 | 1.8 | 6.4 | 1.1 | 6.7 | 100.0 | |

Table 5.5: Data from the Second Stage (12 to 18 years)

Metropolitan France — 1977-78

| | | Algerians | Moroccans | Tunisians | Other African countries | Spaniards | Portuguese | Italians | Yugoslavs | Others | Total | Total respondents | % foreigners |
|---|---|---|---|---|---|---|---|---|---|---|---|---|---|
| | | | | | | Foreign Students by Nationality | | | | | | | |
| 1st cycle without CPPN – CPA[a] | Number | 39,572 | 7,929 | 3,977 | 1,772 | 20,856 | 32,208 | 17,298 | 2,249 | 11,082 | 136,943 | 2,410,972 | 5.7 |
| | % | 28.9 | 5.8 | 2.9 | 1.3 | 15.2 | 23.5 | 12.6 | 1.7 | 8.1 | 100.0 | — | — |
| CPPN – CPA[a] | Number | 5,520 | 1,762 | 490 | 103 | 1,975 | 5,941 | 1,724 | 164 | 970 | 18,649 | 172,732 | 10.8 |
| | % | 29.6 | 9.5 | 2.6 | 0.6 | 10.6 | 31.8 | 9.2 | 0.9 | 5.2 | 100.0 | — | — |
| 2nd cycle (long) | Number | 4,798 | 1,031 | 633 | 1,123 | 4,165 | 2,448 | 3,330 | 283 | 4,140 | 21,951 | 784,706 | 2.8 |
| | % | 21.8 | 4.7 | 2.9 | 5.1 | 19.0 | 11.1 | 15.2 | 1.3 | 18.9 | 100.0 | — | — |
| 2nd cycle (short) (technical) | Number | 15,403 | 2,859 | 1,348 | 508 | 7,218 | 11,596 | 6,589 | 536 | 1,629 | 47,686 | 594,368 | 8.0 |
| | % | 32.3 | 6.0 | 2.8 | 1.1 | 15.2 | 24.3 | 13.8 | 1.1 | 3.4 | 100.0 | — | — |
| Total secondary classes | Number | 65,293 | 13,581 | 6,448 | 3,506 | 34,214 | 52,193 | 28,941 | 3,232 | 17,821 | 225,229 | 3,962,778 | 5.7 |
| | % | 29.0 | 6.0 | 2.9 | 1.6 | 15.2 | 23.2 | 12.8 | 1.4 | 7.9 | 100.0 | — | — |

a. Pre-professional classes.

More revealing are statistics that portray foreign children as being one or several years behind academically, or as being oriented in a direction without future, or as coming out of the school system without a diploma and without any vocational training. These statistics sometimes exist for a school, a district or an academy, but they do not exist on a national scale. Although young foreigners constitute 5.7 per cent of the total secondary school population, according to official statistics, they are much more numerous in classes for weak students than would normally be expected (10.8 per cent), and underpresented in grades nearing the end of secondary studies (2.8 per cent).

Until about 1970, the implicit policy of the Ministry of Education, in agreement with public opinion and the Jacobinic tendency of French administration, was to place young immigrants in the classes of French schools in order for them to learn to speak, read and write French. This was not such a problem when these children started their education at the same time as young French children (at the age of six) and even less when they attended French kindergarten (between the ages of three and six). When they arrived in France during the course of their education, an unfortunate practice, which has not yet totally disappeared, was to place them in the primary classes of the school system: consequently, one could see foreign children aged ten or eleven sitting next to six-year-olds in order to learn to read French, or simply to learn how to read, if they had not attended school in their native country. This happened frequently with North African and African children, especially girls. Before 1960, when education was compulsory only until the age of 14, the majority of immigrant children who arrived in France after the age of twelve avoided French education altogether.

## The Present Policy of the Ministry of Education

At present, the educational policy states that, if a young foreigner between the ages of six and twelve arrives in France, he is advised to be placed in a class appropriate to his age and, through supportive teachers sensitive to his needs and deficiencies, he is to be integrated into the classroom. In some schools, foreign students with language difficulties are placed in special classes taught either by a teacher from the school or by an itinerant teacher. Since 1970, whenever there is a sufficient number of foreign children to warrant it, introductory classes have been organised. Here, for up to one year, the children can learn written and spoken French particularly relevant to their daily lives. The teachers in these introductory classes, who are, in theory, specialised in this type of instruction, help the children to function in French by drawing upon their prior knowledge and experience. As soon as the children can 'get by' in French, and before the end of the introductory year, they join children of their own age group in normal classes for certain activities. One of the difficulties of these introductory classes often arises as a result of the age differences among children, who generally range from seven to twelve years of age. Another problem is caused by those foreign students who arrive during the course of the school year. In addition, integration for a young person who arrives in the country after the age of twelve is very difficult and often results in severe problems for the student. So-called adjustment classes exist in secondary education, but they are few and scattered throughout France. Consequently, adolescents often have no choice but to resort to a pre-professional education that yields a limited scope for the future. At present, there are 1,000 classes of these types (introductory and adjustment) spread throughout the country, concentrated heavily in those regions with large immigrant populations.

The ministerial proposal of 1970 which recommended the establishment of these classes also mentioned other possibilities for the academic support of newly arrived immigrant children:

1. special annual 'open' classes (foreign children have common activities with French children from all other classes);
2. special classes for a limited period of time;
3. special integrated courses for late beginners (with seven or eight hours of special teaching a week);
4. the system of streaming groups within a class.

It must be noted that some assistance was provided by public authorities for the financing of special French lessons for isolated children essentially in rural areas and for those adolescents who could not be placed in adjustment classes. Despite these efforts, there are still many newly arrived foreign children who are immediately placed in regular classes with similarly aged children or younger. Children who are not given the benefit of special academic support may be helped intellectually and emotionally by teachers and family, but generally such additional support only allows the child to reach a limited level of academic achievement. If no such support exists for these children, then they will experience difficulties in school that often lead to unfortunate consequences for their professional futures.

**French and Foreign Children**

The Ministry of Education has recently proposed specialised training
for teachers of foreign children. Six centres bearing the name
'CEFISEM' (Regional Centres of Training and Information for the
Education of Immigrant Children) operate in France and have genera-
ted a great deal of excitement. These centres serve to make the teachers
aware of various alternatives to immediate placement of immigrant
children into normal classes. They emphasise a pedagogy centred around
the needs of the foreign populations and respect for their cultures. One
suggestion to teachers is to organise intercultural activities within the
school as a means of stimulating interest about the problems of non-
francophones. CEFISEM is certainly one of the most valuable programmes established by the ministry in the last few years.

The new spirit of school policy *vis-à-vis* immigrants has been expressed in a ministerial proposal of July 1978. The proposal recommends
flexible and creative classroom activities designed to give support to
foreign students. Parents are also urged to involve themselves in the
school life of their children, to develop supportive behaviour towards
them and to avoid pronouncing too quick a judgement on their children's educational development. Above all, the proposal emphasises
the value of native languages and cultures, a subject to be discussed
later in this chapter.

In order to understand the situation of immigrant children in France,
it is necessary to note that the majority of them were either born in
France or arrived in the country when they were very young. For these
children, then, the French language does not present any particular
difficulties. Out of approximately 850,000 foreign children in the
French school system, only 20,000 require special help through introductory or adjustment classes. For the large number of students not
enrolled in these special classes, and for whom proficiency in the
French language is apparently not a problem, characteristic difficulties
still manifest themselves often throughout their school careers.

The question of whether or not a large proportion of immigrant
children in one school affects the scholastic achievement of both foreign and French children requires a close examination in terms of the
residential patterns of immigrants in France. Most immigrant families
are concentrated either in the older districts of large cities among
French citizens of equally low economic status, or in 'disadvantaged'
suburbs that lack the means to support cultural expression. The French
population (except for that portion which is of a lower economic

status and usually exhibits a virulent racism) readily accepts living in
areas heavily populated by foreigners. Consequently, whenever there
are many foreign children in a school existing side by side with socially
disadvantaged French children, and both immigrant and French children
perform lower than the norm, it is difficult to conclude that this poor
scholastic achievement on the part of the French students is due to the
presence of immigrants. On the other hand, foreign children from the
middle class, or in upwardly mobile positions with respect to French
society, who are generally found in small numbers in schools with a
middle-class student population, do not seem negatively to affect the
academic achievement of French students. The difficulties encountered
are almost always of an economic and socio-cultural nature rather than
linguistic or based upon immigrant status *per se.*

## Language and Culture Conflicts

What language do immigrants speak? The answer is not simple. When
adult immigrants come to France they continue, in general, to speak
their mother tongue among themselves. However, this language is not
always their national language. Thus, the majority of the Algerian
immigrants in France speak Berber Kayle; many Spaniards speak Bas-
que, Catalan and Andalusian; the Italians speak Sicilian, Venetian and
Bergamasque; the Yugoslavs speak Croatian and Macedonian. Young
people who arrived as adolescents continue to speak their mother
tongue with their parents, but the same is not always true for children
who either arrived very young or were born in France. Generally, they
understand the language of their parents but often refuse to speak it,
either because they do not feel comfortable with it or because they
consider it inappropriate to express themselves in the language of a
population at the bottom of the social scale. For example, a parent
will ask a question in Arabic and the child will respond in French.
School-age siblings most often use French among themselves. It often
arises out of a fear of family disintegration that French becomes the
language spoken at home, although the parents speak it poorly and
with an accent. Contrary to what certain teachers believe, such a situation does not help the young students at all.

In fact, even the language problem itself must be placed within a
social context. Bilingualism *per se* does not deleteriously affect social
and scholastic adjustment. What does affect adjustment is the way in
which a young immigrant perceives that a language impinges on social

status. In France, the use of English, American, Swedish and Spanish is not only tolerated, but often gives the speaker a superior status to that ascribed to monolinguals. However, the same is true neither for Portuguese and Arabic, which denote populations previously colonised and held in low regard, nor for other languages spoken by populations of low economic status. Therefore, in order to blend into the crowd, to become 'like the others', to forget and make others forget his origin, the immigrant child refuses to learn or to speak the language of his parents. This refusal is a sign of the desire to assimilate, often shared and encouraged by the family.

The question of cultural identity is always raised in relation to second-generation immigrants who have been subjected to two identification models, one consisting of the family (especially the mother) and the other consisting of the society in which they live. These two models are at times far removed from each other. For example, the difference between the social role of women in Moslem society and in European society is striking: the young Algerian girl is pledged by her family to an arranged marriage, a secluded domestic life and numerous pregnancies, while French society offers the same girl, as soon as she enters school, a totally different way of thinking and living. This is, of course, an extreme case of the separation between two cultures, but it occurs quite frequently. Such cultural tensions are not as strong for young immigrants of European origin. In any case, these difficulties, which hamper scholastic achievement and often lead to anxiety sometimes severe enough even to cause attempts at suicide, are inevitably found among those children whose parents have chosen to live and let their children live in a social milieu different from their native culture. Such difficulties are no worse in France than in other countries of immigration; they are well known to sociologists and psychiatrists around the world.

## The Orientation of Young Immigrants

Many young immigrants are motivated by the desire for socio-economic advancement and for assimilation into the society in which they live. The parents of these children left one country in order to find less miserable conditions in another, and often they have been deceived in their expectations (encountering racism, impossibility of ascending the social scale, etc.). As a result, the parents have transfered their own hopes for a better life to their children, who in their parents' eyes must succeed in order to assuage the guilt engendered by renouncing their native country. But, as is reflected in the scholastic problems which immigrant students often encounter, it is quite difficult for children to fulfil such parental hopes, and consequently the children suffer. During periods of economic crisis, such as the one Europe is currently undergoing, jobs become scarce, competition for them increases and upward social mobility becomes difficult. Studies have shown that there is little social mobility among the children of Portuguese and Algerians who have settled in France. As a result both of the difficulties encountered in school and of an economic situation which is unfavourable even for young French people, immigrant youths are offered almost the same inferior jobs with which their parents had to content themselves. Some, however, succeed in climbing the socio-professional ladder: they are often children of European origin from small, well-integrated families, but some are merely driven by a strong desire for integration. Because of their difficulties, immigrant children are frequently made to follow ill-considered academic paths. How are these paths chosen? Are the instruments used adequate? Two methods are employed for such an evaluation: one is through observation of a child's spontaneous behaviour, the other through observation of his behaviour within a controlled context that is either academic, intellectual or socio-affective. Observations made in an academic domain must take into consideration the French language proficiency of the newly arrived child. Educational reports look at such things as the levels of study in a foreign student's country of origin, his age at the beginning of school attendance and the possible ramifications of repeating a class for a second year. It is difficult to judge whether or not a young person under such observation demonstrates the full extent of his knowledge, and therefore it is often necessary to take non verbal information into account. However, the results obtained from such observations do not make evident the possibilities available for the further development of the student. IQs are generally only valid under a given set of cultural conditions that are frequently very different from those that exist in an immigrant's native country. For example, immigrant adolescents of rural or of North African origin often fail cube tests.

For newly arrived immigrant children, with regard to the socio-affective domain, one must keep in mind not only the after-effects of uprooting and its repercussions on the family, but also the differences between education in a child's country of origin and education as it exists in France. In actuality, each immigrant child presents a specific problem and, consequently, it is difficult to pre-establish criteria from which to determine how, generally, to deal with newly arrived foreign students. Research shows that immediate placement of the foreign student into regular classes (when it is deemed that the student cannot benefit from an introductory or adjustment class) leads to, at best, a student's repetition of a class at the same level. More frequently, in the case of adolescents, it results in a dead-end for the student as he awaits working age.

## Courses in Mother Tongues

As previously mentioned, public authorities in France (Ministry of Education, Secretary of State for Immigrant Workers) have been attentive during the past two or three years to the need for establishing courses in mother tongues and creating cultural and intercultural activities. Their aim is to prevent the foreign child from being cut off from his milieu of origin and to prepare him for a possible return to the country of his parents. The policy of urging immigrants to return to their native countries has been an important question since the autumn of 1977.

For many years, the embassies and consulates have favoured the existence of language courses for foreign students which are given after school hours. Since 1975, the Ministry of Education has favoured the creation of these courses, to be given three hours per week during school hours, whenever there are sufficient numbers of children of the same nationality or of the same language, and whenever such a course is desired by the families involved. At first intended for the Portuguese, the measure has now been extended to the principal national languages of the countries of emigration. The courses, called 'integrated courses', are the result of an agreement between France and the countries of origin. According to the terms of this agreement, the emigration countries have the right to choose the teachers, whom they must financially remunerate. The distribution of children in elementary schools who at present benefit from both types of courses is given in Table 5.6.

The courses in mother tongues, whether integrated into the school programme or not, present many problems. Generally, they are wanted more by the parents than by the children, who see in these courses nothing but extra work and an exclusion from the leisure activities which other children, French and foreign, enjoy. These children, when very young, do not always realise the usefulness of such courses. It is not until the children reach adolescence that they recognise both the

Table 5.6:   Distribution of Elementary Schoolchildren who Attend Courses in Mother Tongue

| Students | School Attendance | Public | Private | Total |
|---|---|---|---|---|
| Spaniards | | 39,009 | 2,451 | 41,460 |
| | 50 integrated courses | | | 500 |
| | 350 parallel courses | | | 19,000 |
| | 250 teaching Spaniards | | | |
| Portuguese | | 94,989 | 5,614 | 100,603 |
| | Integrated and parallel courses | | | 40,000 |
| | 296 teaching Portuguese in January 1978 | | | |
| Italians | | 28,483 | 1,192 | 29,675 |
| | 416 integrated courses | | | 6,885 |
| | 247 parallel courses | | | 3,401 |
| | L'AEFI is charged with 189 courses | | | 2,516 |
| | About 100 teaching Italians | | | |
| | About 30 for L'AEFI | | | |
| | or the next school year projects at Lyon and Grenoble for encouraging Italian for children | | | |
| Yugoslavs | | 5,771 | 226 | 5,997 |
| | 77-78: integrated and parallel courses | | | 3,108 |
| | Integrated courses exist in three schools: in Ivry, Aubervilliers and 22, rue Olivier Métra à Paris for 35 students and 1 teacher. About 50 Yugoslavian teachers are in charge of parallel courses. | | | |
| Turks | School attendance | | | 3,002 |
| | Parallel courses | | | |
| | 28 teaching Turks | | | |
| Tunisians | 77-78: integrated courses | | | 1,605 |
| | Parallel courses | | | 1,916 |
| | Teachers: 50 — 1 insp. — 12 | | | |
| Algerians | | 106,504 | 2,760 | 109,263 |
| | 77-78: 185,000 primary and parallel courses | | | |
| | Integrated courses | | | 9,349 |
| | Marginal instructors | | | 26,311 |
| Moroccans | | 26,777 | 711 | 27,488 |

importance of their own cultural identity within French society and the relevance of such courses to maintaining that identity. Unfortunately, the lack of co-operation between foreign teachers who teach these courses and French teachers results in the small number of special courses offered. It is also important to consider that presenting courses in mother tongues, which creates the illusion of a return to the country of origin, can have a negative effect on the family.

## An Atmosphere of Uncertainty

Does education in the mother tongue contribute to the reconciliation of the child to the culture of his parents? Does it help his progress in French and his integration into the school system? These questions are presently being studied. Indeed, many factors add greatly to the complexity of such questions: the family's plans, the concept of immigration, the school atmosphere, the social status given to foreigners and their culture, the individual child's psychology, the attitude of the foreign teacher, etc. Present research indicates the necessity for intercultural activities within schools for French as well as foreign students. The activities promote interest in the country of origin through books, films, slides, musical activities and an introduction to its language. All this could change the conditions of reception of foreign children and lead to positive attitudes towards the teaching of languages. Undoubtedly, it would be best to start such a programme with the co-operation of the immigrant families, instead of creating courses without any preliminary consultation. All this, however, requires a teacher training programme that is presently insufficient.

In conclusion, it can be said that, for some enlightened administrators and a number of well-informed teachers, the real problems of immigrant children in France are starting to become the object of serious thought. It must be added, however, that school is not everything, and that, if a favourable atmosphere did exist in the schools for foreign children (and this is far from being the general situation), it would not be able to remedy totally the present atmosphere of insecurity that exists for immigrants in France and the serious uncertainties which burden the socio-professional future of second-generation immigrant youth. These young people cannot consider going back to the country of their parents, a country they hardly know, and yet often they find it difficult to integrate adequately into French society.

## References

*Books and Pamphlets*

Centre International de l'Enfance. 'Les enfants de travailleurs migrants en Europe.

Santé, scolarité, adoption sociale', a colloquium organised in Paris, 19–22 March, 1973 (ESF, Paris, 1974), p. 152

Charlot, M. (with the collaboration of A. Lauran and A. Ben Dhiab). 'Mon avenir, quel avenir' *Témoignages de jeunes immigrés* (Casterman, Paris, 1978). p. 208

Marchand, F. (ed.) *Manuel de Linguistique appliquée,* vol. 2: *Acquisition du langage. Enfants français, immigrés* (Delagrave, Paris, 1975)

Porcher, L., *La scolarisation des enfants étrangers en France* (Didier, Paris, 1978)

## Special Issues of Magazines

*Cahiers Pédagogiques.* 'La scolarisation des enfants immigrés'. No. 143, April 1976

*Education et Développement.* 'Enfants de travailleurs migrants'. No. 101, June 1975

*Hommes et Migration — Etudes.* 'Les enfants de partout et l'école française'. No. 123, 1975

*Le Français Aujourd'hui.* 'Dans toutes les classes des enfants d'immigrés'. No. 44, December 1978

*Migrants Formation.* 'Adolescents immigrés'. Nos. 29–30, October 1978

*Migrants Formation.* Sélection d'articles sur la scolarisation des enfants immigrés parus dans Migrants-Formation. Nos. 1–28

# 6 THE CHILDREN OF GUEST-WORKERS IN THE FEDERAL REPUBLIC OF GERMANY: MALADJUSTMENT AND ITS EFFECTS ON ACADEMIC PERFORMANCE*

Schole Raoufi

In order to appreciate the educational problems faced by guest-workers' children in the Federal Republic of Germany (FRG), it is essential to emphasise a given set of socio-political and economic conditions determining the way of life of their parents.

Who are the *Gastarbeiter*? The German word *Gastarbeiter* refers to a certain group of foreigners who are 'guest-workers', also referred to as foreign or alien workers, in the FRG.[1] The economic function of guest-workers is to regulate Germany's employment; they play the role of a so-called 'army of reserve workers' for Germany's industry. Whenever the need arises, depending on the whole mechanism of expansion and recession involved in the production process, this foreign labour army can be employed or dismissed immediately. The euphemistic term 'guest-worker' conveys the notion of being entitled to integration into German society but, in reality, these foreign workers are treated merely as objects whose fate is determined by the fluctuations of the economic health of the nation.[2] Over the past years, this term has lost its literal meaning. Statistics show that only 41 per cent of foreign workers intend to return home.[3] The majority stay longer than initially intended, and meanwhile their children might be born in the host country. Experience has shown that the longer their duration of stay, the stronger their wish to remain permanently in the FRG. Generally, one grows accustomed to the new and becomes estranged from the native environment. It is therefore not surprising that each year only one out of every six foreigners returns to his home country. Among guest-workers, 35 per cent have lived six or more years in the FRG; 25 per cent have remained longer than ten years.

## Pull and Push Forces of Emigration

The process of migration largely depends on socio-economic factors. Workers emigrate for various reasons: in order to escape chronic unem-

113

ployment, to fulfil their desire for upward mobility, or to escape political or religious pressures. Recruitment of foreign workers to the FRG is based upon a steady demand for an increased labour force due to a fall in the birth-rate, a shortened working week, longer vacations, higher educational norms, upward social mobility of native workers, as well as control of inflation. In order to balance out supply and demand in the force, the government of the FRG has formally signed agreements with other countries regulating recruitment and mediation of foreign workers: Italy (in 1955), Spain (1960), Greece (1960), Turkey (1961), Morocco (1963), Portugal (1964), Tunisia (1965) and Yugoslavia (1968). Six main countries (Italy, Spain, Greece, Yugoslavia, Turkey and Portugal) supply 82 per cent of all foreign workers in the FRG.

Guest-workers are forced to leave their home countries due to economic necessity, as pressures from poverty and unemployment become unbearable. They occupy the lowest strata of German society, and almost 90 per cent find themselves in the lowest income brackets. They receive employment in the new country by performing menial tasks which Germans do not like to do.[4] A high proportion of guest-workers are to be found in jobs involving hard physical work, low pay and even lower social status. The following data support this proposition: of all the workers employed in street cleaning, more than 92 per cent are guest-workers. Similar figures obtain for other undesirable occupations which often involve night shifts, such as lavatory attendants (52 per cent), garbage removers (47 per cent), janitors (46 per cent) and hotel and restaurant workers (34 per cent).[5]

Additional complicating factors contributing to the low chances guest-workers have for upward mobility arise out of:

1. a transition from less developed agrarian regions to industrialised urban settings;
2. their low degree of educational and vocational training, which is at least partially a function of a certain degree of illiteracy;[6]
3. their poor command of the German language, because of which they miss an important function of social communication.[7]

Being marked as ethnic minority groups with marginal status, they are trapped in a circle of ghetto existence, educational misery and low social status.[8]

Problems of interethnic relations between Germans and foreigners are especially exacerbated during times of recession and in phases of high unemployment.[9] Contempt and prejudice on the part of Germans are often felt by foreigners. This naturally contributes to their segregation into an underprivileged status.

An Italian correspondent for a large German car industry reports of cases where Italian workers were employed for about eight or nine years in the FRG, spoke fluent German and were qualified in every way. They could not climb the ladder of promotion because managers, as well as trade unions, feared the possible opposition of German workers if senior positions were given to Italian workers. 'One took into consideration the "sensitive feelings" of German workers.'[10]

Frankfurt is the German city with the highest percentage of foreigners (of 635,000 citizens in Frankfurt, 121,000, 19.1 per cent, are officially foreigners, not including 20,000-30,000 illegally residing foreigners).[11] There are approximately two million foreigners working in the FRG. Table 6.1 indicates their proportion according to their countries of origin.[12]

Table 6.1: Proportion of Foreigners Working in FRG

Employees contributing to social insurance as arranged according to nationality and sex:

| Nationality | Total | % |
|---|---|---|
| Germans | 18,255,366 | 90.5 |
| Foreigners | 1,920,895 | 9.5 |
| Turks | 520,989 | 2.6 |
| Yugoslavs | 387,222 | 1.9 |
| Italians | 279,096 | 1.4 |
| Greeks | 173,097 | 0.9 |
| Spaniards | 107,518 | 0.5 |
| Portuguese | 62,328 | 0.3 |
| Others | 390,645 | 1.9 |
| Total | 20,176,261 | |

The nature of prevalent housing conditions is an additional determinant in explaining the distribution of adaptation problems among guest-workers. The situation in this area leaves much to be desired, as it in no way matches the standard enjoyed by Germans. The guest-workers must either find shelter in unhealthy boarding houses provided by their employers or else try to find accommodation on their own. Scarcity of available housing in big cities is a well-known fact; but guest-workers are additionally handicapped in their search for accommodation since they often experience rejection by landlords and

German neighbours due to their non-German origin. In this respect, the foreigner's fate is similar to those collectively labelled 'homeless and marginal people'.[13] One cannot describe the present living conditions of foreigners in any other words than 'a prolonged emergency solution'. They are living in residentially segregated areas consisting of collective barracks and miserable old houses, unfit for human habitation. These overcrowded buildings are in urgent need of restoration.[14] Furthermore, high rents are demanded while adequate water and toilet facilities are sorely lacking. Houseowners see in foreign workers and their families a potential for exploitation. In reaction to such residential discrimination in the FRG, Nikolinakos comments: 'Although foreign workers belong to the lowest income group, they very seldom get the advantages granted by law for living accommodations to their German colleagues of the same income range.'[15] He concludes, 'the state has in reality sanctioned the development towards a ghetto',[16] since no concrete public policy exists for housing foreign workers within German communities. An official inquiry points out that 89 per cent of the guest-worker families asked were not satisfied with their living conditions.[17] Evidence suggests that German occupants tend to move out as soon as foreign workers move into a residential district. Ghettos exist in cities like Cologne, Berlin, Frankfurt and Munich. Undoubtedly, this is one indicator of the social isolation and cultural distance that exists between aliens and natives.

## Prejudice

The German term *Auslaender*, meaning foreigner(s), has received an increasingly negative connotation. It is used in an abusive tone, intending to insult foreigners as 'second-class citizens'.[18] Although every fifteenth inhabitant in the FRG is a foreigner,[19] *Fremdenfeindlichkeit*, a term used to signify a situation in which foreigners are made the objects of hate and prejudice, is still widespread. Words like *Kuemmeltuerke, Spaghetti-* or *Knoblauchfresser, Kameltreiber*, etc. reflect the stereotyped German attitudes towards foreigners.[20] Guest-workers are cast off as outsiders due to stigmatisation by certain outward traits and appearances: particular language accents, facial features, colour of eyes and hair, manners of dressing (their colourful clothing is unusual for German taste) and alien behavioural habits, i.e. standing around train stations and women following men at half-foot distances. Their physical and social characteristics deter Germans from developing with these foreigners relationships on equal terms.[21] As the convention of German city councils *(Deutsche Staedtetag)* cautiously puts it, 'the German people have not yet adequately learned to establish with other peoples partnership relations which are free from hierarchical tendencies'. In this connection, Ernst Klee points out that it is not uncommon for a people who not long ago were raised with the consciousness of belonging to a better race, and who in this century have already inflicted forced labour upon millions of aliens, to conceive of foreign workers as being inferior to them. 'Not all signs saying "foreigners unwanted" have yet been removed from restaurants and dance halls'; (some) social workers have complained about these signs hanging in doctors' waiting rooms. The fear of foreign infiltration *(Ueberfremdung)* is spreading through German society.[22] It is known that German workers avoid contact with foreigners and their families. If contact is actually made, it is in a discriminating or at least condescendingly jovial manner, in order to stress already existing differences between themselves and the aliens.[23] Results of the latest survey reveal how widespread prejudices are, even among Germans with higher education: 40 per cent reject having an alien worker for a son-in-law; 30 per cent refuse to accept an alien worker as a boss.[24]

Thus one should not be surprised by the scarcity of activities which guest-workers share in their leisure time with Germans: only 20 per cent have contacts with Germans, only 15 per cent are members of a club, only 23 per cent have a German girlfriend, only 27 per cent have been enrolled in language courses, 63 per cent have never associated with a German family, 62 per cent seldom or never read German newspapers, only 29 per cent watch TV daily, only 34 per cent watch TV several times a week, and only 24 per cent hear daily German language courses on the radio. As figures show, programmes associated with home culture are more popular: 52 per cent listen daily to radio programmes from home countries, 49 per cent listen daily to radio programmes for guest-workers and 25 per cent listen several times a week to radio programmes for guest-workers.[25]

## German Aliens Act

It is evident that there is not much public interest in the social welfare of aliens in the FRG. Such an apathy is manifested in ways such as: lack of assistance in finding adequate housing, lack of support in remedying their socio-cultural isolation and, last but not least, lack of opportunity to raise their low social status, due to employers' disinterest in promoting alien workers.

German authorities knew as early as 1969 that 70 per cent of all alien workers had been living longer than seven years in the FRG. Despite this, the authorities continued systematically to cultivate a consciousness that guest-workers were here for only a provisional stay. This, in turn, partly answers the question why guest-workers are not eager to learn German and thus have only a poor command of the language. Their rightful question remains unanswered: why should they learn proper German if they are to be temporary residents only, subject to deportation at any time? Integration of the guest-workers, if any, was conceived as a temporary affair. The official declaration made by the German government, stating that the FRG is not a country for immigration, supports this.[26] Integration based on a time limit *(Mitbuerger auf Zeit)*, no matter how long the limit, results in psychological dynamics quite different from the ones that are a product of permanent immigration. If this is so, then it reveals only shortsightedness on the part of the official policy towards foreign workers *(Fremdenpolitik)*, since it was constructed on a false assumption — that the problem of foreign workers was not to become a permanent one. Already in 1971, the German charity organisation *Zentralrat des Deutschen Caritasverbandes* has confirmed that for many foreigners Germany has *de facto* become an immigration country. The basic political declaration has long ceased to be in accordance with reality. Disregard of this evidence by the government has led to inadequacies which cannot any longer be tolerated.[27]

Although widely criticised by various trade unions, interest groups and political organisations, as well as challenged through alternative drafts, the German Aliens Act remains essentially unchanged.[28] Foreigners have to depend largely upon the judgements of the officers *(Ermessensspielraum)* who have the right to issue, renew or refuse to renew the residence and/or work permits of foreigners. They also decide on matters of deportation or expulsion according to personal, political and economic factors, as well as the interests of the labour market. It is no wonder that many foreigners perform pseudo-marriages with Germans in order to find a permanent solution to their problems of residence.

As long as no major modifications are made, the German Aliens Act continues to be 'the most effective tool for the manipulation of migratory policies'.[29] According to existing legal regulations, residence permits are awarded usually for a limited time of one or two years.

This means that alien workers are denied the benefits of residence permits, thus having no guarantee of the right to reside. Their stay in the FRG depends entirely on demands established by industry. Consequently, the majority of foreign workers live in a state of continuous anxiety. It must be remembered that their existential fears are based on and justified by a precarious situation: whether or not their residence and work permits can be prolonged, whether or not they have to leave the country, and whether, even if their permits *can* be prolonged, their eventual deportation will be ordered.

Needless to say, under these circumstances integration efforts on the part of aliens become ineffectual. The anxiety that develops from lacking a definite assurance regarding their further duration of stay extends beyond the effect it has on adults. The insecurity involved in living with packed suitcases ready at hand for the next move inhibits them from making any farsighted plans for their children's education. It is often the case that children who are attending German schools must break up their educational training in order to return home because their parents are not employed any more or have changed their plans. This reflects their social situation, which often leads to non-fulfilment of both raised hopes and educational goals.[30] Figure 6.1 indicates major factors hindering acculturation of foreign workers in the FRG.

### The Children of Foreign Workers

Out of an estimated four million foreigners living in the FRG, about two million are employed (as of 1978); of the remaining two million non-workers, about one million constitute adult family members and the remaining one million are children and adolescents. It is difficult to give exact figures, because the German Aliens Act does not require a residence permit for persons under the age of 16. However, each year 130,000 non-German babies are born in the FRG, while the German birth-rate of one million has dropped drastically to about half a million. For example, in the city of Frankfurt, in 1978, the birth-rate was 6.3 babies for every 1,000 German residents and 16.4 babies for every 1,000 aliens.[31] Consequently, every second child in Frankfurt has foreign parents. In certain city districts, the non-German birth-rate is about three-quarters of all babies born. At the same time, an estimated rate of 50,000 foreign adolescents come of working age every year. Statistics for all of Germany indicate that every third baby has a foreign nationality. 400,000 foreign children, or 10.3 per cent of all foreigners,

Figure 6.1:   Major Factors Hindering Acculturation of Foreign
Workers in the FRG[a]

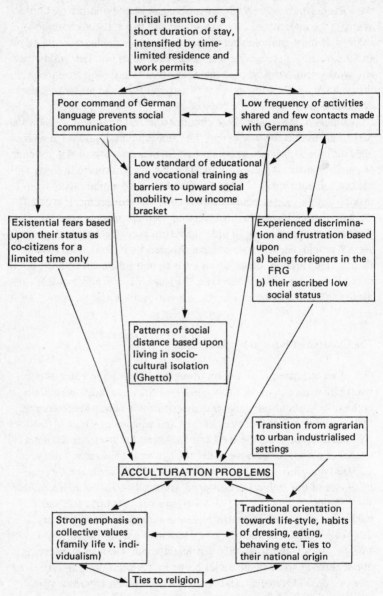

a.  For further explanations see S. Raoufi, *Problems of Cultural Adaptation
among Iranian Families in Southern Germany — empirical research based
upon case studies*, to be published in 1981.

are below the age of six.[32]

Up to 95 per cent of foreign children under the age of six remain at home and are looked after by family members. Only 5 per cent attend public kindergarten.[33] Thus, a majority of them experience socialisation in the streets. Often, this does not even lead to communication between German and foreign children, owing to inhibiting prejudice held by parents of both nationalities.[34] Guest-workers evaluate the role of pre-school education negatively because they fear religious indoctrination and possible alienation of children from their parents and home culture. In any event, there are insufficient numbers of kindergartens and a grave shortage of competent staff able to work with children who cannot speak German.

At present, the number of kindergartens is quite insufficient for accommodating German children, let alone immigrants. As a result, 15 per cent of immigrants send their kindergarten-age children to other relatives or families during working hours.[35] Instead of creating additional places in the kindergartens, it is interesting to note that the social welfare committee for the city of Cologne has made a recommendation for either the deportation of mothers with children or the issuing of only a one-year work permit to married men.[36]

In 1977, about 410,000 foreign adolescents came of working age; only 41 per cent had managed to pass the secondary school final examination (as contrasted with 82 per cent of German children).[37] There is an alarmingly high rate of failure (60 per cent) among foreign workers' children during the obligatory nine years in regular German schools. Even more discouraging are the figures which reveal that 65-75 per cent of foreign adolescents receive no vocational training and will therefore have very little opportunity of finding apprenticeship or employment. Only a very small proportion (6.3 per cent) who successfully complete secondary school can attend continuing schools, let alone higher education. The voices of members of Germany's conservative political party can already be heard lamenting. The German society acknowledges only superficially the lack of vocational qualifications, unemployment, isolation, alienation, ghetto formation and rejection among foreign children and youngsters who are growing up in Germany. It is not likely that these children who are suffering now are going to tolerate the same conditions in the future.[38] Since a low level of academic performance is directly linked to a low level of integration, we must first explain the background of the latter before we can classify the major factors which lead to the former (i.e. the high rate of failure).

At this point, we must distinguish three major unsatisfactory conditions of education which affect these children's low level of integration:

1. Owing to widespread prejudice among Germans, these children experience discrimination through either the marginal status to which they are assigned or their assignment to the role of outsiders. The mere fact of being together under one roof with German children does not necessarily lead to integration. The child's weakness in articulating his thoughts, feelings and experiences in the German language makes him conscious of his role as an outsider. Not being able to participate fully in class, he is in a state of communicating isolation, or 'ghettoism', although he is together with German children in one classroom.[39] This leads to the formation of cliques and segregation. Another possible consequence is that German parents take their children away from the school which is attended by foreigners.[40] As Pommerin stresses in her study, most foreign workers' children are seen as 'foreign elements' *(Fremdkoerper)* in German regular classes; often they are either ascribed the role of class clown or they become resigned or aggressive outsiders.[41] Even if they speak German and attend German schools, one reality remains unchanged: they are still complete strangers in the German environment.[42]

2. In comparison with other German pupils, foreign children start with a low level of competence in German. In one study, language difficulties were cited by immigrant children as being a major problem.[43]

To deal with immigrants, a dual strategy of education is practised in the FRG. One type is called the German system of regular classes, which offers either many stages of special admission and reception or introductory, transitional and preparatory classes.[44] All the instruction is given in German, and only a minimal amount of time is left for the immigrant children to learn their mother tongue. The other type is the school system in which two-thirds of the instruction is given in the child's mother tongue. German is taught here as a foreign language eight hours per week. The Bavarian government has offered this educational system since 1973. The classes are supervised by the Bavarian government, requiring 25 children of one language group in order to set up a class, in which instruction will be administered by the consulates of the respective countries. The pros and cons of these two educational systems have been the issues of long debates and heated arguments among educators of foreign children in Germany. To this extent, it is of special importance that a comparison of the advantages and disadvantages of each educational system be made before proper remedial measures can be taken. Contrary to the many recommendations advocating the German regular classes, the present author supports the method of teaching immigrant children in their mother tongue. The following problems appear to crop up when immigrant children are placed in German regular classes:

a. As already stated, immigrant children enter the German school system from an unequal starting position. They have a harder time in school than the Germans because of their linguistic handicap, but since it is assumed that their basic knowledge of German is equal to that of the rest, no allowance is made for this. Furthermore, a socio-cultural gap separates pupils and teachers.[45] For example, Greek parents feel that their children do not perform well at school because of:

|      |                                                 |                |
|------|-------------------------------------------------|----------------|
| (i)  | linguistic difficulties                         | 69.7 per cent  |
| (ii) | discrimination among peer groups                | 46.8 per cent  |
| (iii)| inability of the parents to help their children | 57.0 per cent  |
| (iv) | neglect of foreign children by German teachers  | 24.2 per cent  |

b. Other apparent disadvantages of the German regular classes are the problems inherent in the German school system itself: overcrowded classes, use of outdated teaching methods, lack of teachers and their discrimination against children of lower social classes in general.[46] As teachers speak only German, they are not prepared to communicate with foreign pupils, and *vice versa*. Consequently, these pupils are condemned to non-participation in class discussion. Furthermore, the school situation is aggravated by the fact that pupils of different nationalities are placed together in one classroom. Preparatory classes are too overcrowded and too short, and 'there is also a risk of remaining in this class without being transferred to normal schooling'.[47]

c. The additional instruction in the children's mother tongue has either not materialised or, once implemented, has led to a double burden on the children. It is likely that their knowledge of their native language is inadequate and, as a result, they are more or less illiterate in both languages *(Weder-noch-Unterricht)*. Pommerin confirms in her study that foreign workers' children are either under- or overworked, since the teacher's orientation is towards an average performance.[48] Indeed, on the basis of his studies on communication and linguistic problems among foreign children and adolescents, Bendit concludes that:

> For children and youngsters whose cultural integration process has not yet been completed, deficient linguistic ability to communicate can lead to conflicts of which the grave consequences can be social and cultural disorientation and loss of identity. Almost always the result of this is severe obstacles in both languages.[49]

d. Discrimination against children, especially those from lower classes, leads to a further hindrance in their integration. Why is it that, even if they are put into special preparatory or transitional classes, most of them 'cannot acquire the required amount of knowledge to be transferred...?'[50] It is too simplistic to argue that foreign workers' children are less intelligent than German children. One has to keep in mind the double burden they are carrying: being expected to learn two languages at the same time, and being put in a disadvantageous position because of their lower social class status.[51] On the other hand, as Pommerin observes,

> children of diplomats, whose acquisition of a second language is affected by favourable socio-economic and institutional conditions ... embody the 'well-liked foreigner' who will be liked and accepted in his peer group, and not seldom becomes the darling in a class group. Their ethnic strangeness and its accompanying characteristics then seem attractive when represented by members of the elevated middle or upper social classes.[52]

To sum up, the child is made to sit in the German regular class and he must listen but he cannot speak. His knowledge of German hardly improves, and he is destined to become a drop-out. Experience shows that more than 60 per cent do not manage to reach the 9th class! It is to be expected, then, that they will not find an apprenticeship, will be unemployed, or will be forced to work as unskilled labourers. The question still remains to be answered: why do we persist in applying this model of German regular classes if it has not proved to be successful?

Let us now compare the main advantages of schools administered in each child's mother tongue:

a. The foreign child's personality is not subjected to disturbing influences from outside. The child is encouraged to make full use of his mother tongue since he is living with and learning from his foreign parents, with whom he shares fundamental cultural values and identifies fields of communication and interaction. It is difficult for the child who speaks his native language up to the age of six to develop his personality through a foreign language. When placed in a German school, he is suddenly stopped from expressing his thoughts, feelings and experiences in his own language. Instead, he is forced to speak German using a restricted vocabulary.

One cannot compare the linguistic situation of children to that of adults. Language mediates for children relevant processes of socialisation, i.e. formations of personality and identity, whereas the cultivation of cultural forms of adults has already been completed to a great extent.[53] Holtzmann clearly points out that

> if a child is forced to express himself, not in his own mother tongue but in a foreign idiom, before he has mastered his own language, he is being robbed of a portion of his personality, and that contravenes article two of our statute. It contradicts law as well as human rights, if children are forced into instruction which is so heavily impregnated with the German language and culture that only five hours per week are left over for instruction in the language and culture of their original homeland.[54]

This is why Savvidis has referred to the schools administered in the mother tongue as an oasis and a place of refuge for a great number of already psychologically disturbed guest-workers' children. There, it is reported, 'they have mutual respect for one another, and from the beginning take pleasure in learning and living in Germany. Besides, the school serves as a protective haven for all newcomers, and eases the overcoming of adaptation problems.'[55]

b. Emphasis is put on the mother tongue and German is taught as a foreign language. Experience shows that a method of teaching German as a second or foreign language can be adapted to the needs of foreign workers' children, thus enabling them to pick up German much more easily. Compared to foreign children in the German regular classes, those in the schools administered in their mother tongue have acquired a better knowledge of German, at least in part because teachers did not assume any previous knowledge of the language.

The Greek school in Munich can be cited as one successful model of bilingual education, combining kindergarten, primary, secondary and high school. It was established in 1969 by Dr Savvidis. It has a present enrolment of 3,500 pupils, who come from average guest-worker families. The Greek school must share buildings with German schools, owing to the unavailability of sufficient school space. This means that their classes are scheduled for later hours of the day, which has a tiring effect on pupils. Nevertheless, the success rate in passing secondary school final examinations is as high as 80 per cent. Here we see, for the first time, results quite different from those obtained in German regular classes. The majority of pupils continue into high school and some even enter institutions of higher learning.[56]

c. The German school has failed to provide equal educational and vocational opportunities for immigrant children. Real equality of opportunity can be achieved primarily through using the mother tongue as the medium of instruction in addition to consistent teaching of German as a compulsory foreign language.[57]

d. The central question continuously burdening the minds of parents is whether their children should be educated in the mother tongue or in German regular classes. Their decision not to place them into the latter form of schooling is not so much influenced by a fear of possible 'Germanising' as it is by the apprehension that alienation between parents and children might occur. Different linguistic capabilities might create barriers of communication which can separate them in their value systems, habits and modes of behaviour.

Compulsory attendance at German schools makes an attempt at integration through the forced replacement of the mother tongue by German. At the same time, there is a lack of any firm assurance of a permanent stay in the country. Parents do not see the relevance of what a child learns at a German school to what will be needed upon return to their country of origin. Even if the child has a diploma from the school, it does not necessarily open doors for professional training or employment back home.[58] In short, it cannot be assumed that integration into regular German classes is a realistic alternative if existing laws regarding the concept of immigration remain unchanged.

3. These immigrant children are subjected to a process of resocialisation and cultural conflict. Consequently, in a search for their identities, they exhibit psychosomatic symptoms.

It is to be regretted that neither psychologists, educators, school administrators nor sociologists have yet made scientific investigations into the self-concept and self-esteem of foreign workers' children and the relationship of these to their educational, vocational and social aspirations and expectations in the FRG. Although a detailed study and analysis of these aspects of their behaviour would be of immense value, no psychological tests have yet been developed to measure their ability, aptitude and achievement. Research on these questions is non-existent in the FRG.[59] So far, the contributions of the social sciences have been mostly limited either to legitimising or to denouncing the interest of the economic system in recruiting the labour force. Little attempt has been made to set up a special, theoretical frame of reference in the fields of social work and education.[60] We can only refer to one study carried out by Gaertner-Harnach and others, which is based on a representative sample of 1,107 foreign and 1,455 German pupils. The findings reveal that foreign children suffer grave psychological disturbances which are expressed in the form of aggression directed against themselves and a tendency towards self-punishment. It is reported that the frequency and the average severity of behavioural disturbances of foreign children are greater than those of Germans. The author clearly identifies the most significant difference to be in the area of affective disturbances,

> such as anxiety, insecurity, oversensitivity, depression, difficulty in concentration and difficulty in establishing interpersonal relations. We interpret these results as demonstrating that foreign children are frequently so strongly affected by the burden which the migration and consequent socio-cultural stress puts upon them, that they are no longer capable of problem solving. Instead, they react by withdrawing and turning against themselves and not against their social environment. Thus, they internalize the stress and conflict. There are also frequent attempts, although to a lesser extent, to get rid of these difficulties through diffused or hidden acts of aggression.[61]

We may thus conclude that the foreign child is largely isolated and seldom experiences social recognition. He is not provided with sufficient emotional support to cope with his present and future problems in life. The psycho-social insecurity of the foreign child arises and increases because neither his own family, the school, the teachers, nor his German friends are able to eliminate the unfavourable social conditions and their effects.[62] Often the resultant reactions take the form of either an attempt to deny one's own national origin or an exhibition of an extreme nationalistic attitude. The rise of ethnic group identification which follows as a result of discrimination has been amply demonstrated by Simpson and Yinger (1953) and Rose and Rose (1949). Broadly speaking, the parents have already undergone an identity crisis while the children are still in the midst of a search for identity, standing between two worlds, not knowing who they are.

Other factors associated with their parents that negatively affect the child's educational performance may be briefly related:

1. since some parents have serious reservations about the German environment in which they find themselves, they do not encourage the development of the child's bilingual identity;[63]
2. the authoritarian style of upbringing, i.e. Koran classes among Turkish foreign workers;[64]
3. the preference of boys over girls as demonstrated by differential treatment — for example, parents discourage their girls from attending school, while they encourage them to babysit and clean the house;[65]
4. inability of parents to assist their children in homework;
5. inadequate living space, so that pupils are unable to study at home.[66]

Children who are brought up 'between two societies', meaning between two different conflicting sets of cultural norms, are capable of functioning in neither society. They lack the social patterns of orientation which are necessary for survival in a society which is, to a great extent, unknown to them. How can they handle the consequences of intercultural conflict, such as behavioural insecurity, loss of orientation and diffusion of identity, without becoming psychologically overburdened for life? As Boos-Nuenning has correctly observed:

> The foreign child needs to be socialized in such a way as to distinguish between the value system of the FRG and that of his homeland, and to apply the corresponding norms in a meaningful and constructive way to each. The present process of socialization does not accomplish this goal. The foreign family is not capable of providing help since it is exclusively or largely rooted in the values of its home culture. The school also does not succeed in mediating between the two cultures and in allowing the foreign child to develop a bicultural personality.

Furthermore, she points out that 'they require a special socialization process which reduces existing defects of socialization, but not in the sense that a total assimilation into the FRG occurs. Instead a new goal and concept of socialization needs to be developed for this group'.[67]

Previous discussions of integration into the educational system of the FRG have not taken into account the effect of intercultural conflicts on the process of instruction. Instruction should be focused in such a way as to enable foreign pupils to master the permanent, intercultural conflicts to which they are subject and to incorporate a bicultural consciousness into their personality. Indeed, this bicultural identity could represent an exciting way of socialising children.

Because of the substantial discrepancy between what the child is taught in school and the reality of his own situation, his motivation to learn is considerably impeded. Even for those few foreign children who have passed secondary school final examinations, future opportunities do not depend on achievement at school alone, 'but also on the social process of allocating status'.[68] In 1975, the rate of unemployment in the city of Duisburg, for example, was 51 per cent among young foreign males and 72 per cent among young foreign females.[69] Unemployment is usually accompanied by poverty and inactivity; gambling, drinking and dancing become a therapy for boredom; feelings are aroused of being discriminated against, of frustration and anger. How long will these young foreigners, especially those who are born here and identify the FRG as their home, tolerate being treated as mere objects by the authorities, or be content with their role as foreigners?[70] We strongly support Schrader's prognosis that in the next few years we will observe reactions on the part of foreign youth which are not dissimilar to those of the Puerto Ricans and blacks in Manhattan, if we do not succeed in eliminating discrimination in professional and vocational training.

The foreign youth will manifest reactions which will not be tolerated by society, if they are denied professional and economic participation. The discrepancy between individual life aspirations and actual social opportunities can lead to reactions which Merton termed 'rebellion'.[71] Hidden acts of aggression, referred to earlier in the study by Gaertner-Harnach, could conceivably take a more open and serious form, as recent findings in criminology have indicated.[72] Compared to Germans, foreigners under the age of 21 have a lower delinquency rate in almost all categories of crime, but in certain types of crimes such as theft foreign adolescents between the ages of 12 and 18 show a higher delinquency rate than Germans in the same age groups.

Given this complex background of linguistic problems, discrimination, failures in school and unsuccessful searches for vocational training, the formation of street gangs, the increase in alcohol consumption and rising crime among the foreign youth are to be understood within their social contexts.[73] Not infrequently, foreign adolescents who are convicted of crimes are deported immediately after serving their prison sentences. They are given no chances to rehabilitate themselves. Combined efforts on the part of the government, trade unions, employers' associations, welfare agencies, churches and private groups are needed to prevent unemployed young foreigners from becoming a sort of sub-proletariat, or what some have called 'a social time bomb'.[74] Figure 6.2 reviews the above-mentioned factors affecting the low academic performance of foreign workers' children in the FRG.

## Conclusion

Even though public opinion today holds the view that foreign workers who stay permanently overburden the social infrastructure, refusal to invest money in the expansion of school facilities and staff, as well as additional training for school teachers, is a perfect example of 'false saving'.[75] It will certainly be much more expensive for the FRG to deal with the behavioural disorders resulting from defective schooling. Investment in the educational future of these children is actually a type of capital investment that will more than pay off in future economic growth. Perhaps understanding the source of misunderstandings can lead to more effective communication. Further investigations are necessary to learn about the foreigners' cultural mores, their needs and their aspirations.

We should keep in mind that 'without the foreign workers, the German economy would not have been able to make the progress it has made, nor that it can do without them in the future'.[76] In view of the expected increase in the demand for foreign workers, the expected continuation of the current decline in the German birth-rate and the higher birth-rate of foreign families in Germany, these problems are likely to become even more serious.[77]

It must be noted, however, that changing the school situation is a necessary but not a satisfactory condition for the minimisation of adjustment problems encountered by the children of foreign workers in the FRG. That is to say, making changes in the schools alone will not solve the problems. Reflecting on the importance of the school and its

Figure 6.2: Factors Affecting the Low Academic Performance of Foreign Workers' Children in the FRG

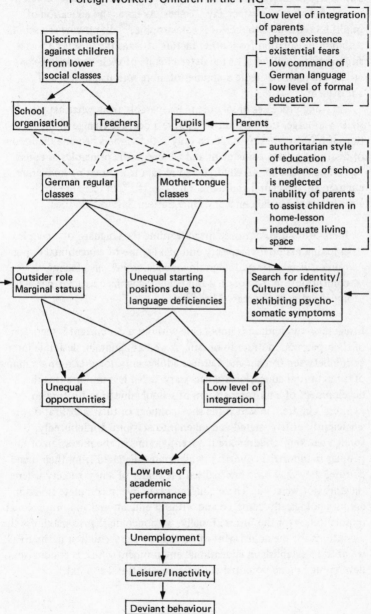

relationship to society at large, Schrader confirms that 'the German school does exactly what is done in society, it follows social developments, but does not effect any changes. As far as the education of pupils is concerned, the result is catastrophic.'[78] Improving the school situation in isolation from other factors, such as the unsettled social situation of the parents or the determinants of their linguistic behaviour, will perhaps create a number of more serious problems of adjustment.

Learning processes in school are inseparable from what happens in society at large. It is possible to achieve a decisive change in the situation of foreign workers' children only if the schools become mediators of institutionalised adjustment and adhere to the principles of equal rights and duties for all children and refrain from treating immigrant children as 'accidental and temporary guests'.[79] In response to the already controversial concept of integration, Savvidis clarifies:

> Integration does not only mean learning the language of a people, enjoying material prosperity and making use of educational opportunities in a country; integration means, rather, also feeling comfortable in the country and being recognized as a partner with equal rights in all areas of life.[80]

Integration of children is impossible without a concurrent integration of their parents. In order to obtain, as well as maintain, desirable interaction between foreign and German adolescents, long-term programmes of intercultural education are necessary.[81] No less important is the development of a uniform system of school education for foreign workers' children, in which the shortcomings of their socialisation are sufficiently differentiated and taken into account. Undoubtedly, foreign workers' children are innocent victims of the migration of peoples in industrial countries: while being alienated from their own culture, they may have internalised the values of a new society where they are not welcome. These children often live in complete isolation, are psychologically damaged and without educational and professional opportunities for the future. Finally, we conclude that to maximise the conditions for the adjustment of foreign workers' children in the FRG, we need to establish an educational environment which is conducive to developing human potential within a multicultural context.

*The author is grateful to Dr Breitman, Dr Bargatzky and Mr Gaida for their help with parts of the translations and to Mr Kiefl for his technical assistance in drawing the sketches. The responsibility for style and content is entirely with the author.

## Notes

1. In this connection it should be pointed out that not all foreigners living and working in the FRG fall under the category of guest-workers. For a detailed analysis, see S. Raoufi, 'Distinguishing Criteria between Guest-workers and Iranians in the FRG', in S. Raoufi, *Problems of Cultural Adaptation Among Iranian Families in Southern Germany – Empirical Research Based upon Case Studies* (to be published in 1981).

2. N. Katsarakis, 'Probleme Kultureller und Gesellschaftlicher Integration griechischer Arbeitnehmer in der BRD', dissertation, Aachen, 1974.

3. A. Schrader, B.W. Nikles and H.M. Griese, *Die zweite Generation, Sozialisation und Akkulturation auslaendischer Kinder in der BRD* (Athenaeum, Kronberg, 1976), p. 21.

4. J. Kuehl, 'Die Bedeutung auslaendischer Arbeitnehmer fuer die BRD', in H. Reimann and H. Reimann (eds), *Gastarbeiter* (Goldman, Muenchen, 1976).

5. *Sueddeutsche Zeitung (SZ)*, 2-4 June 1979.

6. See T. Ansay and D. Martiny, 'Gastarbeiterfamilie in Recht', in T. Ansay and V. Gessner, *Gastarbeiter in Gesellschaft und Recht* (Beck, Muenchen, 1974), p. 174.

7. Compare statistics in M. Damanakis, *Sozialisationsprobleme der griechischen Gastarbeiter Kinder in den Grund-and Hauptschulen des Bundeslandes Nordrhein-Westfalen* (Henn, Kastellaun, 1978), p. 120.

8. See S. Castles and G. Kosack, *Immigrant Workers and Class Structure in Western Germany* (Oxford University Press, London, 1973).

9. S. Raoufi, 'Replies to Disadvantages Related to the Presence of Guest-workers in the FRG', in Raoufi, *Cultural Adaptation Among Iranian Families.*

10. E. Klee, 'Gastarbeiter als Subproletariat', in E. Klee (ed), *Gastarbeiter, Analysen und Berichte* (Suhrkamp, Frankfurt, 1975), p. 33.

11. *SZ*, 2-4 June 1979.

12. *Sonderdruck Sozialversicherungspflichtig beschaeftigte Arbeitnehmer* (30 September 1976), p. 683.

13. Helmut Essinger, *Soziale Rand- und Problemgruppen* (Koesel, Muenchen, 1977), p. 33; see also H. Loesch and K. Wahl, *Familie und Sozialisation bei Auslaendern und Obdachlosen*, Materialien Zum 2, Familienbericht der Bundesregierung (DJI, Muenchen, 1977).

14. About the effects of overcrowded living conditions, see V. Gessner, 'Das soziale Verhalten der Gastarbeiter', in Ansay and Gessner, *Gastarbeiter in Gesellschaft und Recht*, pp. 30-2.

15. M. Nikolinakos, 'Economic Foundations of Discrimination in the Federal Republic of Germany', in H. Van Houte and W. Melgert (eds), *Foreigners in our Community* (Keesing Publishers, Amsterdam, no date).

16. Ibid., p. 87.

17. Ibid., p. 85; see also *Der Spiegel*, no. 43 (October 1970), and *SZ*, 23-26 December 1978.

18. See H. Katsoulis, *Buerger zweiter Klasse – Auslaender in der BRD* (Campus Verlag, Frankfurt, 1978). For closer examination of institutionalised discrimination against guest-workers, see Nikolinakos, 'Economic Foundations of Discrimination'.

19.    Bundesminister fuer Bildung und Wissenschaft, *Pressemitteilung* (14 March 1979), p. 4.

20.    See F. Franz, in Klee, *Gastarbeiter, Analysen und Berichte*, p.38. Compare also Essinger, *Soziale Rand- und Problemgruppen*, pp. 71-4.

21.    See Gessner, 'Das Soziale Verhalten der Gastarbeiter', p. 27; for detailed statistics see Schrader *et al.*, *Die zweite Generation*. See also J. Becker, *Alltaegliche Rassismus, die afro-amerikanischen Rassenkonflikte im Kinder - und Jugendbuch der BRD* (Campus Verlag, Frankfurt a.M, 1977).

22.    Klee, *Gastarbeiter, Analysen und Berichte*, p. 30. Compare for further data on discrimination of foreigners by landlords and restaurant owners, Damanakis, *Sozialisationsprobleme der griechischen Gastarbeiter Kinder*, pp. 122-3, and M. Borris, *Auslaendische Arbeitnehmer in einer Grosstadt* (Europaeische Verlagsanstalt, Frankfurt, 1973), p. 214.

23.    G. Pommerin, *Deutschunterricht mit auslaendischen und deutschen Kindern* (Kamp, Bochum, 1977), p. 21.

24.    Findings from a representative survey in the FRG; B. Panahi, *Racial and Antisemitic Stereotypes held by Germans towards Jews, Negroes and Alien Workers* (Fischer, Frankfurt, to be published in 1981). Compare also prejudices against Jews and foreigners in the FRG, by Essinger, *Soziale Rand- und Problemgruppen.*

25.    P. Arweiler, in K. Bingemer, E. Meistermann-Seeger and E. Neuberg, *Leben als Gastarbeiter* (Koeln und Opladen, 1970), p. 122. See also Schrader *et al.*, *Die Zweite Generation*, p. 34.

26.    'The FRG is not an immigration country. Germany's self-concept is to be a country granting only temporary residence permits to foreigners who, in due course, return to their home countries of their own free will. In the long run, this basic attitude serves the socio-economic interests of Germany as well as the countries of immigration.' Vorschlaege der Bundlaender Kommission,...Hrsg. Bundesminister fuer Arbeit und Sozialordnung II a 5-24200/22, 28 February 1977.

27.    Reprinted in *Weltbild* (March 1977), p. 24.

28.    Franz/Heldmann/Kaspzyk, Majer, Paetzold, 'Auslaendergesetz Alternativentwurf '70, Kritik und Reform', in *Studentische Politik*, 1 (1970). Resolution paper of a seminar held at the Department of Criminology, University of Munich, July 1979.

29.    N. Abadan-Unat, and contributors, 'Turkish Migration to Europe', in N. Abadan-Unat, *Turkish Workers in Europe, 1960-1975: A Socio-economic Reappraisal* (Brill, Leiden, 1976), p. 35.

30.    See G. Savvidis, *Zum Problem der Gastarbeiterkinder in der BRD* (Jugend und Volk, Wien und Muenchen, 1975), p. 28. See Damanakis, *Sozialisationsprobleme der griechischen Gastarbeiter Kinder*, pp. 178 and 201-3.

31    *SZ*, 2-4 June 1979.

32.    Statistiches Bundesamt, September 1976.

33.    Turkish children are reported to have the lowest percentage of kindergarten attendance; see U. Mehrlaender, *Soziale Aspekte der Auslaenderbeschaeftigung* (Verlag Neue Gesellschaft, Bonn-Bad Gotesberg, 1974), p. 207.

34.    A. Langenohl-Weyer/R. Wennekes, 'Auslaendische Familie in der BRD, Die politischen und sozialen Rahmendbedingungen', in A. Langenohl-Weyer and others, *Zur Integration der Auslaender im Bildungsbereich, Probleme und Loesungsversuche* (Juventa, Muenchen, 1979), p. 21; see also CDU/CSU, *Pressemitteilung*, pp. 5-9.

35.    Bingemer *et al.*, *Leben Als Gastarbeiter*, p. 147.

36.    Ibid., p. 147.

37.    Bundesminister fuer Bildung und Wissenschaft, *Pressemitteilung* (14 March 1979), p. 2; see also *Problèmes d'Integration de Jeunes Immigrés dans*

*l'Enseignement Primaire et Secondaire, Province de Liege*, pp. 10-12.

38.   CDU/CSU, *Pressemitteilung, Zukunftschancen der Kinder Auslaendischer Arbeitnehmer* (14 June 1978), p. 2.

39.   Savvidis, *Zum Problem der Gastarbeiterkinder*, pp. 76-7; compare also Pommerin, *Deutschunterricht mit auslaendischen und deutschen Kindern*, p. 56.

40.   *Scala*, no. 4 (1979), p.12.

41.   Pommerin, *Deutschunterricht mit auslaendischen und deutschen Kindern*, p. 57; compare also, S. Harrant, 'Schulprobleme von Gastarbeiterkinder', in Reimann and Reimann (eds), *Gastarbeiter*, p. 157.

42.   Essinger, *Soziale Rand- und Problemgruppen*, p. 76; compare also Schrader *et al., Die zweite Generation*, pp. 198, 200 and 206; sociologically they remain foreigners or become strangers or non-Germans.

43.   U. Mehrlaender, *Soziale Aspekte der Auslaenderbeschaeftigung*, p. 211.

44.   M.S. Bilmen, 'Educational Problems Encountered by the Children of Turkish Migrant Workers', in Abadan-Unat, *Turkish Workers in Europe*, p. 246.

45.   R. Bendit, 'Kommunikations und Sprachproblematik bei auslaendischen Kindern, Jugendlicher und Erwachsenen', in Langenohl-Weyer *et al., Zur Integration der Auslaender in Bildungsbereich*, p. 33.

46.   U. Akpinar, 'Zur Schulsituation der Kinder auslaendischer Arbeitnehmer', in Langenohl-Weyer *et al., Zur Integration der Auslaender im Bildungsbereich*, p. 99.

47.   I. Willke, 'Schooling of Immigrant Children in W. Germany — Sweden — England: the Educationally Disadvantaged', *International Review of Education*, vol. 21 (1975), p. 363.

48.   Pommerin, *Deutschunterricht mit auslaendischen und deutschen Kindern*, p. 57.

49.   Bendit, 'Kommunikations und Sprachproblematik', p.30.

50.   Bilmen, 'Educational Problems Encountered by the Children of Turkish Migrant Workers', p. 246.

51.   See Harrant, 'Schulprobleme von Gastarbeiterkindern', pp. 150-3.

52.   Pommerin, *Deutschunterricht mit auslaendischen und deutschen Kindern*, p. 53.

53.   H. Mueller, 'Sprachfoerderung auslaendischer Arbeiter und ihrer Kinder', in J. Lluch-Ordinaga, W.D. Striening, H. Mueller and A. Lopez-Blasco, *Soziale Eingliederungshilfen fuer auslaendische Kinder*, Studien zur Kommunalpolitik, Band 17 (Bonn, Eichholz, 1979), p. 252-6.

54.   E. Holtzmann, 'Der Gastarbeiter und sein Kind', *Stimmen der Zeit*, (1973), p. 425.

55.   Savvidis, *Zum Problem der Gastarbeiterkinder*, p. 78.

56.   Savvidis, *Zum Problem der Gastarbeiterkinder*, p. 84; also based on interviews with Dr Savvidis, July 1979, in Munich, and with Greek students from University of Munich. It has confirmed that a small group of economically more advantaged Greek families prefer to send their children to German schools.

57.   Savvidis, *Zum Problem der Gastarbeiterkinder*, p. 81.

58.   Langenohl-Weyer *et al., Zur Integration der Auslaender im Bildungsbereich*, p. 29.

59.   Compare for instance, V. Boos-Nuenning, in V. Boos-Nuenning, M. Hohmann and H.H. Reich, *Schulbindung auslaendischer Kinder*, Studien zur Kommunalpolitik, Band 17 (Eichholz, 1976), p. 110.

60.   Schrader *et al., Die zweite Generation*, p. 198.

61.   V. Gaertner-Harnach, Bericht ueber den 29. Kongress der Deutschen Gesellschaft fuer Psychologie.

62.   Akpinar, 'Zur Schulsituation der Kinder auslaendischer Arbeitnehmer', p. 99.

63.   See Schrader *et al., Die zweite Generation*, p. 199.

64.   See C. Zwingmann, 'Nostalgic Behaviour, a Study of Foreign Workers in W. Germany', in C. Zwingmann, (ed.), *Uprooting and After* (Springer, New York, 1973).

65.   See M.B. Kiray, 'The Family of the Immigrant Worker', in Abadan-Unat, *Turkish Workers in Europe*, p. 225-8; Klee, *Gastarbeiter, Analysen und Berichte*, pp. 92-3 and 98; and Pommerin, *Deutschunterricht mit auslaendischen und deutschen Kindern*, p. 39.

66.   See CDU/CSU, *Pressemitteilung*, p. 5; Essinger, *Soziale Rand- und Problemgruppen*, p. 75; and Gessner, 'Das soziale Verhalten der Gastarbeiter', pp. 30-2.

67.   Boos-Nuenning *et al.*, *Schulbindung auslaendischer Kinder*, p. 119.

68.   Schrader *et al.*, *Die zweite Generation*.

69.   *Der Spiegel*, no. 43 (23 October 1978).

70.   See also *Weltbild*, 14 March 1977.

71.   Schrader *et al.*, *Die zweite Generation*, p. 206.

72.   P.A. Albrecht and P. Pfeiffer, *Die Kriminalisierung junger Auslaender* (Muenchen, 1979), pp. 39-40; see also K. Bingemer and R. Neuberg, in Bingemer *et al.*, *Leben Als Gastarbeiter*, article on 'Kriminalitaet', for a view of foreign workers' deviant behaviour as found among all nationalities.

73.   See resolution paper of seminar at University of Munich, July 1979 and Albrecht and Pfeiffer, *Die Kriminalisierung junger Auslaender*, p. 42.

74.   Interview with Mr Hasinger, a German politician, in *Quick*, no. 44 (1978).

75.   See, for example, Essinger, *Soziale Rand- und Problemgruppen*, p. 74.

76.   Nikolinakos, 'Economic Foundations of Discrimination', p. 91.

77.   SZ, 15 September 1978 and 2-4 June 1979; Schrader *et al.*, *Die zweite Generation*, p. 21; projections of the German Ministry of the Economy up to 1985 calculate an increase of the supply of foreign workers between 2.07 and 2.84 million with a median variant of 2.46 million foreigners in 'Die wirtschaftliche Lage in der BRD', *Vierteljahresbericht*, III (1970), p. 16.

78.   Schrader *et al.*, *Die zweite Generation*, p. 200.

79.   See also D. Diamant, 'Auslaendische Arbeiterkinder in der deutschen Schule' in Klee, *Gastarbeiter, Analysen und Berichte*, p. 101.

80.   Savvidis, *Zum Problem der Gastarbeiterkinder*, p. 80.

81.   See Pommerin, *Deutschunterricht mit auslaendischen und deutschen Kindern*, p. 52.

# 7 ASSIMILATION V. INTEGRATION: IMMIGRANT ABSORPTION IN THE ISRAELI EDUCATIONAL SYSTEM

Tamar Horowitz

Israeli society consists largely of immigrants. The immigrants and sons of immigrants of yesterday are the absorbers of the immigrants of today. At the time of establishment of the State of Israel in 1947, some 750,000 Jews resided within its borders. Within four years, their number doubled, and in less than 25 years it quadrupled. This increase in population was almost entirely a function of the addition of new immigrants.

The crystallisation of the educational system is a product of Israel's coping with the various waves of immigration both before and after Independence. Before the establishment of the state, about 90 per cent of the immigrants were of European origin; in the period of statehood only half of the immigrants were of European origin while the other half came from Asian and African countries, the Jewish communities of which had not undergone processes of modernisation. Before 1947, the Jewish educational system in Palestine was fundamentally voluntary and linked with the evolving political system of the Jewish community. After 1947, the system became state supervised and devoid of political and ideological partisan orientation.

This difference between the pre-Independence and post-Independence system is relevant also to the nature of the dilemmas which faced the former and are still facing the latter. In the pre-Independence period the dilemmas were mostly ideological ones, concerned with the issue of communal identity. The question was: to what extent should there be continuity between Jewish education in the diaspora and Jewish education in Palestine; was the objective of the 'Hebrew education' to create a *homo novis* – a new man with a new identity – or should his identity reflect that of a diaspora Jew? This question was linked to the question of language. Should Hebrew be the spoken language of a Zionist state in embryo, or should other spoken languages continue to prevail? A great struggle took place at the beginning of the century over the educational implications of this issue.

This 'struggle of the languages' actually amounted to a *Kulturkampf* over the cultural foundations of the nation-to-be. As a matter of fact, the Hebrew language became the major cultural common denominator

137

of the Jews of Palestine who originated in different countries. It was the sacred language of all Jewish communities, but not a spoken language of any of them. Its transformation into a spoken language played a decisive role in the formation of the Jewish education in Palestine, and indeed it served as its *raison d'être*.

An additional dilemma was whether or not education should remain divided into trends based on political affiliation. Immigration to Palestine in the period of the British Mandate was mainly composed of organised groups affiliated to the various Zionist political parties and movements. The result was that a considerable part of the Jewish community was ideologically committed and highly politicised. It is no wonder that educational institutions, too, were divided according to the main political creeds — labour, religious, and general — the latter consisting of all the non-labour and non-religious Zionist factions. These instruments of political socialisation were challenged by the advocates of a unified educational system.

A third question was whether education should be elitist, oriented towards the fulfilment of pioneering roles, or based on a minimum programme suitable for all students. This dilemma became particularly acute when the non-pioneering waves of immigration arrived from Europe in the late 1930s and during World War II, escaping Nazi persecution.

Another important question concerned the place of the school *vis-à-vis* the non-formal education such as that provided by youth movements. At first, the school and youth movements coexisted, and in a way even complemented each other, but the increased institutionalisation and formalisation of the former and the increased politicisation of the latter ultimately resulted in a gradual development of alienation between these two educational agents. These dilemmas which faced the pre-state educational system were dilemmas of values and identity rather than of logistics or teaching methodology. The response to these questions was a gradual movement towards conservatism in the school system.

With the establishment of the state, most schools were already adapted to middle-class values and were utilising curricula and methods of instruction based on a European model. It is true that some schools, mostly in the kibbutz movement, were still experimenting with progressive education, but they were the exception rather than the rule. Another exception from the rule was that of 'Youth Alyia'. Youth Alyia was established by the Jewish Agency in 1934 as a framework for the absorption of children who, escaping Nazi persecution, arrived in Palestine without their parents. Most of the boarding schools of Youth

Alyia were in collective settlements. Such a placement of the schools reflected the orientation of Youth Alyia which, in addition to providing education, also aimed at the creation of a reservoir of manpower attuned to life in collective settlements. Until the establishment of the state, thousands of children went through the boarding institutions of Youth Alyia in the framework of which many experimental methods of education were tried and eventually implemented.

However, the pre-Independence problems and dilemmas were for the most part rendered irrelevant and obsolete by the nature, composition and social character of the post-Independence mass immigration.

### The Structure and Composition of Immigration, 1948-76

This immigration differed from previous waves of immigration in its size and in its composition with respect to the countries of origin of the immigrants. From May 1948 until the end of April 1975, 1,530,000 immigrants came to Israel, as contrasted with 430,000 who came during the whole of the period of the British Mandate, 1920-48. Immigration after May 1948 was not evenly distributed over the years; it reached its peak during the two-and-a-half years from May 1948 until the end of 1951, with 687,633 immigrants out of a total of 1,600,000 who arrived during the period of 1948-75. In other words, 43 per cent of these immigrants arrived in one-tenth of the total period of time, while 57 per cent arrived in the subsequent nine-tenths. The Jewish population, which numbered about 700,000 in May 1948, doubled within two-and-a-half years. Furthermore, in 1949 alone, 266 immigrants arrived for every 100 inhabitants of Israel (Jews and non-Jews).

After the record-breaking immigration in the first two-and-a-half years of the state, immigration had its ups and downs – down to 55,000 in 1952-54, up to 170,000 in 1955-57, down to 75,000 in 1958-60, up to 229,000 in 1961-64, and down to 61,000 in the years of economic recession, 1965-67.

The wave of enthusiasm that swept the Jewish communities abroad after the Six Day War gave new impetus to immigration, bringing 117,000 newcomers in 1969-71, and a similar number in 1972-73. After the Yom Kippur War there was a serious drop in immigration and in 1975 incoming immigrants numbered only 20,000.

The growth in the population was accompanied by a change in its composition by countries of origin. Immigration before 1948 came mostly from European countries. Immigration after 1948 came almost

Table 7.1:    Immigration in the Years 1948-75

| Year | Total | Year | Total |
|------|-------|------|-------|
| 1948 | 101,837 | 1962 | 61,533 |
| 1949 | 239,954 | 1963 | 64,489 |
| 1950 | 170,597 | 1964 | 55,036 |
| 1951 | 175,245 | 1965 | 31,115 |
| 1952 | 24,610 | 1966 | 15,957 |
| 1953 | 11,575 | 1967 | 14,469 |
| 1954 | 18,491 | 1968 | 20,697 |
| 1955 | 37,528 | 1969 | 38,111 |
| 1956 | 56,330 | 1970 | 36,750 |
| 1957 | 72,634 | 1971 | 41,930 |
| 1958 | 27,290 | 1972 | 55,888 |
| 1959 | 23,988 | 1973 | 54,886 |
| 1960 | 24,692 | 1974 | 31,979 |
| 1961 | 47,735 | 1975 | 20,028 |

Source:    *Know Israel* — Immigration and Emigration — Numbers and
Characteristics, 1978.

equally from Europe — 51 per cent — and Afro-Asian countries — 49
per cent. This was approximately the composition of the great wave of
immigration from September 1948 until July 1951. During this period,
survivors of the Nazi holocaust came from displaced-persons camps in
Europe, as well as the so-called 'illegal' immigrants who had been bani-
shed to transit camps in Cyprus by the British. The years 1949-50 saw
the arrival of tens of thousands of immigrants carried in operation
'Magic Carpet' from Aden to Israel. The year 1951 saw the arrival of
most of the Jews of Iraq.

Only about 25 per cent of the immigrants in 1952-54 came from
Europe. The remainder came mainly from North Africa. Thereafter,
except for the years 1958-60 when a relatively large contingent came
from Roumania and Poland, immigrants from Afro-Asian countries
formed the bulk of the newcomers until the 1967 Six Day War. This
made the proportion of ex-Europeans 63.7 per cent of all immigrants.
Ex-Europeans once again formed the majority — reaching 90 per cent —
of immigrants who arrived in 1973-75. Typical of immigration after
1948 was the arrival of almost entire Jewish communities in a short
period of time. Such was the nature of the immigration from Yemen,
Iraq and Libya. However, waves of immigration from Poland, Morocco,

Egypt and Bulgaria also brought large groups at one time.

A comparison of the contributions of different countries to the immigration into Israel shows that the largest number (over 300,000) came from North Africa. A quarter of the immigration since 1948 came from Europe, with most coming from Roumania (about 250,000 or about 15 per cent of the total immigrants who came to Israel). About 160,000 (10 per cent) came from Poland. Iraq provided the largest contingent of immigrants coming from Asia, with 127,000, 8 per cent of the immigration after 1948. Immigrants from the USSR number about 120,000, most of them coming during the period 1971-75. They include about 25,000 from Georgia, Boukhara and the mountain regions in the east. They made up 90 per cent of the immigration in those years. However, the largest of the Jewish communities in the world, that of the USA, provided only about 40,000 immigrants (less than 3 per cent) between 1948 and 1974.

Table 7.2:   Immigrants by Country of Origin

| Countries of Origin | Number of Immigrants | % |
| --- | --- | --- |
| Total | 1,555,941 | 100.0 |
| Asia | 333,485 | 21.7 |
| Turkey | 56,234 | 3.7 |
| Iraq | 127,404 | 8.3 |
| Yemen-Aden | 50,285 | 3.3 |
| Iran | 60,022 | 3.9 |
| Africa | 401,144 | 26.2 |
| North Africa | 317,929 | 20.8 |
| Libya | 34,769 | 2.3 |
| Egypt and Sudan | 30,903 | 2.0 |
| Europe | 696,405 | 45.5 |
| USSR | 118,773 | 7.8 |
| Poland | 156,478 | 10.2 |
| Roumania | 247,324 | 16.1 |
| Bulgaria | 39,515 | 2.6 |
| Germany and Austria | 14,048 | 0.9 |
| Czechoslovakia | 20,806 | 1.4 |
| Hungary | 24,881 | 1.6 |
| United Kingdom | 14,878 | 1.0 |
| America and Oceania | 101,478 | 6.6 |
| USA | 44,134 | 2.9 |
| Argentina | 27,624 | 1.8 |
| Unknown | 24,469 | |

Source:   *Know Israel* — Immigration and Emigration — Numbers and
        Characteristics, 1978.

Table 7.3: Immigrants by Age and Year of Immigration

| | 1948 | 1949 | 1950 | 1951 | 1952 | 1953 | 1954 | 1955 | 1956 | 1957 | 1958 | 1959 | 1960 | 1961 |
|---|---|---|---|---|---|---|---|---|---|---|---|---|---|---|
| 0-14 | 22.0 | 28.3 | 28.0 | 32.0 | 32.4 | 30.9 | 39.9 | 41.1 | 39.1 | 34.9 | 33.3 | 32.1 | 29.7 | 30.7 |
| 15-29 | 39.5 | 30.8 | 26.0 | 25.0 | 27.8 | 30.7 | 27.9 | 27.9 | 27.3 | 17.3 | 19.3 | 18.4 | 18.2 | 21.8 |
| 30-44 | 25.0 | 22.6 | 22.0 | 16.1 | 17.8 | 16.8 | 16.4 | 16.4 | 17.1 | 23.0 | 22.1 | 22.7 | 21.8 | 19.8 |
| 45-64 | 12.3 | 14.5 | 19.9 | 18.9 | 17.0 | 16.0 | 12.4 | 11.6 | 13.5 | 20.9 | 20.5 | 21.7 | 23.1 | 22.4 |
| 65-plus | 1.2 | 3.6 | 4.1 | 7.1 | 8.0 | 5.6 | 3.4 | 3.0 | 3.0 | 3.9 | 4.8 | 5.1 | 7.2 | 5.3 |
| Median | 25.9 | 26.1 | 27.3 | 24.8 | 23.3 | 23.1 | 20.0 | 19.4 | 20.2 | 27.5 | 27.6 | 29.6 | 31.7 | 27.7 |

| | 1962 | 1963 | 1964 | 1965 | 1966 | 1967 | 1968 | 1969 | 1970 | 1971 | 1972 | 1973 | 1974 | 1975 |
|---|---|---|---|---|---|---|---|---|---|---|---|---|---|---|
| 0-14 | 39.3 | 34.1 | 28.6 | 26.3 | 23.7 | 30.5 | 31.8 | 24.4 | 20.0 | 21.8 | 22.8 | 22.0 | 21.0 | 20.0 |
| 15-29 | 23.4 | 23.6 | 23.0 | 24.3 | 25.9 | 30.9 | 30.5 | 38.1 | 36.7 | 33.6 | 29.0 | 29.0 | 33.0 | 34.0 |
| 30-44 | 16.6 | 17.3 | 18.8 | 16.8 | 16.1 | 14.0 | 15.3 | 15.2 | 17.1 | 17.3 | 18.9 | 18.0 | 17.0 | 18.0 |
| 45-64 | 16.3 | 17.2 | 22.8 | 23.3 | 23.9 | 17.4 | 16.3 | 17.1 | 17.7 | 18.5 | 19.9 | 21.0 | 19.0 | 18.0 |
| 65-plus | 4.4 | 4.8 | 7.4 | 9.3 | 10.4 | 7.2 | 6.1 | 5.2 | 8.5 | 8.8 | 9.4 | 10.0 | 10.0 | 10.0 |
| Median | 20.1 | 21.3 | 29.2 | 29.4 | 30.4 | 22.8 | 22.4 | 23.8 | 26.2 | 26.9 | 28.9 | 30.0 | 27.0 | 27.0 |

Source: Immigration to Israel, 1948-72, Special Series no. 489 (Central Bureau of Statistics, Jerusalem, 1975); Immigration to Israel, 1973, 1974, 1975 (Central Bureau of Statistics, Jerusalem).

Table 7.4:   Immigrants by Occupation and Continent of Origin (percentages)

| | 1950-51 | | | 1953-54 | | | 1955-57 | | | 1958-60 | | |
|---|---|---|---|---|---|---|---|---|---|---|---|---|
| | Total | Asia Africa | Europe America | Total | Asia Africa | Europe America | Total | Asia Africa | Europe America | Total | Asia Africa | Europe America |
| With occupation | 27.9 | 25.0 | 32.2 | 35.1 | 25.2 | 45.7 | 29.7 | 25.2 | 38.9 | 33.4 | 21.4 | 38.4 |
| Without occupation | 61.8 | 66.6 | 54.9 | 59.1 | 69.1 | 49.2 | 63.9 | 67.8 | 56.0 | 59.4 | 63.8 | 54.4 |
| Unknown | 10.3 | 8.4 | 12.9 | 5.8 | 5.7 | 5.1 | 6.4 | 7.0 | 5.1 | 10.2 | 14.8 | 7.2 |
| Occupation total | 100.0 | 100.0 | 100.0 | 100.0 | 100.0 | 100.0 | 100.0 | 100.0 | 100.0 | 100.0 | 100.0 | 100.0 |
| Professional, scientific | 8.3 | 5.5 | 11.6 | 10.8 | 5.5 | 21.1 | 11.8 | 5.1 | 21.5 | 20.6 | 9.3 | 24.1 |
| Technical executives and clerks | 15.0 | 12.8 | 17.7 | 13.8 | 9.7 | 21.6 | 12.3 | 11.5 | 13.4 | 17.2 | 12.3 | 18.6 |
| Traders, agents and salesmen | 19.2 | 22.6 | 15.2 | 12.0 | 12.3 | 11.5 | 7.9 | 10.5 | 4.1 | 7.0 | 13.5 | 5.0 |
| Farmers and fishermen | 5.3 | 5.7 | 4.8 | 6.8 | 5.7 | 9.1 | 4.2 | 5.5 | 2.3 | 1.4 | 2.2 | 1.2 |
| Workers in transportation and communication | 2.6 | 2.6 | 2.8 | 2.3 | 2.6 | 2.1 | 2.9 | 3.2 | 2.4 | 15.3 | 16.6 | 14.9 |
| Workers in construction, quarrying, mining | 2.3 | 2.4 | 2.3 | 4.3 | 5.6 | 1.7 | 4.3 | 5.2 | 3.4 | 3.2 | 3.5 | 3.1 |
| Craftsmen, production workers | 34.6 | 25.9 | 32.9 | 37.8 | 44.2 | 24.7 | 48.9 | 50.6 | 46.5 | 26.0 | 27.0 | 25.7 |
| Workers in sport and recreation | 3.7 | 4.4 | 2.8 | 3.1 | 3.5 | 2.7 | 3.6 | 3.5 | 3.5 | 4.2 | 4.5 | 4.2 |
| Unskilled workers | 9.0 | 8.1 | 9.9 | 9.1 | 10.9 | 5.5 | 4.1 | 5.9 | 2.9 | 5.1 | 11.1 | 3.2 |

Table 7.4 (continued)

| | 1961-64 | | | 1965-68 | | | 1969-71 | |
|---|---|---|---|---|---|---|---|---|
| Total | Asia Africa | Europe America | Total | Asia Africa | Europe America | Total | Asia Africa | Europe America |
| 29.8 | 22.0 | 41.6 | 33.9 | 25.6 | 43.0 | 36.0 | 26.4 | 39.5 |
| 61.7 | 67.8 | 52.5 | 61.4 | 68.8 | 53.4 | 58.6 | 67.7 | 55.3 |
| 8.5 | 10.2 | 5.9 | 4.7 | 6.6 | 3.6 | 5.4 | 5.9 | 5.2 |
| 100.0 | 100.0 | 100.0 | 100.0 | 100.0 | 100.0 | 100.0 | 100.0 | 100.0 |
| 14.1 | 6.8 | 20.0 | 19.2 | 10.3 | 25.4 | 38.4 | 17.4 | 43.7 |
| 15.9 | 12.1 | 18.9 | 19.2 | 18.5 | 19.6 | 19.2 | 21.1 | 18.8 |
| 8.6 | 11.3 | 6.5 | 9.4 | 13.8 | 6.5 | 10.7 | 19.1 | 8.5 |
| 2.1 | 1.5 | 0.8 | 0.9 | 1.1 | 0.6 | 0.8 | 1.7 | 0.6 |
| 2.9 | 3.9 | 2.2 | 2.8 | 3.7 | 2.1 | 2.7 | 3.6 | 2.6 |
| 3.4 | 3.6 | 3.2 | 2.5 | 2.4 | 2.5 | 1.3 | 1.6 | 1.2 |
| 42.5 | 47.3 | 38.7 | 36.0 | 38.9 | 34.1 | 19.8 | 26.5 | 18.1 |
| 5.9 | 5.9 | 5.8 | 6.2 | 6.4 | 6.1 | 4.5 | 4.6 | 4.4 |
| 5.6 | 7.6 | 3.9 | 3.8 | 4.9 | 3.1 | 2.6 | 4.4 | 2.1 |

Source:  Immigration to Israel, 1948-72, Special Series no. 416 (Central Bureau of Statistics, Jerusalem, 1975); Immigration to Israel, 1973, 1974, 1975, (Central Bureau of Statistics, Jerusalem).

Immigration of such proportions inevitably affected the age distribution of the population. Generally speaking, the age distribution of immigrants from Afro-Asian countries differed from that of those coming from Europe and America. When large-scale immigration came from Afro-Asian countries, the proportion of the 0-14 age group in the general population rose. When large-scale immigration came from Europe, there was an increase in the 14-64 and 65-plus age groups. In recent years there has been a marked decline in the number of immigrants in the 0-14 age group, though they still form about 20 per cent of the immigrants. At the same time there has been an increase in the number of old people — reaching about 10 per cent of the immigrants as compared to 4 per cent in the years immediately after 1948.

An examination of Table 7.4 reveals that, beginning in the 1960s, there is an increase in the number of immigrants with occupations — from 25-27 per cent in the years immediately after Independence, to 46 per cent since the end of the sixties. A majority of these immigrants are from Europe and America. The proportion of those with academic education was high — 43 per cent in 1969-71 as compared to 20 per cent in the 1950s and 1960s. The proportion of immigrants with academic background from Afro-Asian countries was between 5 and 10 per cent, reaching its peak of 17.4 per cent in 1969-71. Among those with managerial or clerical occupations, there was not much difference between those coming from Afro-Asian countries — 10-20 per cent — and those of European origin — 13-22 per cent.

The percentage engaged in manual work and industry was high in all groups, about 33 per cent, with more immigrants from Afro-Asian origin falling into this category than from Europe and America.

The education system was thus influenced not only by the rate of immigration, but also by its ethnic composition, by its age distribution and by the educational and vocational level of immigrants.

## The First Phase: Formal Equality

As a consequence of the need to absorb the massive waves of immigration of the 1950s, the Israeli educational system was occupied during its incipient period with solving logistics problems. From a logistic point of view, the system was not prepared for the implementation of the Compulsory Education Act of 1949, which provided free education for children from the ages of five to fourteen (as well as for youngsters aged 14-17 who lacked elementary education), and the State Education Act

of 1953, which abolished the politically oriented 'trends' and established
a uniform curriculum for all. The system lacked facilities and manpower
as well as a suitable curriculum for satisfying the educational needs of
the newly arrived population. While the question of facilities was solved
to some extent by means of improvisation, there was no satisfactory
answer to the manpower question. In 1948, the educational system had
some 6,300 teachers with the output of the teachers' training colleges
being 300 teachers per year.[1] At the end of 1954, some 18,000 teachers
were needed, since the educational system grew during those years from
136,000 students to 350,000. This pressure brought about the mass
production of teachers by means of crash courses and the introduction
of unqualified teachers into the system. But not only was the capacity
to mass produce teachers low, there was also the attrition of teachers
from the system. During the years before the establishment of the state,
when an independent political system and a civil service were non-
existent, one of the major channels of mobility for educated people
was through teaching.

As it happened, the teaching profession in the pre-Independence
system attracted more talented people on the average than its counter-
part in most other countries. With the establishment of the state, the
opening of better occupational opportunities for educated people
resulted in an attrition from the teaching profession. Also, as far as
some of the teachers were concerned, the encounter with the immigrant
children from Asian and African countries was a new and sometimes
traumatic experience for which they were not prepared. The difficulties
in coping with this new situation resulted in further attrition of teachers
not flexible enough to deal with non-middle-class children. The assumption of the educational establishment at this stage was that, if all new
immigrants were allowed to attend schools, and if a uniform obligatory
curriculum was adopted, then the new immigrants would be 'assimilated'
into the social and economic set-up of the state. Moshe Smilansky calls
this the 'Stage of Formal Equality'.[2] This conception of 'formal
equality' is consistent with the prevailing 'melting pot' absorption
policy — namely that the new immigrants should adapt to veteran
Israeli social patterns and life styles, thus abandoning their own cultural
characteristics. The absorption model which guided these attempts at ·
social engineering can be labelled a model of assimilation. However, it
was soon discovered that the universal education and a uniform curriculum could not, by themselves, ensure the full utilisation by the new
population of the educational opportunities afforded them.

Three findings are indicative in this respect:

1. a high proportion of children of Asian and African origin dropped out before completing grades VII and VIII — the two top grades of the elementary school;
2. a relatively high proportion of Asian-African children did not continue their studies at the secondary school level;
3. many of these children who started post-elementary studies did not graduate.

In 1956-57, while their proportion among the entire 14-17 age group was 55 per cent, the proportion of children of Asian-African origin in secondary education was only 18 per cent. The percentage of children of Asian and African origin in the academic secondary schools was even lower — less than 13 per cent (compared with 25 per cent in the vocational secondary schools and 27 per cent in agricultural secondary schools). The very low percentage of children of Asian-African origin in the academic secondary schools as compared with other children in their age group can be attributed primarily to the failure in the 'survey' (Seker) — the qualifying examination for academic secondary education.[3] Consequently, the percentage of immigrant children of Asian-African origin in the vocational and agricultural schools, the entrance to which was not conditioned by success in the 'survey' examinations, was much higher.

An even lower percentage (less than 8 per cent) qualified for higher education, i.e. passed the matriculation examinations for the academic secondary schools given at the end of the 12th grade. The proportion of the Asian-African children in the various grades and types of schools in the year 1956-57 is shown in Table 7.5.

Chaim Adler argues that two sets of factors account for the poor achievement of children of Asian and African origin in the educational system.[4] The first set of factors relates to 'a syndrome of backwardness', while the second is a consequence of the essence of the modern school and the content of its curriculum. The syndrome of backwardness consists of economic, historical and cultural factors.

1. Economic factors — immigrants of Asian and African origin, on arrival in Israel, lacked financial means. They had to undergo the trial of occupational accommodation, which often involved irregular employment because of a lack of necessary cultural prerequisites for coping with the conditions of the modern economy.

2. Historical factors — people of the middle classes have benefited

Table 7.5:    Percentage of Youths whose Fathers were Born in Asian-African Countries in the Relevant Age Group and in Various Types and Grades of Post-primary Schools, 1956-57

| Population | 1956-57 |
|---|---|
| Jewish population aged 14-17 | 55.0 |
| | |
| All post-primary schools | 17.7[a] |
| 9th grades | 22.1 |
| 10th grades | 18.5 |
| 11th grades | 14.4 |
| 12th grades | 8.8 |
| 13th grades (technicians) | — |
| 14th grades (technicians) | — |
| | |
| Academic secondary schools | 12.6 |
| 9th grades | 15.8 |
| 10th grades | 13.8 |
| 11th grades | 9.8 |
| 12th grades | 7.8 |
| | |
| Vocational schools | 25.1 |
| 9th grades | 29.7 |
| 10th grades | 25.5 |
| 11th grades | 20.4 |
| 12th grades | 11.8 |
| 13th grades | — |
| 14th grades | — |
| | |
| Agricultural schools | 26.7 |
| 9th grades | 33.9 |
| 12th grades | 11.6 |
| | |
| Secondary evening schools | — |

a. Data for 1956-57 include only academic, vocational and agricultural schools, not continuation classes in collective settlements nor part-time schools.

Sources:    M. Smilansky, 'The Social Implications', *Child Welfare Research Quarterly*, (in Hebrew), *Megamot*, 8 (1957), pp. 233-6.

from educational opportunities since the Industrial Revolution, while the provision of education to lower strata is a relatively new phenomenon. The exposure of the middle classes to education for such a long period of time affected their pattern of socialisation in a manner that facilitated performance in the school system and eased their adjustment to its values. By contrast, when children of the lower classes were given access to educational institutions, they often lacked the motivation for the intellectual effort necessary for success in the educational system. The historical factor is also prominent in the context of the student's educational cycle; if a lower-strata student fails at an early stage of his school experience, this failure is likely to deter him from making further efforts towards higher school achievement. Since most of the Asian and African children were of lower socio-economic background, the general factors discussed above, regardless of immigration status, continued to depress their academic performance.

3. Cultural factors – immigrants from Asian and African countries, in their countries of origin, were subject to the influence of value orientations incompatible with the 'Modern Man' orientation as described by Kluckhan.[5] This orientation emphasises 'doing' as opposed to 'being'; control over nature as opposed to submission to it; planning as opposed to fatalism. It is thus futuristic in the sense that man is required to postpone immediate gratification in order to have control over his fate. The modern system of education is anchored to this orientation, and therefore attuned to those who are predisposed towards it.

The content of the school curriculum is at the root of a second set of factors which, according to Adler, accounts for the poor performance of immigrant children in the education system.[6] The Israeli school system has been a system generally for the middle class. The system (particularly during the 1950s and early 1960s) has not adjusted its organisation, curriculum and methods of teaching to the change in its student population. Indeed, it has been the student who has had to adjust himself to a context which he often fails to comprehend.

Referring to this phenomenon, Chaim Adler comments:

The curriculum, the story with the names of its heroes, the problems to be solved in the maths session, the observations to be made for the study of 'natural sciences', all those are taken from the mental world of the middle class. We teach civics as a result of an assumption that all students share a basic confidence in the regime and it being necessary, we teach history on the assumption that all students share the same conception of time, continuity and chain of events, and we teach geography while assuming that all children have the capacity and the tendency to translate the three dimensions of their immediate world into the two dimensions of the map.[7]

**The Compensatory Phase**

During the late 1950s and early 1960s, a new approach emerged. Its adherents advocated the adoption of a new educational pattern more suited to teaching Asian and African immigrant children. They maintained that, instead of trying to adapt the children to the system, the programmes and methods of teaching should be adapted to the children's need, thus enabling them to cope more adequately with the system. It was argued that compensatory methods should be introduced for this purpose. At that stage the assumption of the advocates of this new approach was that the existing set-up of schools should not be changed. Instead it should utilise new methods aimed at helping these children who were labelled, in the terminology of this approach, 'culturally disadvantaged'. This term did not apply to all children of Asian and African origin; those among them who did not show signs of the 'backwardness' syndrome were not categorised as 'culturally disadvantaged'.

However, for the majority who were considered disadvantaged the system offered a special treatment which aimed at closing the educational gap in a manner that would enable them eventually to function as regular students. The administrative conception of a disadvantaged student was as one whose probability of succeeding in the 'survey' (Seker) examination was low. An analysis of the 'survey' results during the late 1950s and early 1960s showed that immigrants of Asian-African origin, whose families were large and whose fathers' education did not exceed eight years of schooling, were most likely to fail in the 'survey'. Hence, a criterion was adopted for classifying children as disadvantaged based on country of origin, size of family and father's education and, consequently, schools were provided with additional resources according to the proportion of such children among their student population.

Two strategies of compensation were adopted in the context of the new approach.

1. Special treatment was granted to gifted children of Asian-African origin. Children defined as gifted were children who passed the 'survey' (Seker) examinations but were not likely to continue their studies at the secondary level in their localities. This category included children who had no suitable academic school in their area, as well as children whose parents preferred to send them to work in order to supplement the family income. There were also gifted children who did well in the 'survey' (Seker), but still suffered from the results of insufficient

educational opportunities in the past. For these children boarding institutions were established, attached to existing prestigious secondary schools. This strategy was strongly criticised on the grounds that the gifted children were being cut off from their home environment and alienated from their background. In addition, it was argued that creaming the elite from the schools in their own area would result in a further decline in the capacity of these schools to maintain the drive required for the educational achievement of the remaining culturally disadvantaged children.

2. A second strategy involved the provision of compensatory programmes within existing schools. In the framework of this strategy, a variety of programmes were developed for the different levels of schools:

a. programmes for the kindergarten, which were based on the assumption that bridging the scholastic gap would be easier if it began at the kindergarten level;
b. language programmes based on the assumption that development of linguistic capacity would facilitate change in patterns of thought;
c. enrichment programmes for differing ages aimed at broadening the intellectual perspective of the children;
d. a prolonged school day with extra curricular activities.

But, in spite of all these efforts, it looked as though the output of the programmes was not in proportion to the input.

### School Structure Reform and Integration

Since the mid-sixties a new conception has been formulated, according to which immigrants from Asian and African origins should not be perceived as a separate group, but rather as one of the many groups within the educational system. This conception, designed to help immigrant children of Asian and African origin, gave rise to the school reform programme. The reform had two aspects:

1. The first was an administrative change in the school structure: instead of a two-level school composed of eight years of primary school and four years of secondary school, a three-level school was established. The three new levels were: six years of primary school, three years of intermediate school and three years of high school. The purpose of this

administrative reform was to bring about a change in the school set-up with regard to scope, curricula and atmosphere.

2. The second was the introduction of a system which would facilitate the encounter between various population groups, as a vehicle for integration. Two key concepts related to integration were 'motivation' and 'opportunity'. Both the majority and the minority were expected to raise their level of motivation. The motivation of the majority should have been one of acceptance, expressed in the creation of a climate conducive to the absorption of members of the minority groups. The motivation of the minority group should have been derived from the desire to resemble the majority group. The 'opportunity' referred to in the context of the above-mentioned approach was the opportunity for an encounter between various population groups. The assumption was that opportunity creates a stimulus. This stimulus can be on a cognitive level, resulting from an encounter with students of high intellectual level or from the opportunity to study according to curricula intended for a population of high intellectual level. The stimulus can also exist on a social level – a stimulus to establish interpersonal relations with students of a different social group, leading to an encounter with the values and life patterns of the dominant group. Simultaneously, the dominant group was expected to become acquainted with the values and life styles of the minority.

The subject of reform and integration was widely researched by Israeli social scientists. But, despite the variety of methods and research approaches employed, the conclusions of the various researchers were similar. It turned out that:

1. The administrative manipulation which brought about the introduction of the heterogeneous classroom did not in itself improve the achievements of children of Asian and African origin. On the other hand, the integration did not result in a regression in the achievements of either the Asian-African students or the dominant group of children of European origin.[8] It should, however, be noted that integration was limited to an administrative manipulation and no curricula and special teaching methods were developed for the heterogeneous classroom.

2. For the Asian-African students, the encounter with such a situation fostered in them a low self-image. This decline in self-image could, however, be interpreted as a functional, more realistic perception of their

situation *vis-à-vis* the European students.[9]

3. Positive intergroup relations developed between children of Asian and African origin and children of European and American origin. These relations did not bring about a rejection on the part of Asian and African children of their families.

Following the intergroup encounter, the children of African and Asian origin became acquainted with the central values of Israeli society, which imply a reduction in communal consciousness and an increase in the level of aspiration and Internal Locus of Control.[10]

The case for the proposition that integration brings about higher academic achievement remains 'not proven'. This situation could be attributed to the fact that the conditions in which integration was implemented were far from optimal, since no special methods and curricula for the heterogeneous classroom were developed.

Another innovation of this period was the introduction of special programmes such as 'Moreshet' (heritage) aimed at the cultivation of the unique traditions of the various ethnic communities in Israel. Various anthologies of short stories were published, reflecting the particular cultural heritage of the various Jewish communities. It was assumed that spreading the knowledge of the unique contribution of each group would both provide children of oriental background with a better understanding of their cultural tradition and help them to recover their pride lost in the process of absorption.

## Immigrant Children from Europe and America

The absorption of immigrant children into the educational system was not confined to those who came from Asian and African countries; immigrants also came from Europe as well as from North and South America, and their proportion among the total number of immigrants increased considerably in the late 1960s and 1970s. Indeed, no less than two-thirds of the immigrants of this period came from these countries. The number of school-age immigrants from the Soviet Union alone exceeded 30,000. Yet, because the cultural background of these children did not foster as many difficulties as that of children of Asian-African origin, the focus of the educational establishment was concentrated primarily on the problems of the latter.

Indeed, in the educational literature of the 1950s and early mid-sixties, there are hardly any references to the absorption of immigrant children from Europe and America. It was only with the new waves of immigrants from Europe and America in the late sixties that attention was first paid to the absorption problems of immigrant children of non-oriental background. However, the increase in immigration from South America, North America and particularly from the Soviet Union in the late 1960s and 1970s induced the educational authorities to start looking into the problems involved in the educational absorption of children from these countries, whose adjustment to the system was less difficult than that of oriental children.

A special unit was established in the Ministry of Education to deal with such immigrant children. The local authorities also developed special services for them, including a clinic for psychological counselling. Another institution which took care of immigrants from the Soviet Union in particular was 'Youth Alyia'. This institution was especially suitable for this task, as children from the Soviet Union were more prepared for boarding education, which is not an unfamiliar phenomenon in the Soviet Union. Thus, immigrant parents from the Soviet Union were less reluctant to send their children to Youth Alyia educational institutions. The absorption of children from the Soviet Union into Youth Alyia constituted a change in orientation on the part of this institution, which in the 1950s and early 1960s absorbed children mostly with social and family problems. Another innovation associated with the arrival of the new kind of immigrants was the introduction of a new status definition — that of an immigrant student. The term 'immigrant student' was applied to any child in the educational system for three years after his arrival in Israel. This status entitled the immigrant student to certain privileges, including concessions in the matriculation examination in language and eligibility for intensive instruction in Hebrew in the framework of the Ulpan (language school) system.

The main assistance for these students, then, concentrated upon providing them with linguistic skills. They were also given some instruction in Jewish history and the history of the State of Israel. The underlying assumption of this approach was that, once these students mastered the basic knowledge of the Hebrew language and became better informed about the foundations of Judaism and the State of Israel, then the necessary conditions for their absorption into the Israeli society would be met. An additional assumption which guided the policy makers was that students of European and American origin were not likely, in the long run, to have serious difficulties with their studies. Any problems that they might have had were considered temporary, since the schools in the countries from which they came were not essentially different in organisation or educational methods from Israeli schools.

These assumptions were proved to be basically correct. Nevertheless, some difficulties emerged in contexts other than that of academic achievements. These difficulties arose as a result of:

1. adjustment to the regime and school climate;
2. adjustment to the relatively free teacher-student relations;
3. an alienation between Israeli students and immigrant students.

Despite the positive attitude towards integration exhibited on both sides, such an integration did not actually materialise. A high degree of insecurity and anxiety was found among a considerable number of students from Europe and America. The Horowitz and Frenkel study on the absorption of immigrant children from English-speaking countries and the Soviet Union indicated that the absorption problems of immigrants from these countries were not necessarily related to language difficulties, but were rather of a social nature.[11] Moreover, there were differences between the processes of absorption of students from the Soviet Union and from English-speaking countries.

The English-speaking students adjusted better to school than the Russian students in all areas and at all levels. They were better accepted by their Israeli peers, since their culture was closer to that of the Israelis. Indeed, the Israeli teenage culture recently underwent processes of Americanisation with pervasive popularity of pop music and other symbols of the American youth culture. The English-speaking students adjusted rather easily to the Israeli school discipline, since they too came from permissive schools, not much different from the Israeli ones. Their degree of anxiety was low compared to that of children from the Soviet Union; they also identified with Israeli society and Judaism not necessarily on the basis of experience in Israel, but rather as a consequence of previous Jewish background. The students from the Soviet Union adjusted well from a scholastic point of view, but their level of anxiety was high. Many felt that, by emigrating to Israel, they were cut off from their native environment, and family and friends. Their level of identification with Israeli society and Judaism was rather low. These Russian students also found it difficult to adjust to the school, which seemed to be too permissive. Their behaviour in school was teacher oriented rather than peer-group oriented. The Israeli children, for their part, did not accept the students from the Soviet Union into their milieu in the same way that they accepted the English-speaking students. Both Israelis and Russians were aware of the social distance and the degree of alienation between them.

Special adjustment problems characterised students who emigrated from the Asian parts of the Soviet Union — the Georgians, the Bucharians and the Caucasians. These problems were similar, in some respects, to the problems of the Oriental Jews in the fifties. Nevertheless, it seems that among the Georgian and Bucharian groups there were also students whose scholastic and social profile was closer to that of other students from the Soviet Union. These were, for the most part, sons of professionals.

In retrospect, the absorption of children of Asian and African origin and the absorption of children from Europe and America represented two different problems of immigrant absorption. In the first case, absorption involved a dual transformation: on the one hand, the immigrants had to adjust to the system; on the other hand, the absorbers themselves had to adapt to the immigrants by introducing organisational and educational innovations into the system. In the second case, that of immigrants from Europe and America, the changes in the system were minimal and it was the immigrant children who had to develop their own resources in order to adjust themselves to the new educational and social environment. From the viewpoint of the educational system, however, the main challenge to its integrity was posed by the immigrants of oriental background. Their absorption served as an incentive for the introduction of changes in the system on various levels: organisation, curricula and value orientations. Thus, in response to the challenge of cultural diversity, the Israeli educational system, through a process of 'trial and error', reshaped its structure.

## Notes

1.    E. Yaffe, 'Manpower in the Educational System — Their Training and Status', in H. Ormians (ed.), *Education in Israel* (Ministry of Education and Culture, Jerusalem, 1973), pp. 335-52 (in Hebrew).

2.    M. Smilansky, 'The Challenge of Disadvantaged Children in the Educational System', in Ormians (ed.), *Education in Israel*.

3.    The survey (Seker) is a test which contains elements of achievement tests in Hebrew, arithmetic, geometry and verbal reasoning.

4.    C. Adler, 'The Role of the Educational System in the Integration of Immigrants', in *The Integration of Immigrants from Different Countries of Origin in Israel*, a symposium held at the Hebrew University, 25-26 October 1966 (The Magness Press, Jerusalem, 1969), pp. 17-23 (in Hebrew).

5.    F. Kluckhan and L. Strodtbeck, *Variations in Value Orientation* (Harper and Row, New York, 1961).

6.     Adler, 'The Role of the Educational System'.

7.     Ibid., p. 19.

8.     A. Lewy, 'Class Composition and School Progress', *Megamot*, XXIII, 3-4 (1977), pp. 88-97 (in Hebrew); Y. Eshel and Z. Klein, 'School Integration, Academic Self-Image, and Achievement of Lower-Class Elementary School Pupils', *Megamot*, XXIII, 3-4 (1977), pp. 135-45 (in Hebrew); A. Minkovitch, D. Davies and Y. Bashi, *The Evaluation of Educational Achievements in the Elementary School in Israel*, Research Report to the Van Leer Foundation, Jerusalem, 1977 (in Hebrew).

9.     Eshel and Klein, 'School Integration, Academic Self-Image, and Achievement of Lower-Class Elementary School Pupils'; J. Bashi, 'Effects of Ethnic Class Composition in Self-Concept', *Megamot*, XXIII, 3-4 (1977), pp. 124-33 (in Hebrew).

10.     M. Chen, A. Lewy and D. Kfir, 'The Possibilities of Interethnic Group Contact in the Junior High Schools: Implementation and results', *Megamot*, XXIII, 3-4 (1977), pp. 101-23 (in Hebrew); H. Hadad and R. Shapira, 'Commanding Resources and Social Integration', *Megamot*, XXIII, 3-4 (1977), pp. 166-73 (in Hebrew); Y. Amir, 'Ethnic Interactions and Intergroup Attitudes and Relations: A Review and Re-evaluation', *Megamot*, XXIII, 3-4 (1977), pp. 41-76 (in Hebrew); J. Levin and M. Chen, 'Sociometric Choices in Ethnically Heterogeneous Classes', *Megamot*, XXIII, 3-4 (1977), pp. 189-205 (in Hebrew); Sh. Sharan, E. Cohen and D. Elchanani, 'Modifying Status Relations in Israel Youth Through Expectation Training', *Megamot*, XXIII, 3-4 (1977), pp. 146-58 (in Hebrew).

11.     T.R. Horowitz and E. Frenkel, *The Adjustment of Immigrant Children to the School System in Israel* (The Szold Institute Publications, Jerusalem, 1976) (in Hebrew).

# 8  EDUCATING IMMIGRANT CHILDREN IN THE MIDDLE EAST

**Arpi Hamalian**

## Introduction

The name Middle East has become a conventional term designating the whole area extending from the Atlantic coast of Morocco and Mauritania eastward across North Africa to Afghanistan, encompassing more than 22 countries. This area is now regarded as a broad cultural unit, primarily in terms of its overarching Islamic civilisation, although there is tremendous diversity in the area in terms of languages, ethnic groups, political organisation, religious sects and cultural traditions. The estimated total population of the area was 164 million in 1968.[1]

Mass migration has characterised the life style of most people in the Middle East since antiquity. Internal wars, conquests, the rise and fall of major world powers centred in the Middle East have contributed to the fluctuating and migrant life style. The Middle East has survived over ten thousand years of continuous movement of its inhabitants from one part of the area to another with very few breakdowns until the most recent times.

Between the two world wars, arbitrary national boundaries and new states were established in the Middle East and large nationalist movements spread between the years 1925 and 1930. This new trend elicited exchanges between large population groups such as the Greeks and Turks. Repression, genocide and resettlement of other groups was carried out in many areas, for example against the Armenians in Turkey and the Berber peoples of Morocco and Algeria. The colonisation of Palestine by immigrant Jewish communities from Europe brought about clashes with the British and the indigenous peoples, mostly Arab peasants. Within ten years after World War II, national independence had been achieved by Syria, Lebanon, Iraq and Jordan. The Algerian revolution had started, Morocco, Tunisia, Libya and Egypt had been declared sovereign states and Israel had been established. Except for Israel, industrialisation of the newly defined Middle Eastern economies was minimal. This situation changed slowly, especially where foreign economic enterprises controlled Middle Eastern economic resources. By the mid-1960s, most countries in the Middle East were moving towards secularised and industrialised polity models with nationalist regimes. By the early 1970s, the Middle Eastern societies were well on their way to transition to modern organisation. However, this has been a slow and lengthy process, since various forms of new population movements, such as rural-urban and migrant and refugee movements, have disrupted the efforts of individual countries in building modern nation states.[2]

The newly constituted Middle Eastern countries, in their efforts to achieve national power and unity, placed great hopes and expectations on expanded national education systems. From the very beginning, however, these national education systems had to make adjustments for different migrant, refugee and minority groups. The extent and the seriousness of the problem of educating immigrants and refugees vary from one country to the other, but no single country in the general area defined as the Middle East has been spared the difficult task of providing acceptable education for immigrants, both children and adults.

It should be remembered that, although the region lies almost entirely within the Muslim World, non-Muslim communities are preponderant in Israel, Lebanon and Cyprus, with striking effects upon population dynamics and structure. Moreover, while the region designated as the Middle East covers much of the Arab world, these three small countries are largely non-Arab, as are the two big northern countries of Turkey and Iran. Furthermore, some of the countries of the Middle East are at present mainly emigrant countries, such as Cyprus, Lebanon and Southern Yemen, and some are immigrant countries, like Israel, Libya and Kuwait. In general, however, it is becoming more difficult to migrate internationally within the region, so that intranational migration is more voluminous. Most of the countries of the area are, therefore, progressing towards an increasing measure of demographic individuality and, in view of rising nationalism, most problems related to education as they occur are likely to find solutions only at a national level. Reasons for emigration from, and immigration to, these different areas of the Middle East also vary. Emigration has long been a relief to population pressure in Lebanon, which has provided a major emigration stream since 1860. People of Lebanese origin abroad now exceed two million and their remittances have helped Lebanon to enjoy a higher *per capita* income than most countries of the Middle East. The population of Kuwait, Bahrain, Qatar and some of the Trucial States have been utterly transformed by immigration, especially as male immigrants greatly outnumber females. Immigrants into Kuwait now outnumber Kuwaitis, raising the total population from 206,000 in 1957 to 491,000

in 1966.[3] In a similar example, unofficial sources suggest that there
are 1.3 million expatriate workers in Saudi Arabia: 80,000 are from
the Far East (including 40,000 South Koreans); 300,000 from India
and Pakistan; 400,000 from North and South Yemen; 350,000 from
Egypt; 50,000 from Europe and the United States; and 120,000 from
other Third World countries including Arab states to the north. These
figures compare with a Saudi workforce of one million. Until the
middle of 1978, the Saudi economy also relied on a floating population
of casual labourers. Many of these were employed without work permits, having come in on pilgrimage or business visas and overstayed
their time in the hope of making a fortune before being found out. A
great number of these immigrants are concentrated in oil company
compounds, where special educational facilities are provided based on
American, British or other European models depending on the main
office site of the particular company. Non-Saudi Muslims send their
children to religious schools or to the Saudi government schools. Most
of these 'guest-workers' do not bring their families with them when
they first arrive. However, more and more women and children are
joining the numbers of guest-workers, and the education of the children is on a very random basis, especially since a great number are
working in camps in the desert.[4]

There are other factors influencing the pattern of the present-day
immigration waves in the Middle East. Religion has been a main reason
for immigration to Israel, and war a main reason for the exodus of
refugees from present-day Israel into Jordan, Syria, Lebanon and other
Arab states. Jordan, for example, has been torn apart by the conflict
between Jordanians and Palestinians, the latter more numerous than
the former.

In illustrating some of the problems involved in the education of
immigrant children in the Middle East, I shall draw specific examples
from different countries, on a random basis. This is done to illustrate
the complex nature and extent of the problems encountered, since it
is not possible to give in one chapter a comprehensive and systematic
account of the education of immigrants in more than 22 countries
included in the Middle East. Furthermore, there are many problems
with locating comparable data since population data for the region are
far from comprehensive and statistics available often have a very low
level of reliability and/or validity. This chapter will focus on the education of a special category of immigrant — the refugee. It is generally
accepted that refugees contribute the largest category of migrants on a
world-wide scale. The concept developed after World War I when

Fridtjof Nansen supervised international efforts to help Armenians flee-ing the Turks and Russians fleeing the revolution. The definition used by the United Nations High Commissioner for Refugees excludes any who have fled or been forcibly removed within the boundaries of a single state (such as the case of the refugees in many African countries) or who have been 'return' migrants, such as Algerians of French origin expelled to France. There are few social-psychological studies on refu-gees which attempt even an elementary theoretical formulation and examination. Since the end of World War II, more than 60 million persons have been officially classified as refugees. The importance of this fact is illustrated by comparison with the usual estimate of total emigration from all of Europe of 60 million between 1800 and 1950.[5]

## The Education of Palestinian Arab Children Inside and Outside Israel

### Palestinians Outside Israel: Background

Although, typically, refugee immigrants are victims of their own poli-tics, the original Palestinian refugees illustrate the case of people who are uprooted because they have failed to withstand an influx from the outside. Strife with the immigrant Jews led to the 1948 flight of hun-dreds of thousands of Palestinians, mainly Arabs. For nearly thirty years, the United Nations has struggled for the integration of these refugees through an agency which is called the United Nations Relief and Works Agency for Palestine Refugees (UNRWA).[6]

Founded in December 1949, UNRWA had, in addition to relief, a major objective: creating employment to bring about permanent re-settlement of the refugees in the Arab countries to which they fled. These efforts have failed since, and today the agency is engaged in the direct administration of programmes of relief, health and education. The *raison d'être* of UNRWA is, therefore, to provide services to Pales-tine refugees, that is, persons or the descendants of persons whose normal residence was Palestine for a minimum of two years preceding the Arab-Israeli conflict in 1948 and who, as a result of that conflict, lost both their homes and their means of livelihood. No precise census of the Palestinian people has been taken, but those among them with refugee status must represent a substantial part of the total. Of the persons who fall under the established definition of Palestine refugees, 1,757,269 are registered with the agency. The registrations are distri-buted as follows: Lebanon (211,902 refugees), Syrian Arab Republic (198,435), East Jordan (682,561), West Bank (310,268), Gaza Strip

(354,103). These figures do not necessarily mean that the actual population is where it is registered. The refugees move and do not always inform the agency; there is no inducement to provide this information unless they are receiving services. Since one of the services is education, the maximum number of refugees who could even in theory receive all services is limited to the school population of about 307,000, or approximately 17.5 per cent of the total number of registered refugees.[7] UNRWA provides services to eligible registered refugees directly, not through governments, whether the refugees are in the camps or not. The governments in the area of operations have reported that they provided assistance separately to refugees, costing almost $ 80 million in 1978 alone. The total expenditure of UNRWA for that same year was about 1.5 billion.[8]

## UNRWA Educational Services

Conducted in collaboration with UNESCO, UNRWA's educational expenditure grew from $ 300,000 in 1950 to $ 76.8 million in 1978. The education and training services are provided by approximately 10,975 employees (mostly teachers). The education staff in each field is headed by a Field Education Officer — an UNRWA local staff member — working under the professional guidance of the Director of Education and of the specialist staff of the Department of Education at headquarters.

The services provided include:

1. the general education programme, under which about 307,000 refugee children receive elementary and preparatory education in 617 UNRWA/UNESCO schools;
2. the vocational and teacher training programme, under which 4,540 trainees are trained at eight UNRWA training centres;
3. a programme of subsidisation of secondary education, under which some 7,000 refugee pupils are assisted, by means of book allowances or cash grants, in their education at government or private secondary schools;
4. a university education scholarship programme under which 339 refugee men and women are educated at universities in Arab countries;
5. a modest programme of pre-school and youth and women's activities and adult training in crafts;
6. Participation by the agency in the financing and staffing of a regional institute of education, through which teachers appointed to posts

in UNRWA/UNESCO schools receive in-service professional and other kinds of training. The institute also provides extension services (without UNRWA participation) to government educational systems in the Near East.[9]

At the elementary level of instruction, which comprises the first six years, and at the preparatory level, comprising the next three years, UNRWA schools accommodate most of the refugee children, while government and private schools with financial assistance from UNRWA admit still others in these age groups. At the secondary level — the last three years of general education — UNRWA has no schools of its own, reliance is entirely on government and private schools assisted by grants-in-aid from UNRWA. In 1977-78, a total of 306,968 pupils were enrolled in the 617 UNRWA/UNESCO elementary and preparatory schools in Lebanon, the Syrian Arab Republic, East Jordan, the West Bank and the Gaza Strip. They were served by a teaching force of 8,986. A further 78,167 refugee pupils were known to be enrolled in government and private elementary, preparatory and secondary schools in the same areas, and approximately 40,000 non-eligible children were in agency schools.[10]

There are at least four acute problems facing the education of the Palestinian Arab children in the five regions mentioned above.

*Limited Number of Classroom Places.*   Double-shifting of schools has been, and continues to be, a problem for UNRWA schools because of both the steady growth in the school population and the agency's lack of funds for school construction on the scale required. In 1977-78, double-shifting was necessary in 450 schools (73 per cent of the total).[11]

*Curriculum and Textbooks.*   The UNRWA/UNESCO school system is not self-contained. Laterally, it is dependent on government and private schools to supplement the agency schools where additional places are needed. Horizontally, it depends on the host government and private schools to ensure the secondary education of the Palestinian children. Therefore, UNRWA has the problem of structurally relating to the curricular patterns of the respective national systems as well as to the substantive question of curricular content.

Accommodation between UNRWA's educational system and the systems of Egypt, Jordan, Lebanon and Syria, respectively, developed over the years from empirical adjustments of an *ad hoc* nature. In Lebanon, UNRWA has always enjoyed, and still has considerable freedom to choose its own textbooks, while in other host countries, until the June War of 1967, the practice had been to employ the same syllabi and textbooks used in the government schools. The subordination of an international system to local national curricula was brought into prominence by Israel's occupation of Gaza and the West Bank. The educational system of UNRWA remained under Egyptian and Jordanian school administration except for East Jerusalem, which in effect was annexed to Israel. However, the Israeli government, through the Israeli Foreign Office, protested in July 1967 to UNRWA that textbooks used in agency schools taught hatred of Israel and incited students to violence.

In June 1968, the UNESCO Executive Board appointed a commission of outside experts to examine the textbooks used in UNRWA/UNESCO schools and to make recommendations which the Director-General would submit to the member states concerned for their assent and co-operation. Buehrig discusses the delicate situation of an international agency *vis-à-vis* the education of a particular refugee group in territories under the jurisdiction of national systems, and he concludes:

> Dependence on the respective national systems for structural completeness presents a problem but not the main one; more difficult is knowing what to teach about the identity and aspirations of the national community to which the system ministers. Strictly in the area of methodology, a country might willingly license an international organization to establish a model system of education, but it can hardly be expected to do so for the substance of its national history, which indeed may include an important religious component. The complexities become truly formidable in Gaza and the West Bank where the authority of an occupying power renders tripartite a bilateral relationship already confused as to the respective prerogatives of international organization and the indigenous society.[12]

Not only do the Palestinian children not have the proper textbooks to study their own history; most of the time they are not allowed to study the history of the particular countries where they have been settled as refugees for over 30 years. Since all the countries involved in the dilemma of the education of refugees are in the process of reorganising their national educational system, the situation is even more confusing. *The Continuing War and the Number of Effective School Days.* The reality of a continuing war or series of incidents between Israel and one or other of the countries where the Palestinian refugees are found illustrates the fact that it is not the curriculum alone which perpetuates the

memory of the lost homeland in the minds of refugee children. The
textbook issue came into light on the occasion of the 1967 June War.
Another major war took place in 1973, and many incidents and isolated,
aggressive activities occur almost daily in the area, disrupting the regular
operation of schools and severely affecting the number of working days
in the UNRWA/UNESCO schools. In 1977-78, these schools lost
between 10 and 120 days each, depending on their location.[13]
*Discontinuities between the UNRWA/UNESCO Schools and the
National Schools and Universities.*   After receiving the first nine years
of their general education in UNRWA/UNESCO schools, with peers
belonging to the same background as themselves and teachers trained
specifically for their condition, the Palestinian pupils are transferred
into the national systems of the countries of residence. Here they are
looked upon as 'refugees' and are acclaimed sometimes as 'heroes' and
at other times as 'strangers', 'free loaders' or even 'traitors' by their
peers.

Therefore, for most refugee children, their first contact with children
of the countries of adoption begins with entrance into high school.
Most of the time there are important discrepancies in background preparation due to different textbooks and content material studied at the
UNRWA schools. Some Palestinian pupils take the situation as a challenge to prove the excellence of Palestinian background through
individual achievement. Others still see their personal mobility and
success in life at stake and try hard to obtain high grades and scholarships to university and then transfer to 'Western' 'free' and 'equal'
country and nationality status. There are also those who are overwhel-
med by the gap between their academic and personal backgrounds and
those of their new peers at high school. These pupils lose all motivation
and drop out sooner or later. Furthermore, the psychological motivation to achieve in order to continue academic careers is undermined by
several structural difficulties which are peculiar to the refugee children,
such as irregular examination dates and locations as well as special
quotas for entrance to university faculties.

## Palestinians Inside Israel: Background

The other side of the coin is as interesting. What happened to those
Palestinian Arabs who did not leave Israel? For the most part they were
living in villages in border areas and therefore their status will change
from 'local' to 'migrant' to 'refugee' depending on the political developments in the area and between Israel and the neighbouring Arab
countries. In a word, they became 'immigrants in their own land' from

a sociological point of view. Those who stayed became overnight a minority in their own land and, what is even more important, they became a special type of minority: they belonged to the potential 'enemy' group and, therefore, were excluded in a planned and systematic way from many structures and institutions of the society at large, such as schools, political parties and the army. Forced residential segregation was also carried out until 1967 as part of state policy, restricting the geographic areas where Arabs could live as well as the hours during which they could circulate. The official rationale for subjugating Arabs to military administration was the maintenance of security. The Arabs who remained within Israel's boundaries could not psychologically accept the new political and socio-cultural reality. They were defeated and became subordinated to a group who had won the war against them and had turned into a numerical majority at the same time.[14]

The present-day situation is interesting, since Arabs as a group have been increasing in absolute numbers as well as in relation to the majority. In 1948, when the Israeli State was established, there were 156,000 Arabs in Israel accounting for less than 7 per cent of the total population. In spite of the many waves of Jewish immigrants to Israel, the ratio of Arab to Jew kept increasing. In 1958, Arabs comprised 11 per cent of the Israeli population and, in 1976, almost 15 per cent (500,000 Arabs). The Jewish population has increased at an average annual rate of 2.7 per cent, while the Arab population has increased at the rate of 4 per cent per annum.[15] According to Landau, this high rate is due to many factors:

1. a very high birth-rate of three times that within the Israeli Jewish sector;
2. a significant decrease in infant mortality due to the improvement of health services;
3. family reunion policies through which almost 40,000 Palestinian Arabs entered Israel to rejoin their families from whom they were separated during the war and prior to the establishment of the state;
4. the very low emigration of Arabs from Israel.[16]

Many other factors will continue to put the demographic and political balance in jeopardy in Israel, one of the examples being the annexation of East Jerusalem. Because of this constant increase of the Arab population and the fact that the increased population is geographically concentrated in distant areas, Arabs in Israel are developing a 'sense of uniqueness'. Landau describes it as follows:

> It is not surprising that the ... increase among the Arab minority in
> Israel strengthens their sense of uniqueness and adds weight to their
> demands as a unit. The Nature of these demands is also influenced
> by the relatively young age of the Arab minority members ... More
> than half the Arabs in Israel were born after the establishment of the
> State. Because of that, a recognizable part of their political behavior
> is conditioned by the dynamics of (their) life in Israel.[17]

The educational system of Israel is one of the interface arenas where
the exposure to these dynamics is greatest. Sami Khalil Mar'i describes
the situation of Arab education in Israel as follows:

> The lack of political power in the Arab minority in Israel is not the
> sole reason for the lack of autonomy of Arabs over their educational
> system. Although it is a major reason, it reinforces other existing
> political, legal, and administrative factors, all of which can be con-
> sidered responsible for the majority's control over the minority's
> education. The lack of autonomy in education is being used to
> prevent or at least delay the emergence of political organization and
> movements among Arabs in Israel.[18]

### Goals, Policies and Realities of Arab Education in Israel

The Law of State Education of 1953 specifies the aims of education in
Israel as follows:

> To base education on the values of Jewish culture and the achieve-
> ments of science, on love of the homeland and loyalty to the state
> and the Jewish people, on practice in agricultural work and handi-
> crafts, on pioneer training and on striving for a society built on
> freedom, equality, tolerance, mutual assistance, and love of man-
> kind.[19]

At the same time, the Israeli Knesset (Parliament) specified the goals of
education in Israel. The goals of Arab education were not referred to at
all. The Yadlin Document published in 1972 was the first effort to
address this issue. The goals specified in this document are:

1. education in the values of peace;
2. education for loyalty to the state by emphasising the common

interest of all its citizens and the encouragement of the uniqueness of Israeli Arabs;

3. forming of a plan to make the economic and social absorption of Arabs in Israel easier;
4. educating females for autonomy and for the improvement of their status.[20]

In 1973, a committee of seven Arabs and seven Jews, headed by Dr Matty Peled, was formed by the Director-General of the Ministry of Education and Culture to recommend plans and policies for Arab education during the 1980s. The reaction of this committee to the Yadlin Document was the following:

> The limitations of these guidelines are found in not giving an answer to the question of contradiction in the life of the Arab citizen in Israel between his identification with the Arab nation and his interest in living in peace in the State of Israel — a contradiction which stems from the political reality overwhelming Israel. It is clear that the cry for loyalty by orders cannot be a basis for positive education in the school, and the emphasis on important social problems such as the question of female education, etc. cannot be a substitute to the discussion of the basic problems in the existence of the Arab in the State of Israel.[21]

Administratively, the Arab educational system is controlled by the government at all the key points. All decision-making positions are occupied by Israelis or by a nominee from the government. For example, Arab teachers in Israel have a separate division within the Israeli Teachers' Union. An Arab representative within this division commented that 'the head of this division is not only non-Arab, but he is the only appointed (non-elected) head in any division of the Teachers' Union in Israel'.[22] In his analysis of the politicisation of the Arab education system in Israel, Khalil Nakhleh suggests that 'political, rather than pedagogic criteria are considered paramount in hiring and firing on all levels of the system'.[23]

*Elementary School Level.*    In 1973, the total Arab population in Israel was 497,200 as compared to the total population of Israel in that year of 3,307,600. The potential elementary school population (5-14 years) was 670,700 of which 23.2 per cent (148,900) were Arab children. However, only 18 per cent were actually in elementary school. This illustrates the discrepancy in the application of the compulsory elementary education law. In the Jewish population, elementary school enrolment exceeds 99 per cent, while among Arabs it is at 82 per cent (85 per cent for males and 78 per cent for females).[24]

The average pupil-to-teacher ratio for the Jewish sector was 22.7 in 1974, while in the Arab sector it was 32.8. To close the gap, 1,500 Arab teachers were needed. The classrooms in the Arab sector were also crowded. In 1973, Kupileivitch suggested that 1,720 classrooms needed to be built for Arab children, since 40 per cent of the classrooms in the Arab sector had more than 35 pupils each as compared to 20 per cent in the Jewish sector.[25] Furthermore, special education is almost completely neglected for the Arab sector. In addition to these factors related to the quality of educational facilities, there were only four 'schools for the working youth' for Arab drop-outs in 1974, as compared to 90 such schools for the Jewish sector.[26] These schools provide training through night classes and are particularly important to Arabs who have a high drop-out rate. Although there are 30 regional pedagogical centres in Israel to serve the schools, there are no such centres for Arab schools. Although Arab teachers are encouraged to use the centres, the curricular material developed is not relevant to the needs of the Arab children, mainly due to language differences.

Mahmoud Me'ari prepared a detailed comparative survey of school curricula in the Arab sector in Israel. The data collected showed that Arab students are directed to study Arabic language and literature in such a way as to de-emphasise their value and importance as compared to Hebrew language and literature. The picture is the same in other value-loaded subject-matters such as history and religious studies.[27]

*High School Level.*    Although the Arab adolescents constitute almost 20 per cent of the total Israeli 14–18-year-old population, their percentage of enrolment in high school is less than 10 per cent. This means that only 50 per cent of the total potential Arab students are enrolled in high school. The reasons for this are the limited high school programme options available to Arabs and a high drop-out rate. Furthermore, the vocational and agricultural programmes in the Jewish high school are high-quality programmes compared to such programmes in Arab schools.[28]

*Teacher Training Institute.*    In Israel, kindergarten and elementary school teachers are prepared at the university level. By 1948, there were only two Arab teachers' institutes in Palestine. However, at the establishment of the State of Israel, these remained on the West Bank and were not accessible to Arabs living in Israel. In 1958, an Arab teachers' seminary was established by the Ministry of Education and Culture in Jaffa. That year there were 2,768 Jewish students enrolled in teacher seminaries and only 40 Arabs in the seminary in Jaffa. Another Arab seminary was established in 1968, and by 1974 the enrolment for both was 587 Arab student teachers. This represented only 7 per cent of the total student-teacher population in Israel, while Arab schoolchildren in 1974 totalled more than 22 per cent of the total Israeli elementary school population. Therefore, about 40 per cent of the teachers in Arab schools are unqualified; the schools employ unqualified high school graduates to meet their increasing demands.[29]

*Individual Achievement Levels.*    Until 1968, a national scholastic achievement test (Seker) was given to all eighth-grade pupils in Israel for two purposes: to screen those who should be allowed to continue to secondary school and to determine the distribution of scholarships. In 1967-68, Seker was abolished and a reformed middle school was introduced. This was done to allow a better selection by postponing the screening procedures until the end of high school, at which time pupils are tested nationally by a matriculation exam (Bagrout).[30] By the introduction of Bagrout, Norm B, a lower standard of the Seker was also cancelled. Eighth graders from Sephardic and Arab background usually passed Norm B rather than the Seker. However, it was more difficult to get into high school with Norm B. Even after the introduction of the Bagrout, the average rate of success has been 80 per cent. Observers and researchers attribute this gap to the lack of relevance of the curriculum for the Arabs in Israel. They also think that the lower success rate is due to the lack of motivation of Arab students in Israel who do not see much opportunity at the university level and in the occupational world.[31] In a 1972 study John Hofman discovered that more than 50 per cent of Arab high school students (N − 213) thought they had no future in Israel.[32] In a later study, Hofman found that over 90 per cent of the Arab students questioned (331 out of 367) thought the same. Forty per cent of the Jewish students questioned (123 out of 306) reached the same conclusion regarding their Arab counterparts' future.[33]

A pilot study was carried out to determine the level of intellectual functioning demanded by the Bagrout in Israel for both Arabs and Jews and by the Tawjihi in Jordan and the West Bank. The evaluation was conducted according to Benjamin Bloom's taxonomy of educational objectives in the intellectual domain. The quality of student-teacher interaction in both settings was also analysed by the same objective. It was discovered that the Tawjihi was compatible with the quality of student-teacher interaction based primarily on rote learning and memorising of the required material, while the Bagrout relied more on analysis and synthesis of materials covered in a course.[34]

Based on several years' experience, some improvements are being attempted by the Israeli government in its approach to the Arab educational system in Israel. The Bagrout tests are being replanned to make them more suitable to the different cultural and personal characteristics of Arab and Jewish students in Israel. The quality of the instruction in the high schools is improving due to increasing numbers of qualified teachers entering the Arab high schools. However, the morale of the Arab high school students in Israel is deteriorating. Although the results from various studies exhibit much variation and inconsistency, they are consistent in one respect. Arabs in Israel express a significant inferiority in their readiness to invest energy.[35]

*Educational Policy and the Integration Process.* Since the creation of Israel, one of the highly emphasised goals of the State of Israel, as the embodiment of Zionist aspiration, is Mizug Galuyot, the integration and melting of the different geocultural Jewish groups into one unified nation. Education has been continuously suggested as the means to meet this goal.[36] These reforms were discussed in detail in Chapter 7.

Comparable efforts to close the gap between Arabs and Jews are few and are limited to some experimental situations. One example is the attempt at integration by the founder of Haifa University and the mayor of Haifa, Aba Hushi. He established an integrated Jewish-Arab high school in 1965. Arabs enrolled enthusiastically since they saw a chance for better-quality education and easier access to university. Jewish parents protested and, therefore, a compromise was reached. Instead of completely integrated classrooms, parallel but separate classes were established for Arabs and Jews. One Jewish student expressed his reluctance as follows: 'My father would throw me out of the home if I brought home a Moroccan Jew; what do you think would happen if I brought home an Arab?'[37] Fear of intermarriage seems to be one of the major reasons cited. Professor John Hofman of Haifa University studied readiness for social relations at this high school and found out that

In view of what seems like an equal opportunity to meet members of the opposite national group, it is difficult to understand why 81 per cent Arabs and only 26 per cent Jews in mixed high schools claim to have the opportunity to meet the others socially ... At least in part (it could) be assigned to cognitive functioning: most likely, the minority is more aware of the majority than Jews are of Arabs.[38]

He also suggests that peers, parents and teachers are not generally viewed as encouraging contact with Arabs.

In 1971, Yohanan Peres carried out a similar study using a wider sample. He found similar results: 'Arabs reject Jews less than Jews reject Arabs'.[39] However, in a repeat study in 1976, although the general direction of the findings stayed the same, Arab students' interest in Arab-Jewish social relations had decreased and the Jewish students' readiness to accept such relations had increased.[40]

The Palestinian Arab minority is as opposed to the integration system in general as is the Jewish majority. The majority is afraid mainly of the loss of independence by allowing the minority to enter areas earmarked as being of primary importance for national security. In the same way, the minority would like to preserve in the young generation as much feeling of national identity and differentiation from the Jewish population as possible. The minority has not abandoned the dream of recovering the 'homeland'. Furthermore, the maintenance of a segregated educational system to perpetuate segregation of Arabs and Jews is only the continuation of a long tradition of using the educational system for nationalistic purposes. Western-type formal schooling was introduced into Palestine during the nineteenth century and spread mainly to the elementary education level during the latter part of that century. Three systems coexisted: Turkish government schools in which Turkish was the language of instruction and which tried to oppose the burgeoning nationalistic tendencies of Arabs; the Christian school system which emphasised the language and culture of the sponsoring European countries such as England and France; and the Arab-Muslim private school system which introduced Arab nationalism.[41]

Although teachers have always been the leaders of the local communities in Arab society, their role has started to diminish in importance in the modernising Arab villages in Israel. Furthermore, since teachers are appointed by the Education Department which is controlled by the Israeli authorities, they are seen as having dual allegiance both by themselves and by the population at large. A young teacher describes the situation eloquently:

> I am absolutely going mad ... When I educate my pupils towards loyalty to the state I am considered a traitor ... and when I emphasize the national character of my pupils and try to nurture in them a sense of national pride, I am told I am a traitor.[42]

The case of the Arab Druze education is also interesting. The main Druze settlements are in Lebanon and Syria, but Druzes have inhabited

Palestine for over four hundred years and today they represent about 1 per cent of the Israeli population. Most are farmers in western and central Upper Galilee and on Mount Carmel, while a few live in Haifa. The Israeli government has pursued a policy of desegregation with the Druze schools. The Druze schools in the Haifa and North districts already belong to respective Jewish district educational administration bodies. The move to integrate the Druze schools was mainly a political one to separate the Druzes from the rest of the Arab community. An Arab scholar from a Druze group, Nabih El-Kasem, has suggested that the aim of such an administrative move is to 'blur and distort' the Arab national identity of the Druze group.[43]

W.B. Fisher, who coined the expression 'demographic shatter belt' for Jordan, describes Lebanon as 'an ecumenical refuge'.[44] We shall now turn our attention to the Lebanese experience in educating immigrant children.

## Educating Armenian Children in Lebanon

### Background

It is often claimed that Lebanon is half-Christian and half-Muslim. Each half is in turn subdivided into several sects.[45] The educational system in Lebanon is a clear reflection of the stratified social mosaic. Each sect has its own autonomous private schools. There are private and public as well as national and foreign schools, using different languages as media of instruction (mainly Arabic, French and English) and patterning their programmes after French, Anglo-American, or mixtures of both programmes. About two-thirds of the students in pre-university education attend private schools with diverse programmes, philosophies of education and languages as media of instruction. The rest, mostly poor and Muslim, attend public schools, which have much lower standards than have private schools. Statistics on sectarian distribution have been collected yearly by the Ministry of Education but kept strictly confidential.[46]

### Immigration Patterns of Armenians to Lebanon

The present Armenian community in Lebanon is constituted largely of the survivors of the massacres and deportations by the Ittihad Ve Terake government during the First World War. These massacres and deportations were later continued by the Turkish nationalist government of Mustafa Kemal during 1921-22. The Armenian refugees who arrived in

Syria-Lebanon could not settle in Lebanon at the time because of the famine there during the war. However, after the war, the Lebanese-Armenian community began gradually to grow.[47]

The contemporary Armenian community of Lebanon which is being discussed in this chapter was formed by the following four main waves of migration.

1. The evacuation of Cilicia by the French and its return to Turkey in 1921 forced the Armenian survivors of the 1915 massacres to migrate in large groups to Syria and Lebanon, among other countries. This brought to the area some 200,000 Armenians.
2. After the entry of the Turkish forces to the Sanjak of Alexandretta and until its final annexation to Turkey, i.e. between 1937 and 1939, some 45,000 Armenians migrated again to Syria and Lebanon.
3. In March-April 1948, thousands of Armenians from Palestine poured into Lebanon as a result of the Arab-Israeli conflict.
4. After the Union of Syria and Egypt in 1958, large groups of Armenians came to settle in Lebanon from the neighbouring Arab countries.

The number of Armenians in Lebanon is now given as 180,000. This is a conservative estimate. A large number of them already possess Lebanese nationality. The Armenians consider themselves Lebanese citizens equal in all respects in rights and duties and responsibilities to the other ethnic and sectarian groups in Lebanon. They participated at the formation of the present-day modern Lebanese State in the mid-forties and have since then participated in all aspects of Lebanese life. They have proportional representation in the Lebanese Parliament based on the sectarian quotas established for that purpose. All three Armenian communities possess a dense network of Armenian educational, athletic, social, political and cultural institutions. Part of the educational organisation of each of the three Armenian communities is a large number of schools to educate the children of the community.

### The Armenian Educational System in Lebanon

When the Armenian immigrants first arrived in Syria and Lebanon, the educational system was extremely elitist and therefore limited in scope. Armenians brought with them a well-established tradition of public education as reflected in the Armenian Constitution, which internally governs the life of Armenians in all the Armenian communities of the world and secures an equal right to education for both male and female children.[48] Therefore, with some help from international agencies, other

Armenian communities in the world and some foreign missions and donations, the Armenian community organised a school network for the refugee Armenian children.

*Goals of Armenian Education.*   All Armenian schools in Lebanon are clear about their goal: the preparation of a generation of 'good and conscious Lebanese-Armenian citizens'. A 'good Armenian' is someone born of Armenian parents who perpetuates in himself the 'Armenian spirit'. The 'Armenian spirit' is represented as the sum total of the Armenian cultural heritage. Therefore, to prepare 'good Armenians', the concerned should teach the new generation the language, history, traditions and customs, and the material and non-material cultural heritage. Once the students have internalised these, they are considered 'good Armenians'. However, for the 'preservation of the Armenian nation', it is also important to be a 'conscious Armenian'. To be a 'good and conscious Armenian', the 'good Armenian' should be well acquainted with the 'Armenian problem', or the Armenian question. (In summary, the Armenian question, problem or cause refers to the case of the demand for the retrocession to the Armenians of the Armenian territories lost to Armenia by the treaties of London and Moscow in 1921, when the boundaries between Turkey and the Soviet Union were set.) Once he has met this second requirement, he is still not a complete Armenian. There is one more requirement to be met. Since we can find Armenian communities in almost every country of the world, the 'good and conscious Armenian' is not recognised as such by community standards unless he also meets the requirements of 'good citizenship' of the particular country concerned. Thus, in the case of the Lebanese Armenian community, a 'good and conscious Armenian' is referred to as a 'good and conscious Lebanese-Armenian'.

In order to be able to communicate well with other Armenians around the world in Armenian communities of varying degrees of assimilation, an Armenian should master either French or English. In Lebanon, it is relatively easy to achieve this final and ideal status since the different ethnic and religious groups have their separate and independent existence. Thus, there is a relatively small amount of stress and effort required to pass from the condition of 'good and conscious Armenian' to the condition of 'good and conscious Lebanese-Armenian'. The problem of mastery of French and English is also easily solved, since Lebanon was, until its independence, under a French and British mandate. The Armenian schools, along with the other Armenian organisations, are supposed to socialise the new generation into this mould.

*The Curriculum of the Armenian Schools.*   All Armenian schools apply the complete government Arabic programme. All Armenian schoolchildren should master Arabic, Lebanese-Arab history and Lebanese-Arab culture, in addition to the general Arab history and culture components included in special literature and history courses. In addition to this programme, all Armenian schools have a parallel Armenian programme including all subject-matters, as well as an English or a French programme. Therefore, all Armenian schools apply three full-fledged programmes in three languages, each including all subject-matters found in a regular unilingual school programme. The fourth language, English or French, depeneding on the third complete curriculum of the particular school, is taught as a foreign language starting from first grade. All the other three languages are started at kindergarten. The structures of the school are organised to reflect all the cultures being taught, with appropriate textbooks, teachers belonging to the cultural heritage being taught and extra curricular activities representing the traditions and customs of the ethnic, cultural and linguistic groups. All Armenian schools present their students for the appropriate matriculation examinations administered by the Lebanese government, the French Embassy and the British Embassy. The statistics compiled by all parties indicate that not only do the Armenian students consistently achieve the top grades but the over-all success rate of Armenian students is much higher than the success rate of the student body at large.

## Selected Dilemmas Encountered in Educating Immigrant Children in the Middle East

*Ethnic and Familiar Ties and Boundaries.*   Traditionally, the survival of different groups in the Middle East has depended on the special ethnic balance established between the different communities in each locality. Although education and modernisation have changed the nature of social relations quite radically in most Arab countries, there is still an acute awareness of the *'ird* code (family honour) prevailing in the larger community.[49] This is the basic controlling value which also legitimates the family structure. Family is at the centre of the primordial ties governing the daily life of most countries of the Middle East. Therefore, there is great resistance to integrated school systems. The parents in particular feel that integrated schools will inevitably lead to mixed marriages, thereby undermining the unique features of the ethnic group or the class involved. This preoccupation is cited almost always as the major reason for resisting integration in the school. Cultural plural-

ism is only in terms of a mosaic society as illustrated in the case of
Lebanon and Jordan/Israel.

*Clashes in National and International Ideologies.*   In the case of the
Palestinians, for example, the situation is further complicated by the
fact that part of the population has remained 'on the land' while the
rest has dispersed in different Arab countries. In each country, the
receiving structures were such that some have assimilated the migrants
successfully while others have kept them at the margin of society.
Furthermore, the eagerness and motivation to assimilate on the part of
the different waves of migrants and refugees have been different. As a
result, the emergence of 'varieties of Palestinian nationalism' is obvious.
It is therefore very difficult to design uniform curricula to educate the
immigrants with similar backgrounds in different countries. Furthermore, control of educational matters in some countries like Lebanon is
less centralised and strict than in Jordan or Egypt or Syria, for example.
In addition, within each country there is a different attitude towards
Palestinian nationalism and Israel. For example, in the Arab private
denominational schools in Lebanon, there was never any mention of
Israel until around 1967. However, since there were children in the
same classroom from different socio-political groups and backgrounds,
the geography and history teachers were always confronted with
questions from the class related to political development in Israel. The
hidden curriculum and the informal curriculum were therefore more
important in forming attitudes towards refugees and Israel.

Another fascinating feature of the education of immigrant children
in the Middle East, especially in the case of Palestinian refugee children,
is the special balance struck between national educational authorities
and international agency limitations and requirements, as mentioned
earlier in this chapter.

*Differential Assimilation of Different Waves of Migrants.*   In Lebanon,
for example, children of the 1948 wave of Palestinian refugees were
educated in the Lebanese private denominational and private foreign
schools, along with other Lebanese children. They were willing to assimilate, and most of them had Lebanese nationality. However, the children of the more recent immigrants were educated mainly in the camp
schools, although not everyone in the new wave of refugees settled in
the camps. Lebanon did not bestow citizenship on this new group of
refugees nor were they interested in obtaining Lebanese citizenship.
Since there was no clear pattern of settlement of the new refugees who
were living outside the camps, the distribution of refugee children in
the elementary schools was quite random, and different adaptation

mechanisms and groupings emerged in different schools. At the high school level, however, the Lebanese schools were used by the UNRWA authorities. Since the Palestinian children were bussed to specially designated high schools, they formed a majority in these schools. Thus, the acculturation and integration of these students is expected to be very different from those of the same age group who were not camp residents and were therefore in high schools where they formed only a minority. On the other hand, because of the location of the refugee camps in areas of extreme poverty, many poor Lebanese children frequented the Palestinian camp schools at the elementary level. The confusion in terms of socialisation is not difficult to imagine. However, to date, there have been no serious studies of this 'experimental situation'.

*Schools for a Multicultural Society.*   The reformed programme of the Armenian schools in operation since the early sixties has tried to prepare the young generation for a multicultural society in Lebanon. The curriculum, school structures, teaching body, staff and extra-curricular activities are all designed to provide competencies in the different ethnic, religious and cultural groups and situations in the country. At the same time, acquiring special familiarity with the Armenian heritage has been emphasised. This educational system was designed to prepare individuals to be ready to cope with the demands of a pluralistic multi-cultural society. However, since the social fabric at large remained mosaic in structure, the increasing imbalances in the political power struggle led to the blow-up of the system in 1975.[50] Since the present generation of Armenians was brought up with a pluralistic perspective, they refused to take sides in the conflict which flared up into civil war in Lebanon. All parties involved in the conflict are now blaming the Armenian community for its stand of positive neutrality. The educational system had an important role to play in the changing attitudes. Prior to 1958, the old system of Armenian community schools emphasised mainly the pattern of the 'separate-sectarian' education. Therefore, in the 1958 conflict, the Armenian participation was quite different and more typically sectarian in orientation. In the years between 1958 and 1975, the Armenian schools operated on the pluralistic pattern, and the results in participation in the other spheres of society were different in the civil conflict of the past five years. The important fact to emphasise here is not a causal relationship as such between education and political socialisation, but the realisation that a special concept of pluralism is reflected in the pattern of educational, economic and political cultures of the larger community.

*Social Acceptability.*    Most sociologists and psychologists agree that social acceptability is very important in the process of adjusting to a new group and a new society. There are many studies being conducted on this aspect in different educational situations. However, the models used are mainly imported from Europe and the United States. Some of these studies are mentioned in the section on Arabs in Israel. Clan, tribe and village of origin are all important considerations in the social relations and levels of acceptability in the Middle East. It is almost as difficult to cross clan and tribe lines within a given ethnic group as it is to overcome the boundaries of another ethnic group. Furthermore, within an ethnic group stereotypes are carried over several generations. For example, certain areas in Turkey have had a reputation for being centres of higher learning and Western tradition in education as opposed to others. Teachers are aware of this fact. The first wave of Armenian immigrants to Lebanon came from Turkey. Therefore second- and third-generation Armenian children are still earmarked by their teachers as being more or less highly motivated depending on the area in Turkey from which their grandparents originated. Thus, social stereotypes play an important role in the expectations of teachers and become major determinants of school results for individual children as opposed to individual ability variables.

In the same way, Palestinian children are more or less motivated depending upon the frequency of their movement in and out of majority/minority situations in their schooling careers. However defective the tools for measuring achievement and motivation used in many studies, there are quite startling differences between groups tested under the different conditions. The quality of the social interaction between peers and between pupil and teacher is also important. Palestinian children taught by Palestinian refugee teachers of the same wave are definitely in a different category from those taught by teachers who are well established and can provide success models or from those taught by non-Palestinian teachers who may emphasise the alienation of the refugee children. Furthermore, the type of nationalism being conveyed varies with the nationality of the teacher, whether Palestinian, Egyptian, Jordanian or Lebanese.

*Self-concept and Achievement.*    Although the exact nature of the relationship of self-concept to achievement is not yet established, most studies concur that an adequate self-concept is essential for satisfactory educational attainment at school. In situations like those found in the schools of the Middle East discussed in this chapter, there is not much that can really be done to control some of the factors which contribute to strained and varied attitudinal situations and resulting self-concept effects. Perhaps the type of 'value neutral' educational programme implemented by international agencies is the best solution. Children receive increased recognition for individual achievement, and also the values emphasised in the classroom are of the individualistic variety rather than the 'national/social' consciousness type. This may be one explanation for the seeming paradox between strong motivation and academic aspiration and achievement exhibited by the refugee children who study under the least desirable conditions. However, once again, well-planned and systematic studies are lacking in this area.

*Language Problems.*   Language acquisition appears to be central to the process of integration and assimilation of immigrants. The Middle Eastern situation is interesting in this respect. Multilingualism is part of the way of life in the Middle East and therefore attitudes about the difficulties and hardships of learning one more language are not so crucial as attitudes about the 'exclusivity' of a language and the political power balance involved in the situation. Foreign languages like French and English are welcome almost everywhere in the Middle East because they mean increased mobility and potential solutions to refugee status by facilitating the process of immigration to the West. To illustrate the language problems encountered by schoolchildren in the Middle East, let us consider the maze of language an Arab child has to cope with in school: several Arabic dialects, modern literary Arabic, classical Arabic, French and English. The Armenian child in the Middle East has to cope with at least the following permutations: several Armenian dialects, two branches of modern literary Armenian, classical Armenian, a Turkish dialect, a deficient version of an Arabic dialect, modern literary Arabic, classical Arabic, French and English.

Of course, there are the problems of transfer. Since migrant and refugee populations have been highly mobile for some generations, Armenian children moving from, let us say, a third-grade Syrian Armenian school to a Lebanese Armenian school will be placed according to proficiency in the 'official' language, in this case Arabic. Usually, they are at least a grade ahead of their Lebanese counterparts in Arabic, but they are at least three grades behind in French and English.

Although there have recently been many studies trying to establish categories of classifying language deficiencies — from total, to partial, to dialect impediments — in an effort to design remedial programmes, it is obvious from the above illustration that the situation is extremely complicated in the Middle Eastern case. A fresh outlook on the problem is needed. Maybe we should look for different adaptive cognitive functions from those being examined so far in the existing literature.

## Conclusion

The dilemmas involved in the process of 'educating immigrants' appear therefore to be even more numerous in the particular case discussed in this chapter than in the case of specific nation states with less inter-dependence than the countries of the Middle East. Since it has been documented in the related theoretical literature that refugee and migrant populations will stay much more mobile than regular popula-tions for a longer period of time and sometimes for three or four successive generations, it may be that an education such as the one designed and accepted by an international agency emphasising compet-ence in skills as opposed to socialisation into a particular national system is the best solution for the time being. It will provide the indi-vidual child with the tools for survival in different environments. From the point of view of immigrant and refugee 'nations' who are preoccup-pied both with maintenance of their identity and with the best possible solution for adaptation to the new environment, it should be remem-bered that schooling should not be taken as the only educational and socialising institution which may achieve the desired outcome.[51]

## Notes

1.    J.I. Clarke and W.B. Fisher, *Populations of the Middle East and North Africa: A Geographical Approach* (University of London Press Ltd, London, 1972).

2.    L.E. Sweet, 'Middle Eastern and North African Peoples and Cultures', *Encyclopaedia Britannica*, 15th edn, vol. 12, pp. 167-71.

3.    Clarke and Fisher, *Populations of the Middle East and North Africa.*

4.    MEED Special Report, 'Strict Society Keeps Rein on Growing Work-force', *Middle East Economic Digest* (June 1979), pp. 7-8.

5.    W. Petersen, 'International Migration', *Annual Review of Sociology*, vol. 4 (1978), p. 550.

6.    UNRWA, Reports of the Commissioner-General of the United Nations Relief and Works Agency for Palestine Refugees in the Near East, 1 July 1977 – 30 June 1978, General Assembly, Official Records, 33rd Session, Supplement no. 13 (A/33/13) (United Nations, New York, 1978).

7.    UNRWA, Reports (A/33/13), pp. 1-3.

8.    Ibid., p. 65.

9.    Ibid., p. 3.

10.    Ibid., p. 12.

11.    Ibid., pp. 12-13.

12.    E.H. Buehrig, *The UN and the Palestinian Refugees: A Study in Non-territorial Administration* (Indiana University Press, Bloomington, Indiana, 1971), pp. 165-6.

13.    UNRWA, Reports (A/33/13), pp. 12-13.

14.   J.M. Landau, *The Arabs in Israel: A Political Study* (Ma'arqchout, Tel Aviv, 1971), p. 19 (in Hebrew). (A prior English version is published by The Royal Institute of International Affairs and Oxford University Press, London, 1969.)

15.   S.K. Mar'i, *Arab Education in Israel* (Syracuse University Press, New York, 1978), p. 2.

16.   Landau, *The Arabs in Israel.*

17.   Ibid.

18.   Mar'i, *Arab Education in Israel*, p. 5.

19.   Law of State Education, 1953, para. 34(4), quoted in Joseph S. Bentwitch 'Arab Education in Israel', *New Outlook*, 6(6) (July-August 1963), pp. 19-23.

20.   Mar'i, *Arab Education in Israel*, pp. 52-3.

21.   Ibid., p. 53.

22.   Ibid.

23.   Ibid., p. 64.

24.   Ibid., pp. 19-20.

25.   Ibid., pp. 23-4.

26.   Israel Ministry of Education and Culture Division of Curricula, 'The Regional Pedagogical Center in Service of Teachers', pamphlet (Jerusalem, May 1975).

27.   M. Me'ari, *A Comparative Survey of School Curricula in the Arab Sector in Israel*, a supplementary report to the Final Report of the Committee for the Planning of Arab Education for the 1980s (Jerusalem, January 1975) (in Hebrew).

28.   Mar'i, *Arab Education in Israel*, pp. 21-2.

29.   Ibid., p. 23.

30.   Ibid., p. 132.

31.   Ibid., pp. 133-4.

32.   Ibid., p. 137.

33.   J. Hofman, 'Readiness for Social Relations Between Arabs and Jews in Israel', *Journal of Conflict Resolution*, 16(2) (1972).

34.   Mar'i, *Arab Education in Israel*, pp. 138-43.

35.   Ibid., pp. 142-3.

36.   M. Smilansky, 'Coping of the Educational System with the Problems of the Disadvantaged', in H. Ormians (ed.), *Education in Israel* (Ministry of Education and Culture, Jerusalem, 1973) (in Hebrew); Mar'i, *Arab Education in Israel*, Ch. 5.

37.   Hofman, 'Readiness', p. 247.

38.   Ibid., p. 244.

39.   Y. Peres, 'Arab-Jewish Relations', in J. Hofman (ed.), *Proceedings of the Convention on the State of Research on Human Relations Between Arabs and Jews* (University of Haifa, Haifa, 1971), p. 13 (in Hebrew).

40.   J. Hofman, 'Readiness for Social Relations Between Arabs and Jews in Israel, 1975', research report (Institute for Research and Development of Arab Education, University of Haifa, Haifa, 1976) (in Hebrew).

41.   Mar'i, *Arab Education in Israel*, Ch. 1.

42.   Ibid., p. 37.

43.   N. El-Kasem, *The Reality of the Druzes in Israel* (Dar El Aitam, Jerusalem, 1976), pp. 184, 236 (in Arabic).

44.   Clarke and Fisher, *Populations of the Middle East and North Africa*, 'Contents'.

45.   H. Barakat, *Lebanon in Strife* (University of Texas Press, Austin, 1977), p. 26.

46.   Ibid., p. 42.

47.   A. Hamalian, 'Lebanese-American: A Study of Generational Differences

in Assimilation', unpublished MA thesis (American University of Beirut, Lebanon, 1971). The information in this section of the paper is derived from this thesis.

48.   For an English translation of this constitution see H.F.B. Lynch, *Armenia: Travels and Studies* (Longman, Green and Company, London, 1901).

49.   P.C. Dodd, 'Women's Honor (El-'Ird) in Contemporary Arab Society', paper presented at the Seventh World Congress, International Sociological Association, Varna, Bulgaria, September 1970.

50.   Barakat, *Lebanon in Strife*.

51.   A. Hamalian, 'National Integration in Multi-Ethnic Societies: The Differential Role of Schooling and Non-formal Educational Agencies', *Compare*, vol. 9, no. 1 (1979), pp. 33–44.

# 9 UNPOPULAR VIEWS ON POPULAR BELIEFS ABOUT IMMIGRANT CHILDREN: CONTEMPORARY PRACTICES AND PROBLEMS IN SWEDEN

**Lars Henric Ekstrand**

## Immigration and Action Taken in Swedish Schools

### A Historical Note

For centuries Sweden has been receiving immigrants. Blacksmiths, glass blowers, miners and merchants were called in from Belgium, Germany, Holland and Scotland by various kings to improve skills within trades which were in need of developing. At the beginning of the twentieth century, Italian stone cutters came to southwestern Sweden. From 1851 to 1930, when immigration became larger than emigration, around 152,000 Swedes emigrated, mainly to North America. During this period, however, the population rose from 3.6 million to 6 million.[1]

### The Pattern of Modern Immigration to Sweden

As a country receiving immigrants in the modern sense, Sweden's experience goes back to the 1940s and thus is very short in comparison to such countries as Australia, Canada and the USA. The development of immigration to Sweden during the twentieth century is shown in Figure 9.1. Most of the emigration shown after 1945 is return migration of immigrants. About 20-25 per cent of immigrants who go back home return to Sweden a second time. In 1966, immigration to Sweden became regulated. However, there is no regulation of migration between the Scandinavian countries, and around 50 per cent of the immigrants come from Finland. In 1975, the ten countries from which the most immigrants came, besides Finland, were Denmark, Norway, Yugoslavia, Greece, the USA, Great Britain, Turkey, West Germany and Italy, in that order. The general pattern of migration since World War II, both nationally and internationally, has been a movement in response to the demand for manpower, brought about by industrial expansion. Hence, immigrants in Sweden are not evenly distributed over the country, but concentrated in industrial cities and towns in central and southern Sweden.

The birth-rate in Sweden is extremely low.[2] Most immigrants are

Figure 9.1: Emigration and Immigration to Sweden during the Twentieth Century

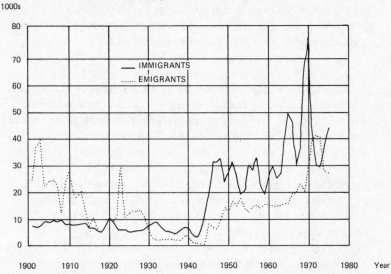

Source: Sweden's official statistics, *Information i prognosfrågor* (Information In Projection Issues 1976: 3, Population Projection for Sweden 1976 — 2000) (Central Bureau of Statistics, Stockholm, 1976).

young, and the birth-rate among immigrants is higher than among the population in general. Thus, immigration has contributed to a small increase in the total Swedish population. As immigration is expected to lessen, projections point to a decrease in the total Swedish population by the turn of the century. Thus, immigrants to Sweden not only take the heaviest and least-paid jobs, but also essentially regulate the population size. Of the 8.2 million inhabitants in Sweden, 700,000 are or have been foreign citizens, while 550,000 persons were born abroad.[3] About 25 per cent of all children born in 1978 have immigrant parents.

By international standards, racism does not seem to be a problem in Sweden. The immigration of coloured people is very small indeed. There is much talk in Sweden about discrimination against immigrants but, in an international perspective, the situation so far is rather idyllic.

*Immigrant Children in the Swedish Comprehensive School (Grades 1-9)*

The definition, in the official statistics, of an immigrant pupil used to be 'a pupil from a home where at least one of the parents is of foreign origin and speaks a native language other than Swedish'. This definition excluded native linguistic minorities in Sweden (Finns, Lapps, Gypsies).[4] This definition is broad and has frequently been questioned. The reason for the broad definition is that any immigrant pupil has a right to tuition in his home language. This right is sometimes limited by practical conditions, such as supply of teachers and the like.

The total number of immigrant pupils by the above definition was 63,000 in 1975 (the first year when statistical data were collected), 78,000 in 1976, 85,000 in 1977, and 88,000 in March 1978. This does not mean a heavy factual increase, but merely that the headmasters were not aware of the broadness of the definition, nor had they worked out efficient local procedures for collecting data. Presumably, the real number has been rather stable these four years. There are just over one million pupils in Swedish comprehensive schools, of whom about 8.5 per cent are immigrants. Of the 85,000 immigrant pupils, 18,439 (22 per cent) speak Swedish as their native language. Finnish-speaking pupils account for 39 per cent, Yugoslavian pupils 7.5 per cent and German and Danish pupils 5.5 per cent. In 1977 (January), 28,834 pupils took advantage of the home language tuition, while 4,709 pupils who wanted to do so could not be given the opportunity. This means that roughly 40 per cent of the pupils were interested in learning their home language.

Table 9.1 shows the number of pupils aged 7-15 who are not Swedish citizens and have moved to Sweden from abroad. The median number in the post-war period is roughly 2,700. Allowing for emigration, this gives a median estimate of roughly 1,000 pupils. Multiplying by a factor of 9 (grades) yields an estimate of 9,000 pupils in the comprehensive school who were born abroad, compared to an over-all total of around 80,000-90,000 immigrant pupils. Thus, a majority, or about 90 per cent of those who are regarded as immigrant children, were born in Sweden.

Due to a change of definition in 1978 from the language habits of the parents to those of the child, an immigrant pupil is now defined as a child whose language of interaction at home is other than Swedish. The total number of immigrant pupils consequently sank from 88,000 in March 1978 to 81,000 in November 1978. The projection for the next few years is that the net immigration of pupils of school age will diminish strongly, while children with another home language, born in Sweden, will increase. We now begin to speak of third-generation children, and no doubt definition and statistics will continue to change.

Table 9.1: Yearly Immigration to Sweden of Children of School Age

| Year | Number | Year | Number | Year | Number | Year | Number |
|------|--------|------|--------|------|--------|------|--------|
| 1946 | 3,178 | 1956 | 2,324 | 1966 | 4,249 | 1976 | 4,583 |
| 1947 | 4,630 | 1957 | 3,160 | 1967 | 3,061 | 1977 | 4,391 |
| 1948 | 5,603 | 1958 | 1,978 | 1968 | 3,654 | 1978 | 3,211 |
| 1949 | 2,301 | 1959 | 1,804 | 1969 | 7,301 | 1979 | 3,473 |
| 1950 | 1,299 | 1960 | 2,580 | 1970 | 8,615 |  |  |
| 1951 | 2,590 | 1961 | 2,940 | 1971 | 4,617 |  |  |
| 1952 | 1,164 | 1962 | 2,453 | 1972 | 3,109 |  |  |
| 1953 | 1,409 | 1963 | 2,570 | 1973 | 3,195 |  |  |
| 1954 | 1,121 | 1964 | 3,772 | 1974 | 3,736 |  |  |
| 1955 | 2,372 | 1965 | 4,423 | 1975 | 4,649 |  |  |

Sources:  Sweden's official statistics, *Statistisk årsbok* (Statistical Yearbook),
1946-73 (Central Bureau of Statistics, Stockholm); *Befolkningsföränd-ringar* (Population Changes), 1974-77 (Central Bureau of Statistics, Stockholm, 1971).

## Immigrant Students in the Upper Integrated Secondary School

In the autumn of 1976, there were 221,000 pupils in the secondary school, which comprises all government and private schools, the latter constituting only a small proportion. The secondary school is organised into 22 options of two or more years.[5] In January 1977, there were 10,542 immigrant pupils (broad definition) or roughly 4.8 per cent of the total population.[6] The proportion of pupils who go directly from the comprehensive to the upper secondary school is 80 per cent of the native and 67 per cent of the immigrant pupils.[7] This does not necessarily indicate, as is often claimed, that immigrant children go less frequently to upper secondary schools. Immigrant children come largely from lower social strata while native children are from all walks of life. The social class difference, therefore, makes any comparisons between the performance of immigrant and native children meaningless.

## Action Taken Within the Swedish School System

During the fifties, the need for organised tuition of immigrant pupils became apparent. A law from 1958, stating that the government could reimburse the local school boards for up to four lessons per week for special purposes, was used to hire teachers for special tuition in Swedish. In 1966, the government increased the support to the local boards to six 40-minute lessons per week for the purpose of teaching immigrant children.

In Sweden, the curriculum is organised centrally and hence it has been fairly easy to establish uniformity all over the country. In the 1969 curriculum, it was stated that the six lessons could be used not only for tuition in Swedish but also for teaching the home language and for giving extra tuition in other subjects using the home language as the medium of instruction. It was recommended that teaching groups be small, three to five pupils. In fact, a group could be any number of pupils and the governmental support would still be paid. Hence, the six-lesson provision represented a powerful economic resource.

Newly arrived immigrant pupils are normally placed into reception classes which are called preparatory classes in Sweden. The pupil attends gymnastics, handicrafts and similar subjects in an ordinary class, but most of his time is spent in the preparatory class where he receives intensive instruction in Swedish and, in recent years, in his mother tongue.

In recent years, home language teaching has attracted increasing interest from all parties concerned. Among immigrant parents, there is considerable diversity of attitudes. Some parents contend that the pupils should not only learn their home language, but also be taught in their home language, as far as grade 6, i.e. to the end of primary school. Not until grade 7, i.e. junior high school, should formal tuition in Swedish start. On the other hand, some parents will not allow their children to take part in home language tuition unless it is arranged outside the ordinary curriculum. Finnish scientists have initiated and supported the first line of action. The idea of the home language as the basis for second language learning, identity and personality development, as well as cognitive and emotional development, appears to have grown into something akin to a religious revival. The opposite attitude may be found among smaller groups, although attitudes among other nationality groups are less homogeneous than in the Finnish group. The home language movement seems to coincide with the development of certain political and nationalistic interests: hence its strength.

For various reasons, regulations for governmental financial support to the local school boards were changed in 1976. Effective from 1977, 1.1 lessons per student are paid for by the government, for home language teaching and study guidance in school subjects by home language teachers. Governmental support for tuition in Swedish is now four lessons per week. By the same decision, local school boards were obliged to organise home language teaching.[8] As a consequence of the changed attitudes, so-called composite classes are being tried. These are classes organised in such a way that some of the pupils are Swedish, and some belong to one other home language group. The immigrant pupils are taught part of the time by the regular Swedish teacher, part of the time by the home language teacher. In some grades (1 and 2) in Malmö in southern Sweden, the proportion of lessons taught by the home language teacher has been as high as 14 lessons out of 22, including time devoted to basic reading and arithmetic. Informal teacher experiences suggest that home language lessons could be fewer, and that basic reading and arithmetic should be taught by the regular teacher. In some places, all but unilingual home language classes are being started, some of which continue even in Grade 7, i.e. junior high school.

*Teacher Training*

For teachers of Swedish as a foreign language, in-service courses have been arranged since the beginning of the 1960s. In 1972, a 160-lesson option called 'Swedish as a foreign language' was introduced in two schools of education and is still available. From 1978, the option has also been offered as a university night course. Within the universities, courses in Swedish as a foreign language have been launched. For home language teachers, summer courses have long been available. In the autumn of 1977, four-semester training courses were launched in three schools of education in Greek, Finnish, Danish, Spanish, Serbo-Croatian and Turkish. The teachers will be qualified to teach in grades 1-9 of the comprehensive school as well as in the upper integrated secondary school. The total number of home language teachers in Sweden at the beginning of 1978 was 2,671 who taught 53 languages in the comprehensive and the integrated upper secondary school. In order to become certified, a home language teacher must take summer courses and have a few semesters of teaching experience, unless he has the new four-semester training. By this criterion, 901 (34 per cent) of the home language teachers were certified by the time the statistics were tabled.[9]

Around 1970 an experiment was launched to train Finnish-speaking, bilingual students as regular primary school teachers. For several years now, such training for Finnish-speaking teacher trainees has been a regular part of the programmes of three schools of education.[10] Since the autumn of 1976, bilingual students with Finnish, Greek or Serbo-Croatian as their native language have been admitted to the regular pre-school training at three schools of education. The students follow the general programme but they are organised in groups, consisting of Swedish and bilingual students. In addition, they have a few special options.[11] University courses in Swedish as a foreign language have existed for several years. Since about 1970, the major universities have given a one-semester course, intended mainly for certified teachers of adult immigrants. A quarter-semester course is given for those majoring in Swedish as a native language.

## Problems of Social and Emotional Adjustment in Sweden and Elsewhere

### *The Frequency of Social and Emotional Disturbances in Immigrant and Ethnic Children*

A high rate of social (relations to friends) and emotional disturbances has often been assumed to exist among immigrant and ethnic children. It is often thought that such children live under strong pressures of various kinds, leading to psycho-pathological states. The belief also exists that immigrants and their children have problems of adjustment in a broader, socio-cultural sense. It is surprising to find that these claims are usually supported by anecdotal evidence and rarely by statistical data. Such evidence is often biased, coming from teachers, psychologists and others who have worked mostly with immigrants and have little experience with native speakers. Only a few empirical studies of the mental health of immigrant children seem to have been undertaken and these do not seem to corroborate the strong claims frequently encountered. For instance, Ekstrand, in a study designed to measure several aspects of bilingual and bicultural adjustment, asked 804 teachers for judgements about the mental health of more than 2,000 immigrant children.[12] As this study will be referred to throughout this chapter, a short description is provided. For more detailed information, the reader is referred elsewhere.[13]

A population of about 2,400 children, who emigrated to Sweden and were given tuition in Swedish in the comprehensive school, was mapped in 1966 by means of a questionnaire to all schools. Questionnaire data from the teachers were obtained for 2,188 pupils and test data were obtained for groups of varying sizes for different tests. There were six tests in Swedish — three reading skill tests and three intelligence tests — measuring the Thurstone R, S and N factors, and teacher assessments on four variables, i.e. 16 measures in all.

The children were distributed rather evenly over grades 1-7, with a diminishing number in grades 8 and 9. Children from 36 nations were represented in the sample. Sixty-two per cent of the pupils came from Finland, 16 per cent from Yugoslavia, 5 per cent from Greece, 2.6 per cent from the USA, 2 per cent from Italy and Hungary, and the rest were distributed over the remaining 30 nations. The 804 teachers were asked to give judgements about their students with respect to academic progress, social adjustment (relations to peers), emotional adjustment, and progress in Swedish. No Swedish control group was studied. The teacher observations were quantified and coded into a five-point scale where 1 is a very bad adjustment and 5 a very good one. The result shows average progress in school ($\bar{x} = 3.0$), better than average social adjustment ($\bar{x} = 3.5$), better than average emotional adjustment ($\bar{x} = 3.5$) and average progress in Swedish ($\bar{x} = 3.2$). These data do not support the common beliefs of particularly poor social and emotional adjustment among immigrant pupils. It must, however, be stressed that the adjustment data are impaired by uncertainties, and that no Swedish control group was examined. Other studies, however, also point in the same direction.

Goldenberg surveyed 264 children of recent immigrants in Montreal.[14] She found that a majority (59 per cent) of the children did not have any problems. No detailed account is given, nor was a control group employed. Rutter *et al.* compared British children with West Indian children in an Inner London borough.[15] Of the West Indian children, 41.2 per cent exhibited some kind of behaviour disturbances compared to 19.1 per cent of the British children. A sample of teachers was interviewed and the information obtained was psychiatrically rated. The results are given in Table 9.2.

Table 9.2: Psychiatric Ratings of Teacher Interview Data

| Disturbance | West Indian children (%) | Non-migrant children (%) |
|---|---|---|
| Emotional | 33.3 | 26.8 |
| Peer relationships | 18.5 | 19.6 |
| Conduct | 22.2 | 8.3 |
| Other | 18.5 | 14.4 |
| Total N | 54 | 97 |

Source: M. Rutter, W. Yule, M. Berger, B. Yule, J. Morton and C. Bagely, 'Children of West Indian Immigrants, I: Rates of Behavioural Deviance and of Psychiatric Disorder', *Journal of Child Psychology*, 15 (1974).

The over-all difference, 38.2 per cent of West Indian children with disturbances as compared to 27.6 per cent of non-migrant children, was not found to be statistically significant. Several factors remain unexplained. It is not quite clear if the non-migrant children were white. If so, there is an additional race variable to be considered. As is seen in Table 9.2, the main difference lies in the variable 'conduct', which may be more related to cultural behaviour differences than to mental disturbances, strictly defined. Also, the variable 'peer relationships' yields a result contrary to the main tendency. The conclusion to be drawn is that there is possibly a moderate difference to the disadvantage of the migrant children. Also striking is the rather high rate of poor adjustment in *both* groups, which may point to the metropolitan environment as a variable to be considered. This possibility will be further discussed later in this chapter.

It has been proposed that Finnish children in Sweden may exhibit more socio-emotional disturbances than do other immigrant children.[16] An investigation of this possibility was carried out in my previously mentioned study, and the results are presented in Table 9.3.[17] Simple analyses of variance were employed. Language and intelligence variables need not be considered, due to the very low correlations with the adjustment variables.

Table 9.3:    Analyses of Variance for Nationality Differences in School Adjustment and Socio-emotional Adjustment

|  | 1. Progress in school | 2. Social adjustment | 3. Emotional adjustment | 4. Progress in Swedish |
|---|---|---|---|---|
| **Nationality** | | | | |
| a) Finnish $\overline{X}$ | 2.91 | 3.45 | 3.45 | 3.11 |
| b) Yugoslav $\overline{X}$ | 2.95 | 3.51 | 3.57 | 3.23 |
| c) Greek $\overline{X}$ | 2.88 | 3.51 | 3.56 | 3.35 |
| d) Spanish $\overline{X}$ | 2.75 | 3.50 | 3.26 | 3.09 |
| F ratio | .469 | .451 | 1.65 | 2.04 |
| P $>$ | NS | NS | NS | NS |
| $100 \times \omega^2$ | .09 | .09 | .59 | .55 |
| df within | 1564 | 1578 | 831 | 1106 |

Source:    L.H. Ekstrand, 'Social and Individual Frame Factors in L2 Learning: Comparative Aspects', in T. Skutnabb-Kangas (ed.), *Papers from the First Nordic Conference on Bilingualism* (University of Helsingfors, 1977), and in *Reprints from Department of Educational and Psychological Research*, no. 227 (School of Education, Malmö, Sweden, 1977).

As seen in Table 9.3, there are no significant differences with respect to socio-emotional disturbances between nationalities. However, nationality explains less than 1 per cent of the variance in these adjustment variables. As can be seen from Table 9.4, language group explains a little more of the variance, probably because of the greater number of degrees of freedom, as the $\omega^2$ is sensitive to grouping of the independent variable. Now the over-all difference becomes significant in all variables.

Table 9.4: Analyses of Variance for Language Group Differences in Adjustment

| | 1. Progress in school | 2. Social adjustment | 3. Emotional adjustment | 4. Progress in Swedish |
|---|---|---|---|---|
| Language group: | | | | |
| a) Finnish-Ugric $\overline{X}$ | 2.97 | 3.51 | 3.59 | 3.25 |
| b) Slavic $\overline{X}$ | 3.24 | 3.74 | 3.83 | 3.49 |
| c) Germanic $\overline{X}$ | 3.10 | 3.59 | 3.58 | 3.28 |
| d) Romanic $\overline{X}$ | 2.91 | 3.54 | 3.45 | 3.12 |
| e) Greek $\overline{X}$ | 2.83 | 3.51 | 3.56 | 3.35 |
| f) Other $\overline{X}$ | 2.88 | 3.90 | 3.50 | 3.55 |
| F | 3.87 | 4.66 | 3.57 | 4.51 |
| P > | .01 | .001 | .01 | .001 |
| $100 \times \omega^2$ | 1.0 | 1.2 | 1.8 | 1.7 |
| df within | 1883 | 1901 | 1000 | 1318 |

Source: As for Table 9.3.

The tendency in academic adjustment is for the Slavic and Germanic groups to adjust the best and the Greek and Romanic groups the worst. In social adjustment, the Slavic and Germanic groups again show the finest adjustment, while the Greek and Finnish groups show the poorest. In emotional adjustment, the Slavic and Germanic groups exhibit the best, while the Romanic and Greek groups show the worst. Thus, there is no consistent tendency in the direction predicted, and differences are small.

Takac compared immigrant and native children in the city of Gothenburg in western Sweden.[18] The types of problems studied are given in Table 9.5. The problems were indicated on class lists by the teachers, according to a check list, without the teacher knowing that the purpose of the study was to compare native with immigrant children.

Table 9.5:   Proportions of Pupils with Specific Types of Problems

| Type of Problem | Swedes % | Immigrants % | Difference |
|---|---|---|---|
| A 1. Health in general | 3.7 | 5.4 | 1.7 |
| A 2. Motor | 5.6 | 5.6 | - |
| A 3. Speech | 4.1 | 7.7 | 3.6 |
| A 4. Alcohol or drugs | .9 | 1.6 | .7 |
| A 5. Hygiene | 1.5 | 4.4 | 2.9 |
| B 1. Self-confidence | 10.1 | 12.0 | 1.9 |
| B 2. Independence | 6.5 | 8.4 | 1.9 |
| B 3. Language | 2.0 | 30.6 | 28.6 |
| B 4. Aggression | 7.0 | 10.3 | 3.3 |
| B 5. Anxiety | 6.8 | 9.7 | 2.9 |
| B 6. Nervousness | 6.5 | 8.0 | 1.5 |
| B 7. Frustration tolerance | 8.1 | 12.7 | 4.6 |
| B 8. Adjustment ability | 5.1 | 7.6 | 2.5 |
| C 1. Family situation | 5.4 | 9.1 | 3.7 |
| C 2. Relations with adults | 3.7 | 3.3 | .4 |
| C 3. Relations with mates | 8.6 | 14.1 | 5.5 |
| C 4. Mobbing | 2.5 | 5.0 | 2.5 |
| C 5. Co-operative ability | 4.4 | 7.3 | 2.9 |
| D 1. Achievement | 12.0 | 16.5 | 4.5 |
| D 2. Attention, concentration | 16.5 | 18.4 | 1.9 |
| D 3. Motivation | 9.2 | 11.1 | 1.9 |
| D 4. Tempo | 10.7 | 12.7 | 2.0 |
| D 5. Initiative | 6.4 | 8.8 | 2.4 |
| D 6. Absence | 4.6 | 6.5 | 1.9 |
| D 7. Reading, writing, arithmetic | 18.7 | 27.1 | 8.4 |

Source:   M. Takac, *Invandrarbarns problem* (Problems of Immigrant Children) (City Council, Gothenburg, 1976).

As seen in Table 9.5, the difference in the percentage of native and immigrant children's specific types of problems is quite small. Language problems (B3, D7), as expected, exhibit the largest differences, and hence explain most of the sum of differences, from which Takac draws his conclusions. In only three variables is the difference larger than 4 per cent.

Most immigrant pupils belong to the working class but are in this study compared to a Swedish group which is undifferentiated with respect to social class. A control of SES might attenuate differences, as many variables, such as hygiene, family situation, achievement and attention, may be SES related. Furthermore, a breakdown by national-ity would have been interesting, as some nationalities may be over-represented with respect to certain types of problems (see discussion below). Differences in area B (emotional adjustment) and C (social adjustment) are surprisingly small, in view of the strong claims often heard. They might have been even smaller had appropriate controls been applied. Many controls are missing in this study.

Sveri studied crimes committed by immigrants in Sweden.[19] Foreign citizens between 15 and 17 years of age had a lower rate of conviction than Swedish citizens, and those between 18 and 20 years of age had about the same rate. In many cases, crime and alcoholism existed before immigration. Suikkila administered a questionnaire to 63 out of 67 Finnish immigrant male students in grades 7-9 (13-15 years of age) in one municipality in Sweden.[20] The students all belonged to families where one or both parents came from Finland, regardless of native language (Finland is a bilingual country and approximately 20 per cent of Finnish immigrants to Sweden speak Swedish). Confessions to petty crimes, such as shoplifting, were lower, but not significantly so, among the Finnish boys. Thus the results of Sveri, as cited above, are confirmed in this self-report study. As strong claims that the native language contributes to mental health have recently been made (see p. 201), it is interesting to find that mental health is positively related to the speaking of Swedish at home. In spite of the data, Suikkila concludes that 'the immigrant youth is a risk group with lower immunity against crime and other forms of deviant behavior than Swedish youth'.

Admission rates to mental hospitals and psychiatric clinics show a notorious over-representation of immigrants.[21] Some studies suggest that the rate of mental illness in the country of origin may explain part of the rate among immigrants. Haavio-Mannila and Stenius found that the rate of anxiety was highest among non-migrant Finns in Finland, next highest among internal migrants in Finland, third among Finnish-speaking immigrants in Sweden, fourth among native Swedes and lowest among Swedish-speaking Finnish immigrants in Sweden.[22] Allardt in part confirmed this when he found a higher rate of anxiety among Finnish than among Swedish women in a comparative survey of Scandinavia.[23] Social adjustment can be taken in a broader sense than hitherto, for we can consider it to be the degree of success in society. This may not be at all related to mental health or ability to form a warm relationship with friends or relatives; these two types of social adjustment are often confused. Some data on social adjustment, in its broader sense, were obtained by the local social authority of the city of Malmö in southern Sweden, a city with approximately 200,000 inhabitants.[24] All children from 0-19 years who had a record with the social welfare districts during the period July-December 1977 were classified with respect to migrant status. The immigrant children were identified through their and their parents' names. Out of 46,700 Swedish children, 670, or 1.4 per cent, had been in contact with the social authorities. Out of 6,300 immigrant children, 324, or 5.2 per cent, had had such contacts. More than half of the contacts were benign, in connection with a child needing day care or an inquiry into alleged alcoholism or marital trouble on the part of the parents. There was an over-representation of Finnish (9.7 per cent) and Danish (6.5 per cent) children. The other immigrant children had 4.7 per cent contacts. In 1976, 8.5 per cent of the Swedish families in Malmö received some kind of social welfare, compared to 46.4 per cent of the Finnish families, 36.4 per cent of Danish and Norwegian families and 29.7 per cent of other nationalities. There are many cases of alcoholism, crime, divorce and other problems among immigrants in Malmö. In most recent cases, the problems have started before immigration. The nearness to Sweden probably explains the over-representation of problems among immigrant Scandinavian families: they attempt to solve problems by migration, it being fairly easy. These facts seem to suggest that social and cultural conditions in the emigrant countries explain many of the problems immigrants may have in the new country. It is astonishing that the act of emigration or the encounter with new conditions are so often put forward as causes of these problems, and that conditions in the native country are so seldom offered as likely explanations. We may conclude that the alarming claims of a high rate of emotional and social disturbances (in a psychopathological sense) among immigrant children seem to be highly exaggerated. If there is a higher rate, the difference is not large but, until further research with better methods of measurement and better control of various contaminating factors has been carried out, no safe conclusions, even as to the existence of a moderate difference, can be drawn. There seems to be a large difference in social adjustment in a broad sense, but the data seem to point to family conditions rather than to individual problems, judging from the low rate of criminality and psychopathological conditions in children. However, recent mass media reports suggest that the rate of criminality among immigrant youth is going up in most industrialised countries. Whether this is a difference between first- and second-generation children, or a variation in general factors, remains to be seen, as well as the duration of this trend. It is likely, however, that second-generation children are at higher risk for various conflicts than are first-generation children.

Having tried to estimate the rate of disturbances *per se*, we will have a closer look at some specific hypotheses about the possible causes of these assumed disturbances. The fact that there seems to be little difference between native and immigrant children quantitatively does not exclude the possibility that such disturbances that do exist may to some extent have a different cause, i.e. there may be a qualitative variation.

## The Possible Influence of Migration Per Se on Mental Health

Not many studies on the effects of migration *per se* on mental health seem to have been undertaken. Pedersen and Sullivan studied parental attitudes towards geographical mobility in the case of disturbed and non-disturbed military children in the USA.[25] The two groups did not differ with respect to number of residences. The normal group had a mean of 9.1 residences and the disturbed group 10.5 residences, the difference being insignificant. While this study is not concerned with crossing national borders or changing language, it does study frequency of relocation *per se* in relation to emotional disturbances. The negative finding with respect to a hypothesised relationship argues for considerable caution in interpreting repeated family relocation as an etiologically significant factor in and of itself in the development of emotionally disturbed children. Kantor has reviewed studies concerning the adjustment of migrant children.[26] The majority of studies on immigration or wartime displacement seem to show very little pathology for children who remain in their families. Disturbances are more frequent if children are removed from the family. The level of social adjustment decreases both from keeping a child completely stationary and from moving him around too much. One or two moves seem to lead to greater social acceptance. The degree of urbanisation both in the areas which the immigrants leave and in the areas to which they migrate, which seems to be of importance in relation to adult migration, has been investigated for migrating children.[27] Children with continuous city residence, country-to-city and city-to-city migration were compared. The three groups did not differ markedly with respect to social relations, school relations, parent-child relations or personality characteristics. Thus, migration *per se* need not bring about maladjustment as an inevitable consequence.

## 'Cultural Shock' or 'Cultural Squeeze'?

The term 'culture shock' has frequently been used to describe how a person experiences confrontation with an entirely different culture. Culture shock is put forth as a possible explanation of mental illnesses such as psychosomatic disturbances and neuroticism among migrants. Ekstrand has used the term to describe a state which must be mastered by the migrant.[28] Serious doubt may, however, be cast on the word 'shock'. In connection with immigrant children in Sweden, teachers report that the children's emotional disturbances do not generally appear until some time after their arrival, and that those who seem to be associated with a positive home background tend to show disturbances (if they do so at all) at a later stage than do children with a poor home background and poor education. Parker, Kleiner and Needelman discuss the concept of cultural shock and state that: '... culture shock either is not a useful explanatory concept, or that it is associated with mental disorder only in particular situations'.[29] Parker *et al.* offer an alternative theory.[30] They assume that more differentiated groupings in an urban society provide a more differential status hierarchy: the urban citizen will perceive greater discrepancies between his own achievements and those of the reference groups on different levels of the status hierarchy. This leads to a lower self-esteem among urban dwellers than among rural inhabitants. On these assumptions they base the following four hypotheses:

1. urban migrants have higher rates of mental disorder than rural migrants;
2. urban migrants have higher levels of goal-striving stress than rural migrants;
3. urban migrants have greater discrepancies between perception of their own achievement and that of their reference groups;
4. urban migrants have lower self-esteem than rural migrants.

They administered a 206-item questionnaire to a sample of mentally ill persons and a representative sample of the Negro population of a large urban centre, and picked urban and rural migrants from the larger groups. The first hypothesis was supported. There was a statistically significant over-representation of mental illness among migrants of urban origin. The findings for hypotheses 2 and 3 were in the expected direction, but not statistically significant. Hypothesis 4 was supported. Combinations of a) high goal-striving stress *or* high scale-striving stress, b) high reference group discrepancy, and c) low self-esteem were manifest in significantly higher rates among migrants of urban origin than among migrants of rural origin. The authors conclude that global variables, such as 'migration' and 'social status', are too heterogeneous to order data pertaining to mental illness. Apart from dispensing with the concept of 'culture shock', the findings suggest that an urban environment might itself create psychopathological disturbances — a theory often reported in the sociological literature.[31] But what about the possibility that, in the long run, cultural differences 'squeeze' immigrants?

## Do Immigrant Children Develop Emotional Disturbances as a Function of Time?

We have found that the data so far available suggest that the rate of psychopathological disturbances in immigrant children does not seem to be very much higher than in native children. We have found that the parents often carry a heavy burden of social problems. There are several indications that these problems, as well as the rate of mental disease, may be a function of the conditions in the country of origin. The social disturbances (in a broad sense) among immigrant children seem to be a function of the parents' problems and thus primarily reflect the parents' cultural background. In fact, despite these problems, the immigrant children seem to do remarkably well, with no high rate of deviant behaviour.

As migration would not be the kind of trauma that causes neurotic behaviour, we would expect some time to pass before disturbances appear. In other words, *if* there is a 'culture squeeze', we would expect an increase in disturbances (or a decrease in mental health) as a function of time spent in the new culture. If not, an alternative hypothesis gains in likelihood: that factors belonging to the background culture, rather than factors pertaining to the process of migration or to the new culture, cause possible disturbances in immigrant children. The judgements of teachers concerning the social and emotional adjustment of the students, mentioned in Ekstrand's study,[32] were plotted against length of residence (LOR) in years. The results are shown in Figure 9.2. Means of at least five pupils were plotted against age. The upper and lower curves are the means ± one standard deviation. Analyses of variance for extreme groups of LOR did not yield significant differences.[33] Furthermore, the $\omega^2$ values were not higher than .001, i.e. LOR cannot explain more than 1 per cent of the total variance in the adjustment variables. Thus, there do not seem to be any systematic changes in social and emotional adjustment as a function of LOR, a result supported by the findings of Bhatnagar.[34] In other words, there are no changes in the mental health of the immigrant children over time, suggesting that the hypothesis of 'cultural squeeze' is not tenable as far as psychopathological changes are concerned. This, of course, does not mean that the emotional life or the personality of immigrant children is not affected by migration and life in a new culture. Such effects surely do exist, but

Figure 9.2    Teacher Judgements of Emotional and Social Adjustment in Immigrant Children Plotted Against Length of Residence

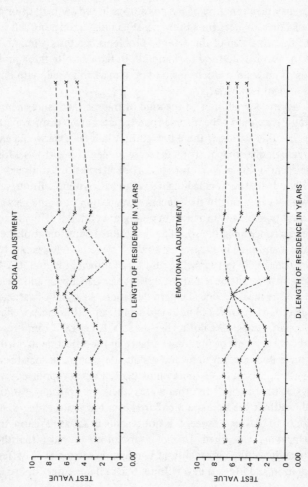

Source: L.H. Ekstrand, 'Age and Length of Residence as Variables Related to the Adjustment of Immigrant Children, with Special Reference to Second Language Learning', in G. Nickel (ed.), *Proceedings of the Fourth International Congress of Applied Linguistics* (Hochschul Verlag, Stuttgart, 1976).

in most cases they seem within the realm of normal, non-pathological variation. The hypothesis that problems of immigrant children are mainly derived from the background culture of the parents gains some support from case studies (published and unpublished) which I have done.[35] In these studies of emotionally disturbed immigrant children, it was evident that the problems existed in the family before migration.

## *Does Lack of Command of Language Create Emotional Disturbances?*

It is generally assumed that emotional and social adjustment is causally connected to language proficiency.[36] Schumann believes that the foreigner's repertoire of problem-solving and other coping mechanisms, which in the old culture are routine matters, require great energy in the new culture, and such a condition 'can produce fear, anxiety and depression'. Language learning may prevent or cure emotional problems.[37]

Toukomaa and Skutnabb-Kangas argue that lack of command of the native language, and not being taught with the native language as the language of instruction, cause an identity crisis which is strengthened by the minority situation.[38] This identity crisis is assumed, in the long run, to create disturbances.

Thus, we have two kinds of assumptions regarding the notion that language is a causal factor in creating psychopathological conditions: new language deficits and native language deficits. This puts the immigrant in a difficult position. It is very hard for an individual to become a balanced bilingual, and such efforts, according to modern stress research, might create the kind of mental overload which produces more or less temporary psychosomatic symptoms. However, a number of studies of the degree of association between emotional and linguistic variables do exist, and we will take a look at some of them.

In my previously mentioned study I computed intercorrelations within and between matrices of correlations for the four domains of measurements: language tests (six variables), teacher judgements of scholastic and socio-emotional adjustment (four variables), oral reading tests (nine variables) and tests of the R, N and S PMA factors (Thurstone classification).[39] The intercorrelations between the language tests were .57 on the average, .52 for the adjustment assessments, .33 for the intelligence tests, and .73, .76 and .75 for the three different measures on each of the three reading tests. These results were all normal and as expected. The intercorrelations between language by adjustment variables were .19 on the average, .26 for intelligence by language variables, .11 for intelligence by adjustment variables, .37 for reading tests by language variables, .12 for reading tests by adjustment variables and .18 for reading by intelligence tests. These coefficients are surprisingly low. On the basis of the suggested relationship between language skills and emotional and social adjustment, one would have expected much higher correlations between language and adjustment variables and intelligence and adjustment variables. Matrices are given in detail elsewhere. For two particularly interesting adjustment variables, the average correlation between 'social adjustment' and the six language tests was .13, and the corresponding correlation for 'emotional adjustment' was .17. In other words, the statistical association is so low as to be negligible; hence, no strong causal relationship can exist.

Lambert *et al.* also found very low correlations between affective measurements (e.g. feelings towards French people, language and culture), some measures of social adjustment (e.g. social dissatisfaction), and L2 achievement.[40] They ranged from -.16 to .25, which checks with the findings mentioned above. Gardner and Lambert found equally low correlations between similar measures.[41] It should be mentioned that these authors draw the opposite conclusion and argue the importance of attitudes, motivation, etc. for L2 acquisition.[42] These conclusions, however, seem to be influenced by the social desirability of the outcome rather than by an unbiased evaluation of the actual figures. Haynes also found low correlations between social adjustment and two measures of language and arithmetic abilities.[43] Bhatnagar found correlations between five measures of adjustment (social acceptability, personal satisfaction, anxiety, objectivity of self-concept, composite score) and academic achievement in the range of .09-.45, with spoken English -.28 -.23, and with IQ .18-.46.[44] We find that measures of social adjustment (in the narrow sense) and emotional adjustment have very little to do with language performance. The various hypotheses cited in the beginning of this section do not find support in existing data. Language skills neither prevent nor cure psychopathological conditions, nor do emotional disturbances (unless debilitating ones) highly affect language learning. Animal experiments such as those of Pavlov[45] and psychiatric experience[46] suggest a 'spill-over' between the affective and cognitive domains in the individual only in extreme cases. If a cognitive conflict is severe and enduring, an emotional breakdown may occur, and *vice versa*, but only if an emotional state was so grave as to require hospitalisation would cognitive functions be impaired. Fortunately, the condition of the immigrant children or their situation is not of this debilitating character.

## Problems Related to Language Learning

### *Is Early Bilingualism Harmful?*

Recently, it has been argued with reference to conditions in Sweden that early bilingualism is desirable neither among immigrant children[47] nor among native children learning second languages.[48] Some even go as far as to suggest that immigrant children should be taught their native language only, and *in* their native language only, until the age of 12-13, i.e. the start of junior high school.[49]

Early studies used to show the superiority of unilinguals in intelligence. When non-verbal measures of intelligence were being used, the difference tended to disappear, and when SES, in particular, was controlled, the difference sometimes went in favour of the bilinguals.[50] Recent experiments seem to indicate the superiority of bilinguals in problem sensitivity and portrait sensitivity,[51] in separating words from their meaning,[52] and in sensitivity to communicative needs.[53] Ben-Zeev reported more verbal transformation, more symbol substitution, equal semantic understanding, lower vocabulary and better non-verbal system understanding in bilinguals (intelligence well controlled).[54] Reports by Torrance,[55] Carringer[56] and Landry[57] indicate higher creativity in bilinguals. Research has also been undertaken concerning the effects of early bilingualism (within the 6-12 age range) on school subjects, including the native language. Donoghue reviews research on the effects of the early FLES experiments on general academic achievement and finds no harmful effects.[58] Her findings are confirmed by Johnson *et al.*, Lopato, Geigle, Potts and Smith in their studies.[59] Malmberg, however, maintains his apprehensions concerning early L2 learning.[60] His suspicions seem to be partly borne out by the research on early English teaching in Denmark.[61] Special-class children exposed to early English teaching were clearly inferior on written tests in Danish to special-class pupils without such training. No such effects could be traced in pupils in ordinary classes. It is interesting to compare the Danish experiments with the Swedish experiments. I was in charge of the evaluation of these experiments, which compared the start of English in grades 1, 2, 3 and 4, respectively. In these classes, the English teaching was completely audio-oral.[62] The teaching was totally imitative, i.e. the instruction was administered by sound tape and still films and the teachers did not take part in the teaching process. The evaluation of possible harmful effects in special classes was done informally. The teachers were in daily contact with the local supervisors who reported to the Board of Education. No harmful effects, but in fact positive social and emotional effects, were reported in this context.

The difference between the Swedish and Danish experiments is that the latter introduced written English in special classes. This seems to have been a less suitable didactic approach, and interference in writing may be easily avoided by means of a prolonged audio-oral approach in special classes.

A current major Swedish experiment in early L2 teaching is the longitudinal EPÅL study, where English is begun in grade 1 as compared to the regular start in grade 3. Holmstrand presents the results when the experimental pupils have finished grade 3 by means of analyses of covariance, in which an initial school readiness test is the covariate.[63] Sex and SES are controlled by keeping groups apart. In arithmetic, there is no difference between experimental and control pupils. The former have more positive attitudes towards school. In Swedish, experimental pupils in social group III (the lowest), as well as experimental girls, do significantly better than the controls, in spite of 80 minutes a week less instruction in this subject. Native-born immigrant pupils do as well as Swedish pupils, while foreign-born immigrant pupils tend to do worse.[64] These tendencies also remain in grade 6.[65] Holmstrand concludes that early L2 teaching seems to have a slightly stimulating effect on the native language.

## Is There an Optimal Age for Becoming Bilingual?

The preceding section suggests that early bilingualism is not harmful. The problem of a possible optimal age for learning second languages remains, however. A number of explicitly formulated theories predict that the early ages are optimum for second language learning. In fact, all theoretical approaches, including the most recent ones, seem to agree upon an early optimum age and to disregard the accumulating contrary evidence. Ekstrand reports 40 studies of L2 learning and age, of which 23 studies indicated that older learners (including adults) are better, seven studies yielded inconsistent results and ten studies indicated younger individuals to be superior.[66] Judging the quality of studies (anecdotal/statistical, design, control, measurements, etc.), it turned out that the ten latter studies were all 'weak', while 21 out of the 23 belonged to the category 'good'. Thus L2 learning ability seems to develop according to the general cognitive development (to which it is also positively correlated on a number of measures) with no early optimum or critical period.

Some authors, such as Cummins[67] and the earlier-mentioned Toukomaa, Skutnabb-Kangas and others, claim that the increasing ability to learn a new language is a basis for postponing it for many years. This, however, is a hasty conclusion, for the following reasons:

1. it takes a long time to develop a language, be it the first or second — not even after 17 years have immigrants a native command of Swedish;[68]
2. small children have ample time for interaction with playmates, thereby learning language;
3. small children learn sentences, grammatical and intonation patterns as unities and not as composed parts, which means that even the first items learned have a very high value as vehicles for communication;
4. immigrant children need to be bilingual in order to develop a bicultural identity, thereby avoiding conflicts and crises;
5. many other children in today's world need a second language;
6. the nearer to balanced bilingualism the individual comes, the greater, probably, is the contribution to the cognitive development — here the time factor is also important, i.e. it takes a long time to develop a language, as well as integrate language and other cognitive components.

*The Relations Between L1, L2 and Cognition*

In a previous section, it was shown that neither nationality nor language group had any great influence on the adjustment domain. As shown by Ekstrand, the influence of nationality and language group is somewhat greater on language variables, although not much.[69] This small but significant influence suggests that the qualitative influence of different mother tongues on the acquisition of a new language is small. Carroll, in the cross-national IEA study, made a similar finding.[70] Lately, it has been argued that native language is the key to the entire development of the child, be it emotional or cognitive. The data on pp. 201-3 indicate that this claim is certainly not true for the affective domain. Cummins, however, argues that language is crucial for the entire cognitive domain.[71] I have not traced any multivariate study that gives a comprehensive account of the relationship between language and other cognitive variables. Looking at single correlations, Ekstrand reports low to moderate correlations between L2 variables and non-verbal primary mental abilities.[72] Cummins finds that correlations between L1 and cognition seem to be of the same magnitude as between L2 and cognition. So far I agree, although I differ in conclusions. Modern basic research on cognition works with more factors, 20 or more, than we have grown used to do, and has revealed more complex interrelations

than we have so far recognised. Considering that we do not use only
verbal types of communication, but also figural and numerical, I would
be very hesitant to ascribe the entire development to just one set of
variables, i.e. language.

The stress put by Cummins and others on the role of language for
cognition is a link in attempts to prove that L2 acquisition is completely
contingent on the degree of L1 development. Ekstrand reports correlations between .20 and .50 between variables of L1 and L2, computed
from very large samples.[73] Cummins found coefficients from fairly
small samples between .40 and .80. Again, considering sample sizes I
would bet on the lower coefficients, which are also more likely in view o
all the various factors that contribute to L2 acquisition (see pp. 207-8).
It should be clear to the reader that all the emphasis put on the relations
L1 - L2 - cognition are attempts to justify unilingual home language
classes not only for first- but also for second-generation immigrant
children, primarily in Sweden and Bavaria, but also lately in other
European countries. In my view, this is an attempt to order data according to a certain ideology, rather than to shape teaching strategies
according to known facts. We will now see what is the outcome of
unilingual classes.

*The Effects of Prolonged Instruction of Immigrant Children with the
Native Language as the Medium of Instruction*

As mentioned previously, it has been claimed by Finnish authors that
immigrant children should have a prolonged period of instruction with
the native language as the medium (first during the entire pre-school
period and then at least during the first six years, but preferably for
nine years), unless the entire development is to be impaired. Swedish
should not be introduced until grade 3, and then only orally. This is
called 'positive discrimination' or 'positive segregation'. Results from
this type of education are beginning to appear, and they are not
encouraging.

Lauren found 31 immigrant youths in 100 psychiatric patients at a
Swedish hospital.[74] All 31 young patients had been born in Sweden. The
five worst, i.e. psychotic cases, had all spoken their native language only
in the family and socially, had attended minority schools and consequently suffered segregation, exactly as prescribed by Skutnabb-Kangas,
Toukomaa, Malmberg, Cummins and others. Only the gravest cases were
admitted to this special clinic for children and young people with severe
mental disturbances. Nelleman found that 1,200 children of Polish farm-
hands in Denmark had quite different experiences at different types of

schools.[75] Those who had gone to Polish schools had certainly preserved more of their background language and culture. On the other hand, they had suffered more discrimination. Many were highly critical of having been put into Polish schools, as they felt that this had made their social careers more difficult. Rist found that unilingual, native-medium education of immigrant children in Bavaria prevented them from undergoing secondary education and vocational training.[76]

It seems that an early, bilingual education where the family provides the first bilingual model, as described by Andersson,[77] and the school provides a second one, would most safely lead to the development of a bicultural identity. 'Positive segregation' seems to put the children of the second generation — who form the majority in Sweden — in a loyalty conflict between the family and the native-medium school on the one hand, and the rest of society on the other. It must be remembered that second-generation immigrants do not know any country other than that in which they were born.

As discussed by Ekstrand, a number of studies in Sweden have shown that pupils in unilingual home language classes in Sweden do not reach fully native-like command of their mother tongue.[78] A number of Scandinavian studies also demonstrate that it is virtually impossible to achieve a completely balanced bilingualism. Test results as well as reaction times will always be inferior in one of the languages. It seems obvious that this fact is due to the social forces of the surrounding society. Instead of putting the child in opposition to these forces by unilingual home language classes, the child should be allowed to join the mainstream of the school and society, while the home language and cultural background is being kept up to a fair, although not native-like, level by means of composite classes or the 2-6 weekly home language lessons which is the prevailing model in Sweden (cf. pp. 185-7 and 187-9). It is true that those authors who favour 'positive discrimination' argue that society should be changed so as to allow immigrant children to function 'on their own conditions', i.e. receive their primary and secondary education (and presumably go to college) in their home language, stick to the often very low SES of their parents (meaning virtually no social mobility), etc. Such a gigantic task is so unrealistic as to appear foolish, but suppose it were possible: according to which of about 100 nations represented in Sweden should the change be made?

*Factors related to L2 Acquisition*

Ekstrand has listed a number of variables, derived from various quantitative studies, which have been shown to have some association with L2 acquisition and has ranked them according to the amount of variance that each seems to explain.[79] While it must be stressed that such a list is neither exact nor complete, it does give a rough picture of the complexity of the conglomerate of social and individual factors that operate in L2 acquisition. The top item is the relation L2 - L3 which indicates a learning-to-learn process, or set formation. Next comes age, indicating maturation as a crucial factor. Then comes native language, which of course is such an important factor that there is no need for boosting it in the debate, verbal intelligence, non-verbal intelligence, urban/rural area, teacher's L2 competence (formal), length of residence, previous experience of the language, radio teaching, sex, school adjustment, language family, nationality, socio-emotional adjustment, SES, aptitude, teacher's sex, teaching method, teaching materials, teacher's basic education and class type (ordinary/special class). We might also add factors of school organisation, motivation, homework, parents' interest and many others. In view of this many-faceted picture, the claims that native language classes will solve all problems appear rather naive.

## Academic Achievement of Immigrant Pupils in Sweden

Wennerström made an extremely well-controlled comparison of immigrant and native Swedish children.[80] Immigrant pupils performed about as well as Swedish pupils, *ceteris paribus*. Further analyses showed SES to create substantial differences in school results, while degree of bilingualism did not. SES, being a much more important variable for school success than bilingualism, has also been confirmed in recent research in Friesland and Wales.[81]

As mentioned above, the proclivity among immigrant students to go to secondary education has been good, in spite of claims to the opposite. Data from the Swedish EPÅL study (cf. p. 204)[82] indicate that foreign-born immigrant pupils do worse than native-born immigrant students, but SES factors probably play a part. Attention should be paid to the difference between naturalised and non-naturalised immigrants, as immigrants from higher social strata become naturalised more often.

As many studies show, immigrant pupils do tend to have language problems, although these often are SES related. Foreign-born immigrant pupils, in particular, suffer a more or less prolonged period of language retardation during the language shift. As discussed above, L1 seems to deteriorate quicker than L2 is acquired. Instruction in the mother tongue during the period in the reception class, as is beginning to be practised in Sweden, does not seem to be a bad idea. Generally speaking, however, the academic achievement of immigrant students seems to be a question more of social and cultural factors than of bilingualism. Action should be taken accordingly, such as trying to engage parents in adult education and other activities, as the family has the earliest and most powerful impact on the child. The importance of the parents' model behaviour is demonstrated in a study by Bhatnagar.[83] If the parents are bilingual, the children do much better academically and socially than when parents try to deny their old language and culture. The children fare worst, however, when the parents stick to the old language and culture. These effects from what Bhatnagar calls 'retractive bilingualism' seem to be equivalent to those produced by 'positive segregation'. As the latter course gains ground in Sweden, the controversy over immigrant education will probably increase, as more and more parents and teachers also realise the disadvantages.

## Notes

1. Sweden's official statistics, *Befolkningsförandringar* (Population Changes), III, 1967 (Central Bureau of Statistics, Stockholm, 1968).

2. Sweden's official statistics, *Statistiska Meddelanden* (Statistical Bulletins), Series B. – *Befolkning och val*, 1978:6 (Population in the Whole Country, the Counties and the Communes), 31 December 1978 (Central Bureau of Statistics, Stockholm, 1978).

3. S. Reinans, 'Har vi en million invandrare?' (Have We One Million Immigrants?), *Ny i Sverige*, 7, 1 (1978), pp. 28-30.

4. Sweden's official statistics, *Promemorior från SCB* (Memos from SCB) 1977:12 (Central Bureau of Statistics, Stockholm, 1977).

5. Sweden's official statistics, *Statistiska Meddelanden* (Statistical Bulletins), Series U – *Utbildning, forskning och Kultur*, v, 1978:24 (Integrated Upper Secondary School), 1977/78 (Central Bureau of Statistics, Stockholm, 1978).

6. Sweden's official statistics, *Promemorior från SCB*.

7. Ibid.

8. National Board of Education, PM, October 1977, *Hemspråksträning, hemspråksundervisning, stödundervisning i svenska* (Home Language Training, Home Language Teaching, Study Support) (National Board of Education, Stockholm, 1977).

9. Ibid.

10. National Board of Education, Special Information P 1, 1978:15 (National Board of Education, Stockholm, September 1978).

11. National Board of Education, *Hemspråksträning*.

12. L.H. Ekstrand, 'Adjustment Among Immigrant Pupils in Sweden', *International Review of Applied Psychology*, 25, 3 (1976), pp. 167-88.

13. Ibid.

14. A. Goldenberg, 'Educational Adjustment of Immigrant Children', *JIAS News* (Autumn 1973).

15. M. Rutter, W. Yule, M. Berger, B. Yule, J. Morton and C. Bagely, 'Children of West Indian Immigrants, I: Rates of Behavioural Deviance and of

Psychiatric Disorder', *Journal of Child Psychology*, 15 (1974), pp. 241-62.
16.    P. Toukomaa and T. Skutnabb-Kangas, 'The Intensive Teaching of the Mother Tongue to Migrant Children at Pre-school Age', *Research Reports*, no. 26 (Department of Sociology and Social Psychology, University of Tampere, Finland, 1977).
17.    L.H. Ekstrand, 'Social and Individual Frame Factors in L2 Learning: Comparative Aspects', in T. Skutnabb-Kangas (ed.), *Papers from the First Nordic Conference on Bilingualism* (University of Helsingfors, 1977), and in *Reprints from Department of Educational and Psychological Research*, no. 227 (School of Education, Malmö, Sweden, 1977).
18.    M. Takac, *Invandrarbarns problem* (Problems of Immigrant Children) (City Council, Gothenburg, 1976).
19.    B. Sveri, 'Utlänningars brottslighet' (Criminality Among Foreigners), en kriminalstatistisk jämförelse mellan svenska och utländska medborgare, *Svensk Juristtidning* (1973).
20.    J. Suikkila, *Normer och normkonflikter bland finska immigrantungdomar och svenska ungdomar* (Norms and Norm Conflicts Among Finnish Immigrant Youths and Swedish Youths) (Institute of Criminal Science, Sociology Department, University of Stockholm, 1977).
21.    L.H. Ekstrand, 'Migrant Adaptation – A Cross-cultural Problem', in R. Freudenstein (ed.), *Teaching the Children of Immigrants* (AIMAV-Didier, Bruxelles, 1978).
22.    E. Haavio-Mannila and K. Stenius, 'Mental Health Problems of New Ethnic Minorities in Sweden', *Acta Sociologica*, no. 4 (1974), pp. 367-92.
23.    E. Allardt, *Att ha, att älska, att vara. Om välfärd i Norden* (Having, Loving, Being. On Affluence in Scandinavia) (Argos, Lund, 1975).
24.    Internal PM, Appendix 1 (Social Welfare Department, City Council, Malmö, 1979).
25.    F.A. Pedersen and E.J. Sullivan, 'Relationships Among Geographical Mobility, Parental Attitudes and Emotional Disturbances in Children', paper presented at the 1963 Annual Meeting of the American Orthopsychiatric Association, New York.
26.    M.B. Kantor, 'Some Consequences of Residential and Social Mobility for the Adjustment of Children', in M.B. Kantor (ed.), *Mobility and Mental Health* (Thomas, Springfield, Ill., 1965).
27.    Ibid.
28.    L.H. Ekstrand, 'Invandrarelevernas mentalhygieniska problem' (The Problems of Mental Health of Immigrant Children), in H. Egidius (ed.), *Mentalhygien* (Mental Health) (Esselte Studium Uniskol, Stockholm, 1975).
29.    S. Parker, R.J. Kleiner and B. Needelman, 'Migration and Mental Illness', *Social Science and Medicine*, 3 (1969), pp. 1-9.
30.    Ibid.
31.    Suikkila, *Normer och normkonflikter*.
32.    L.H. Ekstrand, 'Age and Length of Residence as Variables Related to the Adjustment of Immigrant Children, with Special Reference to Second Language Learning', in G. Nickel (ed.), *Proceedings of the Fourth International Congress of Applied Linguistics* (Hochschul Verlag, Stuttgart, 1976).
33.    Ibid.
34.    J. Bhatnagar, *Immigrants at School* (Cornmarket Press, London, 1970).
35.    E. Einarsson and L.H. Ekstrand, *Fallet Heimo* (The Case of Heimo) (Psykologiförlaget, Stockholm, 1973).
36.    I. Gelinek, 'Migrants' Children', *International Child Welfare Review*, no. 21 (1974), pp. 45-55.
37.    J.H. Schumann, 'Affective Factors and the Problem of Age in Second

Language Acquisition', *Language Learning*, 25, 2 (1975), pp. 209-35.

38.     Toukomaa and Skutnabb-Kangas, 'The Intensive Teaching of the Mother Tongue'.

39.     Ekstrand, 'Adjustment Among Immigrant Pupils in Sweden'.

40.     W.E. Lambert, R.C. Gardner, H.C. Barik and K. Tunstall, 'Attitudinal and Cognitive Aspects of Intensive Study of a Second Language', *Journal of Abnormal and Social Psychology*, 66, 4 (1963), pp. 358-68.

41.     R.C. Gardner and W.E. Lambert, 'Motivational Variables in Second-language Acquisition', *Canadian Journal of Psychology*, 13, 4 (1959), pp. 266-72.

42.     R.C. Gardner and W.E. Lambert, *Attitudes and Motivation in Second-language Learning* (Random House, Rowley, Mass., 1972).

43.     J.M. Haynes, *Educational Assessment of Immigrant Pupils* (NFER, Slough, 1971).

44.     Bhatnagar, *Immigrants at School*.

45.     I.P. Pavlov, *Conditioned Reflexes* (Dover, New York, 1960).

46.     J.R. Smythies, *Brain Mechanisms and Behavior* (Blackwell Scientific Publications, Oxford and Edinburgh, 1970).

47.     Toukomaa and Skutnabb-Kangas, 'The Intensive Teaching of the Mother Tongue'.

48.     B. Malmberg, 'Språkundervisningen leder till språkförbistring' (The Language Teaching Produces Language Confusion), *Sydsvenska Dagbladet*, 13 October 1977.

49.     Toukomaa and Skutnabb-Kangas, 'The Intensive Teaching of the Mother Tongue'.

50.     D. Wagner, 'Some Cognitive Perspectives on Bilingualism in Children', *International Review of Applied Psychology*, 29, 1 (1980), pp. 31-41.

51.     B. Bain, 'Toward an Integration of Piaget and Vygotsky: Bilingual Considerations', *Linguistics*, 160 (1975), pp. 5-20.

52.     A.D. Ianco-Worral, 'Bilingualism and Cognitive Development', *Child Development*, 43 (1972), pp. 1390-1400.

53.     F. Genesee, G.R. Tucker and W.E. Lambert, 'Communication Skills of Bilingual Children', *Child Development*, 46 (1975), pp. 1010-14.

54.     S. Ben-Zeev, 'The Influence of Bilingualism on Cognitive Strategy and Cognitive Development', *Child Development*, 48 (1977), pp. 1009-18.

55.     E.P. Torrance, J.C. Gowan, J.-J. Wu and N.C. Aliotti, 'Creative Functioning of Monolingual and Bilingual Children in Singapore', *Journal of Educational Psychology*, 61, 1 (1970), pp. 72-5.

56.     D. Carringer, 'Creative Thinking Abilities of Mexican Youth', *Journal of Cross-cultural Psychology*, 5, 4 (1974), pp. 492-504.

57.     R.G. Landry, 'A Comparison of Second Language Learners and Mono-linguals on Divergent Thinking Tasks at the Elementary School Level', *Modern Language Journal*, 58 (1974), pp. 10-15.

58.     M.R. Donoghue, 'What Research Tells Us About the Effects of FLES', *Hispania*, 48, 3 (1965), pp. 555-9.

59.     C.E. Johnson, F.P. Ellison and J.S. Flores, 'The Effect of Foreign Language Instruction on Basic Learning in Elementary School', *Modern Language Journal*, 45 (1961), pp. 200-2.

60.     B. Malmberg, *Språkinlärning* (Language Learning) (Aldus/Bonniers, Stockholm, 1971).

61.     J. Florander and M. Jansen, *Skoleforsøg i engelsk 1959-1965* (School Experiments in English 1959-1965) (Danmarks Pedagogiske Institut, Copenhagen, 1969) (stencilled).

62.     M. Gorosch and C.A. Axelsson, *English Without a Book. A Bilingual Experiment in Primary Schools by Audio-visual Means* (Cornelsen Verlag, Berlin,

1964); L.H. Ekstrand, 'English Without a Book Revisited: Towards an Integration of the Optimum Age and Development Hypotheses in Foreign Language Learning', *Didakometry*, no. 60 (School of Education, Malmö, Sweden, 1978).

63.  L. Holmstrand, *Effekterna på allmänna färdigheter och attityder i skolan av tidigt påbörjad undervisning i engelska* (The Effects on General Skills and Attitudes in School of Early Teaching of English) (Department of Education, University of Uppsala, 1978).

64.  L. Holmstrand, *De långsiktiga effekterna på allmänna färdigheter och attityder i skolan av tidigt påbörjad undervisning i engelska* (The Long-term Effects on General Skills and Attitudes in School of Early Teaching of English) (Department of Education, University of Uppsala, 1979).

65.  K. Jansson and Y. Linden, *Social bakgrund och skolprestationer hos invnadrarbarn i Västerås* (Social Background and School Achievement Among Immigrant Children in Västerås) (Department of Education, University of Uppsala, 1974) (stencilled).

66.  L.H. Ekstrand, 'Early Bilingualism: Theories and Facts', *Reprints and Miniprints*, no. 307 (School of Education, Malmö, Sweden, 1977).

67.  J. Cummins, 'Det första språket' (The First Language), *Invandrare och Minoriteter (Scandinavian Migration and Ethnic Minority Review)*, 6, 3 (1979), pp. 12-18.

68.  E. Mägiste, 'The Competing Language Systems of the Multilingual: A Developmental Study of Decoding and Encoding Processes', *Journal of Verbal Learning and Verbal Behavior*, 18 (1979), pp. 79-89.

69.  Ekstrand, 'Social and Individual Frame Factors in L2 Learning'.

70.  J.B. Carroll, *The Teaching of French as a Foreign Language in Eight Countries* (Almqvist and Wiksell International, Stockholm, 1975).

71.  Cummins, 'Det första språket'.

72.  Ekstrand, 'Adjustment Among Immigrant Pupils'.

73.  Ekstrand, 'Social and Individual Frame Factors in L2 Learning'.

74.  K. Lauren, 'Nationellt främlingsskap och tonårsidentitetsproblem' (National Alienation and Teenage Identity Problems), *Socialmedicinsk Tidskrift*, 6 (1973), pp. 359-63.

75.  G. Nelleman, 'Nationale skoler og deres indflydelse på assimilation, diskrimination og mobilitet (National Schools and their Influence on Assimilation, Discrimination and Social Mobility), paper presented at the Vth Nordic Migration Seminar, Oslo, 1979.

76.  R.C. Rist, 'On the Education of Guest-worker Children in Germany: A Comparative Study of Policies and Programs in Bavaria and Berlin', *School Review* 87, 3 (1979).

77.  T. Andersson, 'Parents, Wake Up. Why Deprive Your Child of a Superior Education?', unpublished paper, stencilled, 1979.

78.  Ekstrand, 'Early Bilingualism'.

79.  Ekstrand, 'Social and Individual Frame Factors in L2 Learning'.

80.  G. Wennerström, *Språklig anpassning och studieframgång hos barn till utländska föräldrar* (Linguistic Adjustment and School Achievement Among Children of Foreign Parents) (School of Education, Stockholm, 1967).

81.  J.M. Wijnstra, 'Education of Children with Frisian Home Language. Summarizing Account of an Evaluation Study in the Multilingual Dutch Province of Friesland', *International Review of Applied Psychology*, 29, 1-2 (1981, in press); J.M. Wijnstra, 'Attainment in English in the Schools of Wales', *International Review of Applied Psychology*, 29, 1-2 (1981, in press).

82.  Holmstrand, *Effekterna på allmänna färdigheter och attityder*; Holmstrand, *De långsiktiga effekterna på allmänna färdigheter och attityder*; Jansson and Linden, *Social bakgrund och skolprestationer*.

83.  J.K. Bhatnagar, 'Linguistic Behavior and Adjustment of Immigrant Children in French and English Schools in Montreal', *International Review of Applied Psychology*, 29, 1-2 (1980), pp. 141-58.

# 10 CONTEMPORARY AMERICAN POLICIES AND PRACTICES IN THE EDUCATION OF IMMIGRANT CHILDREN*

**Gail P. Kelly**

This chapter will review educational policies and practices towards recent immigrants to the United States and focuses on the extent to which such policies foster or inhibit cultural pluralism. It will be done through careful investigation of resettlement procedures and educational programmes for three recent immigrant groups: Hungarians, Cubans and Vietnamese. Such an exercise allows us to identify United States policy and its continuity over recent decades and the ways in which domestic and international politics as well as the nature of immigrant populations themselves influence educational policies.

I have chosen to use the Hungarian, Cuban and Vietnamese immigrations to illustrate US policy because they represent some of the largest immigrant groups admitted to the country in the past thirty years. Current legislation prohibits large-scale entry of persons from a single nation. No more than 20,000 persons per year from a given country may immigrate. The 1965 Immigration Act gives preference to professionals who can obtain documentation from the US Department of Labor that their skills are needed in the US labour market and that they will not compete with US citizens for employment.[1] This restriction has put an end to the mass immigrations experienced in the late nineteenth and early twentieth centuries. Vietnamese, Cubans and Hungarians have been the major exceptions. In their cases, Congress waived immigration laws concerning both the numbers to be admitted and their occupational skills. In the case of other recent immigrants, no special educational and social programmes have been instituted. The government has assumed that they would easily integrate into the society, given the small numbers of any one nationality and their employability. Clearly, if one wants to identify American policy, it is possible only in cases where the government has felt it necessary to design programmes. This has occurred in the cases of these three immigrations.

The analysis which follows argues that American school policies and practices towards immigrant children militate against cultural pluralism. Schooling is seen as a means of integrating the immigrant into American political, cultural and economic life. If immigrant children are to become bicultural, given resettlement policies and school programmes, they must do so on their own, with minimal support either from the state or from the school, unless, as in the case of Cuban immigration in its early years, American foreign policy goals are furthered by bicultural, bilingual education.

Before turning to educational programmes, it is important to consider the nature of these immigrations and American resettlement practices.

## Immigrant Characteristics and US Resettlement Policies

The Hungarians, Cubans and Vietnamese came to the United States in large groups, each within a relatively short time period. Although the economic, social and cultural backgrounds of each varied, as did the international and domestic political conditions of the times in which they came, the US government adopted, in most cases, as I will demonstrate below, policies to disperse the immigrants throughout the country and discourage the development of ethnic communities.

The Hungarians entered the country in 1956 after the Soviet Union reoccupied Budapest to prevent the establishment of a non-aligned government. Of the 150,000 persons who left Hungary, 38,000 were admitted to the United States under special legislation lifting the national origins quotas that were part of the then American immigration law. Americans greeted Hungarian immigrants as 'freedom fighters'. The US government used its welcome to Hungarians as propaganda in its Cold War with the Soviet Union. The climate in the US was friendly. In 1956, the American economy was expanding and there was little fear that a large influx of immigrants would adversely affect an American's chances on the job market. This belief was strengthened further by the nature of the immigration itself, for most of the Hungarians who came to the US were professionals and technicians whose skills were sorely needed in the workforce. Because public opinion was so favourable and the immigrants could be used to further American foreign policy, the government had no difficulty in appropriating millions of dollars to assist the newcomers.[2]

When they entered the country, the Hungarians were retained in a refugee holding centre at Fort Kilmer, New Jersey. They were resettled through a sponsorship programme whereby American individuals or groups — churches, businesses, civic organisations — took responsibility for the immigrant's adjustment to the United States and assumed financial responsibility for his/her family. Hungarians were resettled rapidly in disparate parts of the United States. The only area to receive a sizeable number was New York City, where 3,100 were relocated in this city of over 16 million. The Hungarian immigrants of 1956 were not, for the most part, integrated into the pre-existing Hungarian community in the US. This was partly the will of the immigrants, who perceived the earlier Hungarian immigrants as lower class.[3] Besides, in 1956, public policy fostered dispersal of immigrant groups and their rapid integration into American society through isolation and, as I will show later, through sponsorship into the middle classes through education.

The policy of dispersal and rapid integration so evident in the resettlement policies towards Hungarians seemed somewhat abandoned during the early phases of Cuban immigration. Cubans began entering the country in large numbers in 1959 when it became evident that the government that overthrew Batista was Communist. The US government welcomed the 275,000 persons who arrived in Miami, Florida, between 1959 and 1962, perceiving them not as immigrants, but rather as persons seeking temporary asylum. There was no attempt between 1959 and 1962 to resettle the Cubans or to integrate them into American economic or social life. On the contrary, it was US policy to encourage the development of a Cuban community that was unified, both culturally and politically, in the hopes that it could spearhead a counter-revolution and return as a group to Cuba.[4] As a result, Dade County, Florida, in which the city of Miami is located, became a centre for Cubans, with close to 250,000 immigrants taking up residence there. The government provided funds for community centres, the best known being the Cuban Refugee Center of Miami, which served not only as a contact point for incoming refugees, but also ran cultural programmes and ultimately provided a locus for political activities.

After the missile crisis of October 1962, the US government abruptly changed its policies. It was clear that the Castro government was not going to be overthrown in the near future and that the Cubans, so freely admitted as refugees, were indeed immigrants. As an organised community they became a political problem, both domestically and internationally, for while the US was not willing to risk nuclear war to oust Castro, many Cubans were. Additionally, the build-up of the Cuban population in Dade County, where the economy was not expanding fast enough to absorb a quarter of a million persons entering the workforce, had meant an ever-increasing welfare burden. The size of the Cuban community meant that it could exert substantial influence in local politics, much to the chagrin of local residents.

Cuban immigration came to a standstill between 1962 and 1965. In late 1965, the Cuban government agreed to allow anyone who wished to leave to do so – and the US government airlifted approximately 4,000 persons per month to the US. This later group, however, was treated differently from those who had entered earlier. The government made every attempt to disperse the newcomers by discouraging them from entering Miami and resettling them with American sponsors throughout the country. Cubans who insisted on settling in Miami were refused any resettlement assistance, including job training and special programmes. None the less, close to 25 per cent of this second wave joined their compatriots in the Miami area.

The federal government committed millions of dollars to the integration of Cubans into American society. It allocated $42,600,000 in 1966 and $52,000,000 in 1967 alone to various programmes. Behind these expenditures lay real concern about the ability of Cuban immigrants to integrate easily into the American economy. A considerable number of Cubans, unlike the earlier Hungarian immigrants, did not possess skills greatly in demand. Over 31 per cent were unskilled workers. In addition, many were poorly educated: 4 per cent had less than primary education, another 60 per cent had not completed high school.[5] Without special help, US government officials feared a long-term welfare expenditure and a difficult political problem between the well-organised Cuban community in Florida and US citizens in the state. The Cuban assistance programmes were not only well funded – possible under the conditions of economic boom of the 1960s – but also long term, with the government committed to continuing assistance into the 1980s. I will discuss the nature of programmes funded for Cuban immigrants later. At this point, it is necessary merely to point out that the assistance was great and designed to integrate Cubans into American society on an unprecedented scale. However, these programmes, many of which tried to sponsor Cubans into the American middle classes, in the long run proved so costly that Congress used them as a negative referent for designing federal assistance programmes for the Vietnamese who arrived in 1975.[6] In its deliberations, Congress vowed to provide only limited aid to the Vietnamese and to establish policies to avoid creating 'another Miami'.

Resettlement policy towards immigrants clearly depends on American political interests – this was demonstrated in the case of the Cubans. The programmes developed for Vietnamese immigrants underscore the role of the economy as well in shaping policy. One hundred and fifty thousand Vietnamese entered the United States in the midst of the worst economic recession the country had seen since the 1930s. The governors of several states and their Congressional representatives made it patently clear that they did not want large numbers of Vietnamese entering their states; and American labour voiced its concerns about Vietnamese competing with Americans for scarce jobs.[7] Additionally, no state or municipality wanted to deal with welfare costs that would surely follow if Vietnamese located and were unemployed in their communities. Not only did the economic situation mean that Vietnamese would get lesser funding than the Cubans and Hungarians who had preceded them; the political climate of the country also encouraged this. Vietnamese were not perceived as 'freedom fighters'; on the contrary, Americans believed they were corrupt officials of the Thieu and Ky government, unwilling and unable to defend themselves or democratic ideals. A majority of Americans thought the government should not let them into the country.[8] The early 1970s were also a time of detente — and there was little political benefit to be gained by opening the country to refugees from Communism. The government saw the Vietnamese as a political embarrassment and it acted swiftly to minimise their impact on American society and on US foreign policy.[9]

Vietnamese, like the Hungarians, were interned in four camps on the United States mainland to await sponsors. Every effort was made to disperse them throughout the country to prevent the build-up of a sizeable community. Additionally, aid programmes were minimal. The government provided a $ 600 *per capita* resettlement grant to voluntary agencies to relocate them. Job retraining and educational funding was kept to a minimum, despite the fact that, of the three immigrations, the Vietnamese were least equipped to enter the American economy. Only about 35 per cent of these immigrants had managerial, technical or professional skills that could be transferred into the American job market. A sizeable number were poorly educated — close to 20 per cent had less than a primary school training and another 38 per cent had less than secondary education. Five per cent spoke no English; another 25 per cent who claimed some background in the language could not make themselves understood in it.[10]

The results of federal policies were predictable. Vietnamese, indeed, were initially relocated throughout the country. No community comparable to the Cuban one in Miami formed immediately. For the most part, Vietnamese were resettled in nuclear family units, with at most ten or twenty other families from their country in any given community. The federal government hoped this diaspora would speed their assimilation into the society. Congress stipulated that, as of December 1977, all special programmes for Vietnamese be ended.

The resettlement policies and patterns in all three immigrations have similarities which have vast implications for immigrant education. Resettlement policies, except for the brief period in which Cubans were expected to return home, were aimed at integrating the immigrants into American society. Integration meant, first and foremost, living apart from compatriots and not forming distinct subcultures. It meant developing skills useful in the American workforce and it meant, as I will show later, being schooled in American institutions that had little relevance to immigrants' culture. If this was not an explicit, intentional part of US policy, it was ultimately a result. Nowhere is this clearer than in education, for in order for a school system to provide special programmes, not to mention bilingual, bicultural education for immigrant children, there has to be a number of children of a given immigrant group within a school district. Resettlement policies and, as we shall now see, federal assistance programmes for education militated against the development of such programmes.

## Federal Educational Aid to Immigrants

If education has been looked to to integrate immigrant children into American society, as many have seen the schools, it has done so without federal assistance and/or without special educational programmes. In short, the government has not placed a great premium either on immigrant children succeeding in school or on the schools offering special programmes that transmit immigrant cultures. This has historically been the case, and is still the case, as I will show, today. The reasons are many. In the past, ethnocentrism has been a hallmark of American education — the schools were called upon to transmit American values to the next generation and little else.[11] Today, schooling is perceived as the entrée to well-paid jobs, and emphasis in education more and more is placed on schools preparing children for the world of work and attempting to give all children equal educational opportunity. This has, in large part, been a response to the past, where educational tracking, both racial and ethnic, has clearly led to educational inequality and resultant economic inequalities.

Hungarians, the earliest of the immigrants considered in this chapter, were not the focus of specialised educational programmes, bilingual or otherwise, within the American school system. Rather, they were given individual educational assistance in the form of direct grants to be used for college for Hungarian youth who were college students at the time they came to the United States. US government grants were also given for courses to Hungarian MDs, dentists and lawyers to prepare them for entry in the US into the professions they had practised in Hungary. Special funds were also made available for English language instruction. So successful were these programmes that the downward occupational mobility experienced by many Vietnamese and Cuban immigrants did not occur. A survey of Hungarian immigrants taken in 1968, 14 years after their arrival, indicated that most were employed at jobs equivalent to or better than they had held in Hungary. The study further showed that most immigrants had entered the middle classes. Their major social ties were not to a Hungarian community. Many used English in their daily lives and within their families, and identified themselves as Americans.[12]

The size and nature of the Hungarian immigration, as well as government resettlement policies, the willingness to sponsor Hungarians into the middle classes, and the state of the American economy, all contributed to such results. The Cuban immigrants, however, did not have the same experience.

In the initial stages of Cuban immigration, from 1958 to 1962, the government made little effort to integrate the Cubans into American society or the American school system. It acted rather to maintain a Cuban community, for reasons I outlined earlier. The government initially established English language classes for adults through the Cuban Refugee Center and other agencies in Miami. It also provided grants-in-aid to the Dade County public school system, covering 50 per cent of the educational costs for each immigrant child enrolled in the schools. The government, in addition, allocated funds for the hiring of Cuban teacher aides within the classrooms and for special bilingual programmes. Between 1959 and 1962, the government supported a Cuban University of Miami, conducted in Spanish, and special courses at the University of Miami for Cuban students. It awarded grants for retraining Cuban professionals, MDs and dentists to meet US certification requirements as well as for teachers and social workers to serve the growing Cuban community.[13]

These programmes, extending from 1958 to 1962, were clearly not designed to integrate Cubans into the American social fabric; rather, they were geared to retain a community which might otherwise fragment. Little concern was expressed about 'success' according to the standards of the American school system.

Federal educational programmes shifted drastically after 1962 with the realisation that the Cubans were indeed immigrants. The federal government by 1966 developed programmes resembling those it had offered the Hungarians. First, the government in 1966 attempted to divest itself of all special primary and secondary school programmes in Dade County and the City of Miami. The county and city governments, faced with the prospects of losing considerable monies, threatened to expel all Cuban students from school. The federal government then agreed to cover 100 per cent of all schooling costs for the immigrant children and contribute $ 600 per child to a school building fund. It did, however, cease supporting special bilingual programmes and paying the salaries of Cuban school aides. The Dade County and Miami public schools were encouraged to integrate the children into regular school programmes. Simultaneously, government funding of English language classes for adults was stepped up and programmes for job retraining instituted. Higher education programmes for Cubans were also revised. Emphasis was placed on student scholarship and loan programmes, with priority given to students who wished to attend colleges and universities outside the State of Florida. In the first half of 1966 alone, the federal government granted 3,200 loans, totalling $ 1,197,731, for Cuban immigrants.[14]

Job retraining programmes took a different cast. Sums were allocated to integrate Cuban professionals with their American peers. Teacher retraining efforts exemplify this the most. In 1966, the federal government funded nine centres for training Cuban teachers to work in American schools. None was situated in Florida; rather, they were located in Montana, Oregon, Iowa, Indiana, Kansas, Pennsylvania and New Jersey. Their mission was to prepare Cubans to become Spanish teachers in areas of the country where there were shortages of native Spanish speakers.

Despite the lack of federal government support for bilingual, bicultural education, some immigrant schoolchildren did receive such education. This was the case in Miami and Dade County, where there is a large concentration of Cubans and their numbers are large enough to make such programmes economically feasible and for Cuban parents to exert pressure on local school boards to offer them. In other areas, like New York City, where over 3,000 Cubans resettled, bilingual (Spanish-English) education is available; but whatever bicultural education there is, is Puerto Rican-American in content, not Cuban-American. Cubans who attend such programmes are integrated into the educational programmes designed for disadvantaged minorities rather than education which represents either their culture or that of mainstream, middle-class Americans.

Have Cuban immigrant children succeeded in the schools and integrated into American society as the post-1966 programmes intended? The answer to this question is not entirely clear. Little research has been done on Cuban immigrant schoolchildren *per se*, not to mention the educational successes of children in bilingual, bicultural or mainstream American education. We do know, however, that the Cuban community in Miami still exists and is a major political force in the area, and that integration/assimilation of that community into the American mainstream is far from that of the Hungarians who entered only two years earlier.

The discussion thus far has centred on federal policies that encouraged the integration of immigrants into American society. These policies were not only a result of funding programmes that immigrants could choose to participate in or not to participate in; they were an integral part of schooling designed especially for immigrant children. This becomes clearest when we turn to an investigation of federal education programmes for Vietnamese who immigrated in 1975.

The Vietnamese were relocated in much the same manner as Hungarians in 1956. Because their numbers were five times greater than the 1956 Hungarian immigration and because their entry was greeted with hostility, Vietnamese resettlement moved much slower than the Hungarian. Many Vietnamese were held in camps in the US for over five months, awaiting sponsors. In the camps, the federal government, through the Department of Health, Education and Welfare, established its own educational system to prepare Vietnamese for entry into American society. Close to $4,000,000 was expended on these programmes, which consisted of compulsory schooling for children aged six to 18 and adult English language schools.[15] While educational programmes varied in detail from camp to camp, the curriculum was established under federal guidelines. To look at these programmes is to see school practices at a level which, to my knowledge, scholars of immigration have not done before; for educational policies can tell us merely what is intended – they do not necessarily show us the process of education immigrant children receive. The brief discussion that follows is based on extensive field work I conducted in 1975 at one of the refugee centres, Fort Indian Town Gap, Pennsylvania. I attended classes, collected curricular materials and interviewed teachers, curriculum specialists and school personnel as well as camp officials and Vietnamese immigrants.

**The Content of Immigrant Education**

School at Fort Indian Town Gap met daily. For children aged six to 18 it was compulsory. Camp officials, assisted by the military police, rounded up recalcitrant children and sent them to class. Attendance was taken daily and children who were absent were checked on — confirmed illness was the sole legitimate excuse for skipping class.[16] Adult education was not compulsory; however, camp officials strongly encouraged immigrants to attend, warning them that if they failed to learn English they would find neither sponsors nor jobs once the camps closed. Adult classes also met daily in three-hour sessions.

Without exception, the camp schools were staffed and taught by Americans. Vietnamese had no role in curriculum formulation or in the conduct of class except to participate on terms which Americans defined. The primary and secondary schools employed two Vietnamese as aides. They functioned as school disciplinarians. Both spoke English well and were supposed to serve as role models for the children in order to demonstrate that Vietnamese could indeed learn the language. The adult school had no Vietnamese aides.

All classes were conducted in English. In the primary and secondary school, use of the Vietnamese language was forbidden. The two aides initially went from class to class explaining the ban on Vietnamese. 'Speak English only', they warned the children, 'even among yourselves.'[17] Toys were given daily to the few children who managed to pass the six-hour school day without uttering a word of their native tongue. Vietnamese became a forbidden language as well as a language of punishment, for the Vietnamese aides were called in to restore order in class and discipline the children. In such situations, they spoke in Vietnamese.

The language medium of instruction itself stood as an indication of the unicultural nature of this education, designed specially for immigrant children. Curricular content underscored this. The curriculum of the primary and secondary school was designed ostensibly to prepare Vietnamese children for American schools. This involved not only teaching children English, but also teaching them American school procedures and appropriate student behaviour and, according to curriculum specialists, for the child's psychological well-being, about how to interact with their American peers. Thus, the curriculum placed a great deal of emphasis on teaching about the culture with which Vietnamese children would presumably have contact once they entered the American public schools. In the primary grades, it meant teaching about the family; in the secondary school, it involved detailed instruction on adolescent subcultures. A few examples will illustrate that such instruction went beyond describing American culture and, in effect, projected American cultural behaviour as one to which Vietnamese needed to conform in order both to succeed in school and to 'adjust' to America. I will focus here on two units: one taught in the primary grades, the other in the secondary school. Both units were the central themes of classroom instruction for over one-third of the time the camp schools were functioning.

In the primary grades, this unit focused on the family and its activities; in the secondary school, the topic was 'adolescent life'. In both, the materials were couched in 'my-we-our' terminology – 'my family ...' – or with Vietnamese as major actors – 'Thanh went to ...' The materials were not presented as 'the American family does ...' or 'American teenagers ...' The terminology itself was designed to project Vietnamese into the situations depicted, normalising, in effect, what would be fundamental cultural change.

Instructional materials in the primary classes defined the family as a nuclear family consisting of mother, father and two to three children. The household was coextensive with this family.[18] A finger game which children in grades 1-3 recited daily is typical:

This is the mother so happy and gay (point to the thumb)
This is the father who works all day (point to the index finger)
This is the brother so strong and tall (point to the middle finger)
This is the sister who plays with her doll (point to the fourth finger)
This is the baby, the sweetest of all (point to the little finger)
This is the whole family, great and small (point to all fingers).[19]

This image was the only one presented. The curriculum did admit that 'other' people sometimes lived with 'my' family – grandparents, uncles, aunts, cousins as well as nurses, maids and cooks. The curriculum presented 'my' family not only as American in organisation, but also as American in its leisure activities. 'My' family celebrates Christmas, American Independence Day, Thanksgiving Day, Easter, Halloween and Armistice Day; it has picnics, it visits the zoo.

This portrayal of the family seems benign, especially to Americans. On Vietnamese terms it clearly represents major changes in family life, which Americans, through resettlement procedures, were attempting to effect in the face of Vietnamese resistance. Vietnamese families and households were large and consisted of grandparents, aunts, uncles and cousins. Among the immigrants this pattern was evident; for Vietnamese had, for the most part, come to the US in households averaging nine persons. Many households consisted of 40 to 50 persons. The average number of children per family was five, indicating that at least four adults were part of each household.[20] Camp officials attempted to break this non-Western family organisation for resettlement purposes, reckoning accurately that few Americans would step forward to sponsor upwards of 50 persons. Many households were divided into nuclear family units by the government and sent to disparate parts of the country. Vietnamese resisted this. One family of over 30 refused to leave their quarters at Fort Indian Town Gap for fear that Americans would photograph them and find different sponsors for various members of the family.[21] School personnel were not acting benignly in portraying the nuclear family in the school curriculum. They were consciously trying to adjust children to the realities of American policy and prepare them for far-reaching changes in their daily life. 'My' family was, in effect, the new Vietnamese family, remade in the American image.

At the secondary level, the schools also promoted cultural change, but in a different way. They tended to adjust Vietnamese youth to American subcultures that perhaps could be defined as deviant, rather than to mainstream American ideals of youth behaviour. This was clearest in the many vocabulary drills and lessons on adolescent subculture. Included, for example, in one week's vocabulary drill were the following words, all relating to drug taking and juvenile delinquency:

| | | |
|---|---|---|
| Scene | Acetylene Tank | joint |
| stoned | going ape | grammar school |
| Juvenile hall | pot | to stutter |
| groove | a lid (of pot) | overdose |
| cool | convulsions | heroin |
| get high | parole officer | addict |
| 'reds' | 'speed' [22] | |

One wonders whether this lesson's inclusion in the curriculum was based on the assumption that Vietnamese youth, like the youth of urban slums, would inevitably become involved in crime. This same lesson also introduced American colloquial terms like 'gimme', 'aw', 'say baby' and 'you rate'.

Other curricular materials used in class depicted days in the life of Thanh, a Vietnamese immigrant. Thanh was indistinguishable from his American peers. With his two friends, Doug and Brian, Thanh spent his days sipping cokes and munching hamburgers in the local teenage hangout. They gossiped about girls and sports and complained about parental restrictions and most of all about being bored.[23] These portrayals made certain assumptions about Thanh — for in his reactions and his obligations to his family he is no different from his American peers. Thanh becomes a role model for Vietnamese youth, and he stands as an invitation to behave as American teenagers do, autonomously, detached from their families. Adjustment in this case boiled down to accepting American behavioural norms, many of which are objectionable even to many Americans.

The type of education designed for Vietnamese immigrants reveals the essence of American policy towards immigrants that was implied by the federally funded educational programmes for both Hungarian and Cuban children. Not only are federal policies directed towards social and economic integration; they are, as the curriculum of the schools in the Vietnamese camps underscores, directed towards changes in personal and cultural behaviour. Adjustment of the immigrant child to schools becomes inextricably intertwined with remaking the child culturally, preparing him or her to be an American 'kid', not a Vietnamese or even a Vietnamese-American child living in two worlds.

Post-camp education for the Vietnamese has closely paralleled the pattern established first for Hungarians and later for Cuban immigrants who entered the country after 1966. The only difference in the programmes is that the federal government did not allocate sufficient funds to sponsor Vietnamese into the middle classes, partly because of the recession. The government in 1975-76 allocated $12,431,000 for the education of Vietnamese immigrants.[24] These monies were earmarked for special English language classes and were made in the form of direct grants to school districts which could demonstrate that 10 per cent or 100 of their pupils were Vietnamese requiring special services. Because resettlement policies scattered Vietnamese throughout the country, only a handful of schools, several of which are in California, obtained these grants. Funding in 1976-77, the last year in which direct assistance to the first wave of Vietnamese immigrants was given, was specifically for English language instruction through already existing programmes that served not only Vietnamese but also other persons whose native tongue was not English. No federal funds were made available for bi-cultural, bilingual Vietnamese-American education. In California, where a sizeable Vietnamese community has formed, the Los Angeles school system has experimentally introduced such programmes in response to the 40,000 or more Vietnamese who have settled there on their own.

## American Policy and the Future of Immigrants in the Schools

American policy and practice towards the education of immigrants centres on using schooling to integrate immigrants into American society by offering assistance in learning the English language and providing the immigrant with various sorts of job retraining. This was apparent in the cases of Hungarian, Cuban and Vietnamese immigrants who were all the focus of special government programmes. The particulars of the programmes, however, varied not by the size of the immigrations or the immigrant's degree of prior exposure to American culture and industrial society, but rather according to domestic and international political exigencies and the state of the American economy. Hungarians, as I have pointed out, came at the height of the Cold War at a time when US foreign policy goals would best be served by showing that the country welcomed 'freedom fighters' and rewarded them. The reward in this instance was entry into the affluent middle classes — and educational programmes were designed to maximise the immigrants' chances of remaining professionals and technicians. The price was isolation from other immigrants. The American economy could well offer such rewards to this group of immigrants, for it was rapidly expanding, and the skills of many Hungarians were greatly in demand.

The impact of foreign and domestic politics on educational policies is perhaps best illustrated in the case of the Cubans, where educational policies discouraged integration as long as American foreign policy was directed towards ousting the Cuban government with assistance from the immigrants. Once the US recognised the impossibility of its foreign policy goals, educational policy shifted once again to integrating Cubans into American society. The Cuban community, grouped as it was in Miami, was able to exert enough power on a local level to continue what had once been national policy. The onus, however, was on the Cubans. For those resettled outside the Miami-Dade County area, integration pressures were greater. Some, as in the case of Cubans residing in New York, could choose to educate their children in Spanish with Puerto Rican children. However, such choices meant that their children would be integrated into education designed for poor, disadvantaged minorities. In a time of prosperity, like the mid-1960s, the US government was still willing to sponsor immigrants into the middle classes if they abandoned their ethnic communities.

The Vietnamese programmes reflect the impact both of the economic recession and of domestic politics. In this instance, the country simply could not afford to underwrite Vietnamese entry into the middle classes when US citizens themselves were unable to find jobs. No advantage in domestic or international politics could be gained by treating Vietnamese as Hungarians had been treated.

While American policy aims to integrate immigrants through dispersion and education, it is not at all clear that such policies have their desired effect. At the same time, alternative practices have yet to be developed which reflect the perspective of immigrants themselves, for it is by no means the case that all immigrants desire bicultural education or special programmes that would either distinguish them from the American mainstream or more efficiently integrate them into the nation's cultural and social life.

We have seen that American policies seem to have been successful in regard to the Hungarian immigration of 1956. Follow-up studies indicate that they integrated, not into the pre-existing Hungarian community in the US, but into the American middle classes.[25] Cubans and Vietnamese seem to present a different pattern. Cuban immigrants who were able to resettle in the vicinity of other immigrants have not assimilated structurally or culturally into American society and have, in some cases, been able to use the schools to perpetuate their community. From all indications, many Cubans have not entered the middle classes. Why this is the case we do not know. Is it because Cuban children have been unable to adjust to the schools or achieve in them? Or has the nature of the immigrant population itself, containing many poorly educated and lower-class adults, been the cause? Or has the American economy been so tenuous that entry into the middle class becomes impossible, especially for dark-skinned foreign-born persons? These questions certainly need further investigation.

The disjunction between policy intent and outcome is probably most evident in the case of the Vietnamese immigrants of 1975. While American policy aimed at dispersal and integration without the reward of affluence, the Vietnamese rebelled against American policy. Between 1975 and 1977, Vietnamese resettled themselves, moving out of isolation and forming ethnic communities throughout the country. The city of Los Angeles exemplifies such a movement. In 1975, 27,000 Vietnamese were relocated there; but in 1976, 40,000 resided in the city, coming from other resettlement locations in the US. It has been estimated that, by 1980, if current trends continue, the number of Vietnamese in Los Angeles will rise to 100,000.[26] Many Vietnamese self-help organisations have developed in Los Angeles and elsewhere, the functions of which are not confined to job placement and mutual aid. Many hold cultural events – like Tet (Vietnamese New Year's) celebrations – and offer classes in Vietnamese on Vietnamese culture and history as well as tutoring services to school-age children to enhance their chances for academic achievement. In 1977 alone, there were over 150 such organisations.[27]

The regroupment of Vietnamese, the rise of voluntary organisations and the development of bilingual Vietnamese-English education within several California schools indicate a pattern different from that of the Hungarians. So also does the integration of Vietnamese into the American economy. Vietnamese immigrants have, for the most part, experienced downward social and economic mobility in coming to the US. A substantial number, close to 50 per cent of all households, are on public assistance because they are either unemployed or partly employed, or in jobs that do not provide for the basics of life.[28] This economic picture has not changed for the better since 1976, despite the movement of Vietnamese to areas where the American economic decline has not been as severe. The prospects for economic betterment are indeed dim, given the complete absence of federal programmes to assist Vietnamese since 1977 and the high rate of unemployment which is heaviest among racial minorities.

Are American policies desirable? This question has long been debated by American policy makers, educators, scholars and immigrants. While all agree that government policies have for some meant entry into the middle classes, there is less accord over whether affluence and integration require unicultural education and dispersion or whether the toll such policies exact on individuals is too great. Much has been written lamenting both the successes and the failures of American policies and educational practices. Yet little substantive research has been carried out on alternatives and their implications. We know that some first-generation immigrant children 'adjust' well to American schools and to American society; some do not. How 'adjustment' is defined, however, depends on who is defining it. Does 'adjustment' mean that children get good grades, are not delinquent and ultimately make 'good' (presumably defined in terms of their relative status within the American occupational structure)? Is 'adjustment' the lack of problems defined by social welfare workers? Can it be defined in terms of persistence within an immigrant community?

A second set of questions that need to be asked concerning the adjustment of the immigrant child (once that is defined) is what type of educational situations foster or impede that adjustment. Much literature exists in the US arguing that multicultural, bilingual education will speed integration, encourage good school performance and allow the culturally different child to adjust to often conflicting cultural social systems. While the intentions of those who propose such innovations in education are admirable, it has yet to be demonstrated that students who benefit from these programmes integrate better into their own community or into American society than students who are not schooled in them. Further, we do not know whether students receiving bicultural or bilingual education get better grades in the American schools, experience less cultural and personal conflicts, or enter the American mainstream faster than their peers who do not receive such education. Until such research is carried out, it may be easier to condemn current policies and practices than to formulate alternatives that facilitate the adjustment of immigrants — on their own as well as on American terms — to the school and the society.

## Notes

*I wish to thank David Gerber of the Department of History, SUNY/Buffalo, David Kelly of the Department of History, D'Youville College, and Maxine S. Seller, of the Department of Social Foundations of Education, SUNY/Buffalo, for their comments on earlier drafts of this paper.

1.   Michael G. Wenk, 'Assessment of the United States Immigration Policy', *Migration News*, vol. 19, no. 1 (January-February 1970), p. 2.
2.   Philip Soskis, 'Adjustment of 200 Hungarian Refugee Families in New York City', *Migration News*, vol. 17, no. 1 (January-February 1968), pp. 7-13; Philip Soskis, 'Ten Years Later: A Report of the Integration of Jewish Hungarians in the U.S.', *International Migration*, vol. 5, nos 3/4 (1967), pp. 169-75; Alexander Weinstock, *Acculturation and Occupation: A Study of the 1956 Hungarian Refugees in the U.S.* (Martinus Nijhoff, The Hague, 1969); Joseph Szeplaki, *The Hungarians in America 1953-1974* (Oceana Publications, Dobbs Ferry, New York, 1975).
3.   Weinstock, *Acculturation and Occupation*.
4.   US Senate, Committee on the Judiciary, Subcommittee to Investigate Problems Connected with Refugees and Escapees, *Hearings, Cuban Refugee Problem*, 89th Congress, 2nd Session, Parts I, II and III (US Government Printing Office, Washington, DC, 1966). See especially testimony of Dr Ellen Winston, US Commissioner of Welfare, and John Thomas, Director, Cuban Refugees Program, Part I, pp. 95-120.
5.   Richard R. Fagen, Richard A. Brody and Thomas J. O'Leary, *Cubans in Exile: Disaffection and the Revolution* (Stanford University Press, Stanford, California, 1968), p. 17. See also US Senate, Committee on the Judiciary, Subcommittee to Investigate Problems Connected with Refugees and Escapees, *Hearings, Cuban Refugee Problem*, Part I, p. 13.
6.   US Senate, Committee on the Judiciary, Subcommittee to Investigate Problems Connected with Refugees and Escapees, *Hearings, Indochina Evacuation and Refugee Problems, Part II. The Evacuation*, 94th Congress, 1st Session, 15, 25 and 30 April 1975 (US Government Printing Office, Washington, DC, 1975);

US Senate, Committee on the Judiciary, Subcommittee to Investigate Problems Connected with Refugees and Escapees, *Indochina Evacuation and Refugee Problems, Part IV. Staff Reports Prepared for the Use of the Subcommittee*, 94th Congress, 1st Session, 9 June and 8 July 1975 (US Government Printing Office, Washington, DC, 1975).

7.   Ibid.

8.   'Refugees: A Cool and Wary Reception, *Time Magazine* (12 May 1975), pp. 24, 26; Richard T. Schaefer and Sandra T. Schaefer, 'Reluctant Welcome: U.S. Response to Vietnamese Refugees', *New Community*, vol. 4, no. 3 (Autumn 1976), pp. 366-70. Both articles report polls that indicated that only 36 per cent of all Americans believed Vietnamese should be admitted into the country.

9.   Gail Paradise Kelly, *From Vietnam to America: A Chronicle of the Vietnamese Immigration to the U.S.* (Westview Press, Boulder, Colorado, 1977), Ch. 2.

10.   Interagency Task Force on Indochinese Refugees, *Report to Congress* (15 December 1975), p. 13.

11.   Robert A. Carlson, *The Quest for Conformity: Americanization Through Education* (Wiley, New York, 1975); David Tyack, *The One Best System: A History of American Urban Education* (Harvard University Press, Cambridge, 1974).

12.   Weinstock, *Acculturation and Occupation.*

13.   US Senate, Committee on the Judiciary, Subcommittee to Investigate Problems Connected with Refugees and Escapees, *Hearings, Cuban Refugee Problem.*

14.   Ibid., Part I, pp. 94-120, 131.

15.   HEW Refugee Task Force, *Report to Congress* (15 June 1976), p. 80.

16.   Interview with H.M.B., Curriculum Coordinator, Grades K-3, Fort Indian Town Gap Schools (17 October 1975), Tape 9, Side 2, Vietnamese Immigration Collection, SUNY/Buffalo Archives.

17.   Interviews with B.T. and N.T.D., Vietnamese aides, Fort Indian Town Gap Schools (30 October 1975), Tape 31, Side 2, Tape 32 and Tape 33, Vietnamese Immigration Collection, SUNY/Buffalo Archives.

18.   Interview with B.G., Curriculum Coordinator, Grades 4-6, Fort Indian Town Gap Schools (16 October 1975), Tape 21, Side 2, Tape 22, Side 1; Interview with H.M.B., Curriculum Coordinator, Grades K-3, Fort Indian Town Gap Schools (17 October 1975), Tape 26, Side 1, Vietnamese Immigration Collection, SUNY/Buffalo Archives.

19.   Grades 1-3, 'Suggested Schedule' (20-24 October 1975), Fort Indian Town Gap School, Curriculum Guide (mimeo), Grades 1-2, 'Suggested Schedule' (13-17 October 1975), Fort Indian Town Gap School, Curriculum Guide (mimeo), Vietnamese Immigration Collection, SUNY/Buffalo Archives.

20.   HEW Refugee Task Force, *Report to Congress* (15 June 1976), pp. 27, 28.

21.   Interview with J.C., Resettlement Caseworker, United States Catholic Conference (17 October 1975), Fort Indian Town Gap, Tapes 27 and 28, Vietnamese Immigration Collection, SUNY/Buffalo Archives. I accompanied this caseworker on 16 October 1975 to Vietnamese living quarters and watched this individual, along with a Vietnamese interpreter and a photographer, try to convince this family to step outside the barracks to have their picture taken.

22.   Ibid.

23.   Ibid., p. 9, 'Dialogues'.

24.   HEW Refugee Task Force, *Report to Congress* (15 June 1976), p. 80.

25.   Weinstock, *Acculturation and Occupation.*

26.   *HEW Report on Indochinese Refugee Resettlement in Region IX, 1 July*

*1975 to July 1976* (HEW, San Francisco, 15 August 1976, typescript), p. 10; HEW Task Force on Indochinese Refugees, *Report to Congress* (15 June 1976), p. 24.

27.    A list of these organisations may be found in 'To Chuch Ai Huu', *Doi Song Moi*, Bo 2, So 7 (February 1976), pp. 16-17.

28.    'Nhan Dinh cua HEW ve Tinh Trang Dinh Cu', *Doi Song Moi*, Bo 2, So 10 (October 1976), pp. 1, 15. HEW Refugee Task Force, *Report to Congress* (15 March 1976), pp. 48-50.

# NOTES ON CONTRIBUTORS

**Joti Bhatnagar**, Concordia University, Montreal, Canada.

**Ronald Taft and Desmond Cahill**, Monash University, Australia.

**Gajendra K. Verma**, University of Bradford, England.

**Kanka Mallick**, West London Institute of Higher Education, England.

**Martine Charlot**, Agrégée de l'Université, Paris, France.

**Schole Raoufi**, University of Hamburg, Federal Republic of Germany.

**Tamar Horowitz**, Henrietta Szold Institute, The National Institute for Research in the Behavioural Sciences, Jerusalem, Israel.

**Arpi Hamalian**, Concordia University, Montreal, Canada.

**Lars Henric Ekstrand**, University of Lund, School of Education, Malmö, Sweden.

**Gail P. Kelly**, State University of New York at Buffalo, USA.

# SUBJECT INDEX

# NAME (AUTHOR) INDEX